THE BEST-EVER BOOK OF
CAKES

THE BEST-EVER BOOK OF
CAKES

165 utterly irresistible and foolproof cakes to bake
for everyday eating and special celebrations,
shown in 800 delectable photographs

 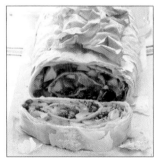 

ANN NICOL

LORENZ BOOKS

Contents

Introduction

For those who love to bake, both young and old, this is the perfect compendium of cakes to make for every occasion. Traditional tried-and-tested cake recipes sit alongside moreish contemporary creations that can be served at any time of day.

Baking produces so much pleasure. There's a real sense of achievement when you create a fresh batch of delicious cakes, and the whole house is filled with the marvellous aroma of baking. Home-made cakes must be the most popular, homely food you could make, and old favourites are always welcomed, but it's also fun to try something new. You'll find an almost overwhelming choice here. Each chapter deals with a different group of cakes, from classic cakes to luscious chocolate cakes and traybakes, covering every type you could imagine.

BAKING SKILLS

If you are a less experienced baker, remember that there are no secrets to making a cake; just follow the simple step-by-step methods to ensure successful results. Baking and cake-making involve several different techniques, and some cakes will certainly require more skill than others, but as you bake the recipes that appeal to you, you'll gradually build up your confidence and

expertise. Use the best ingredients you can afford to buy. Similarly, choose good quality bakeware and utensils. Always choose the correct tin (pan) size, otherwise your cake might not bake evenly or according to the times listed for each recipe. Careful weighing and measuring of ingredients is crucial for success, as is using the precise oven temperatures and exact timings. Gauging whether your cake is fully cooked can become instinctive, but beginners should always test the centre of their cakes just to be sure. All the methods and techniques you need to understand before starting to bake are clearly explained in the first chapter of the book. Step-by-step photographs guide you through each stage, showing how the ingredients should look at specific points of making.

IN THIS BOOK

The recipes included here are made with a wide range of methods and for different skill levels. There are cakes of every kind and for every occasion here, so there is sure to

Below A classic creamed sponge is moist and tender, and makes a favourite tea-time treat.

Below Everyone loves a chocolate cake and this versatile ingredient complements so many other flavours.

be something that will appeal to all ages and palates. You'll find cakes for birthdays, loaf cakes, spicy cakes, nutty cakes or simple plain scones, tea breads and fruit cakes that go well with a cup of tea – and you'll love the sweet ideas for lunchbox treats. Some are quick and easy to make with minimal ingredients, whereas others require a little more time. The Classic Cakes chapter includes the trusted recipes that you will make again and again – Carrot Cake with Cream Cheese Icing, Madeira Cake, and All-in-one Sponge Cake to name but a few. The Spice, Nut and Seed Cakes chapter incorporate blends of spices and other strong flavours to produce cakes with complex flavours. These cakes may well include your favourite flavouring ingredients. Try Pear and Cardamom Spice Cake, or Date and Walnut Spice Cake for everyday eating. Chocolate must be the most popular ingredient in baking, and every type of chocolate appears in the Chocolate Cake chapter – dark, milk and white chocolate, cocoa powder, grated, melted and chocolate chips, or a combination of several of them – offering a superb selection of indulgent treats. Black Forest Gateau, Death by Chocolate and Sachertorte are a few of the classics, but other contemporary batters are included too. Chocolate and Prune Cake, and Chocolate and Beetroot Layer Cake, are perfect for those with adventurous tastebuds.

For special gatherings the Individual Cakes chapter provides the perfect serving suggestions. These cakes can be simple to make, as with Rock Buns, or divine creations upon which you can lavish time and attention, such as on Hallowe'en Horrors. If you enjoy baking for a charity stall or the school fête, you'll find the Traybakes chapter essential. Traybakes are cooked in larger shallow tins (pans) or trays and then cut into squares, making them ideal individual cakes for lunchboxes. The chapter

Above This sophisticated-looking cake is a sponge covered in buttercream and tinted almond paste.

on Loaf Cakes includes plenty of traditional tea-time favourites, as well as contemporary offerings such as Chickpea Cake. A large chapter on fruit cakes includes both delicious and flavourful fresh fruit treats as well as dried fruit and spice combinations. The final two chapters, Dessert Cakes and Special Occasion Cakes, include recipes that require a little extra preparation. A special cake brings a personal touch and can be made as a gift or a stunning centrepiece. There are mouthwatering gateaux and cheesecakes, as well as wedding, birthday and anniversary cakes to be made. Whatever your skill level, taste preferences and occasion, there is sure to be a recipe included that is just perfect.

Below French madeleines are a favourite treat.

Below Fruit and nuts add luxury to cakes.

Below Traybakes are fast to make and economical, too.

Below Nuts and spices add depth of flavour to cakes.

Cake-making basics

This chapter will help you master all the basic preparation that leads to successful baking. Good-quality ingredients are the foundation of well-made cakes, so information is provided on the basics such as sugar, eggs, flour, fats and spices. Using good quality baking equipment is vital for cake-making, but only a few items of bakeware are needed, and the essentials are all described here. Learning how to bake is a key skill and often we find it easiest to make the foods we most love to eat. The many methods of making cakes, such as creaming, all-in-one, rubbing-in, melting and whisking, are illustrated with photographs and described step by step. To finish a cake you may like to add fillings and toppings – recipes for buttercream, chocolate icings, almond paste, royal icing and sugarpaste are all provided. The final section explains what can go wrong and the reasons why.

Left: Eggs, sugar, butter and flour are basic ingredients for cake making. Chocolate is a luxury ingredient.

Essential ingredients

Fat, sugar, flour and eggs are the four ingredients that form the basis of many recipes. To these, a whole array of flavouring ingredients can be added, such as chocolate, coffee, lemon juice and zest, nuts, and dried fruits, to name just a few. Each addition alters the basic cake flavour.

Sugar

Not only added for sweetness, sugars produce the structure and texture that make a cake tasty, so it's important to use the correct type:
Caster (superfine) sugar is available in white and unrefined golden varieties. It blends easily with fats when beaten or 'creamed' into light sponge mixtures.
Granulated sugar may be coarse white or golden and unrefined, and is used for toppings.
Demerara (raw) sugar is golden in colour and has a grainy texture.

Below clockwise from bottom left Caster sugar, runny honey, granulated sugar, demerara sugar, soft light and dark brown sugar, black treacle, golden syrup, icing sugar, and muscovado sugar are all sweeteners with their own clearly defined flavours.

It is often used for recipes where sugar is melted over heat, or as a decorative topping.
Soft light and dark brown sugars cream well and usually form the base of a fruit cake, or are used in recipes where a rich flavour is required. Store them in an airtight container.
Muscovado (molasses) sugar is natural and unrefined, with an excellent dark colour and richer flavour. It makes fruit cakes and gingerbreads extra special.
Icing (confectioners') sugar is sold as a fine white powder or in an unrefined golden form. It is used for icings, frostings and decorations. Store the sugar in a dry place, as it tends to absorb moisture. Sift the sugar at least once, or preferably twice, before you use it, as it may form hard lumps during storage.

Above Eggs and buttermilk.

Golden (light corn) syrup, honey, treacle and molasses are thick liquid sugars. They can be used in cakes made by the melting method.

Eggs

Although eggs are often stored in the refrigerator, better baked results will be achieved if they are at room temperature when they are used. The eggs will then whisk better than those kept refrigerated, and will achieve more aeration. Aeration gives more volume but also allows the eggs to blend into mixtures more easily. Cold eggs will tend to curdle a mixture more quickly.

Medium-size eggs are used in the recipes in this book, unless otherwise stated in the recipe.

Dried egg-white powder gives excellent results and can be substituted in royal icing recipes, or in recipes where you are unsure about the suitability of using raw egg whites. Raw eggs are unsuitable for the elderly, pregnant women, babies and young children.

Flours

Plain (all-purpose) flour provides the structure of a cake but contains nothing to make it rise. Richer cakes that do not need raising agents are made with plain flour.

Self-raising (self-rising) flour has raising agents mixed into it. These create air in the batter to make a cake rise, so self-raising flour is used for sponges and light mixtures that contain little or no fruit. If you have only plain flour, add 12.5ml/2½ tsp baking powder to every 225g/8oz plain flour to make it into a self-raising flour.

Wholemeal (whole-wheat) and brown flours contain bran from the wheat, which provides a good

Above, clockwise from left Baking powder, bicarbonate of soda, and cream of tartar.

Above, clockwise from bottom left Plain, strong, wholemeal, brown, and self-raising flours.

texture with extra fibre. This tends to keep cakes and breads moist and gives a mellow flavour. If you are substituting brown flour for white in a recipe, you will need to add extra liquid, as the bran in brown flour will absorb more fluid.

Gram flour is made from ground chickpeas and retains moisture.

White flours can be kept in a cool dry place for up to six months, but wholemeal flours will not keep for as long because they have a higher fat content. Check the use-by date on packs of all types of flour. Flour is best stored in an airtight container, which should be thoroughly washed and dried before refilling. Don't add new flour to old, as eventually small micro-organisms that look like tiny black specks may form, and will spread into new flour. Make sure all flour is kept dry, as damp flour weighs more and therefore alters the measurements in a recipe, which could lead to failure.

Raising agents

There are a number of raising agents that, when added to flour, make cakes rise. They produce an airy and light texture. As they are added in small quantities, it is important to be

accurate when measuring them out.

Baking powder is a ready-made mixture of bicarbonate of soda (baking soda) and cream of tartar. When liquid is added, the powder bubbles and produces carbon dioxide, which expands with heat during baking and creates an airy texture in the cake.

Bicarbonate of soda (baking soda) is a gentler raising agent than baking powder and is often used to give heavy melted or spicy mixtures a lift. It can create a bitter flavour if too much is added.

Cream of tartar is a fast-acting raising agent that works immediately it touches liquid, so bake the mixture as soon as possible after adding it.

Buttermilk

When added to recipes that use bicarbonate of soda (baking soda), buttermilk acts as a raising agent. The acidity in the buttermilk combined with the bicarbonate of soda produces carbon dioxide, which raises the mixture as it cooks. If buttermilk is not available, make your own souring agent by mixing 290ml/10fl oz low-fat yogurt or milk with 5ml/1 tbsp lemon juice.

SEPARATING EGG WHITES AND YOLKS

When separating egg whites from their yolks, tip the whites into a cup one at a time so that if there are any specks of yolk or pieces of shell in the cup, you can remove these easily. If yolk is present in a bowl of whites it will inhibit whisking and aeration. Even a tiny speck of yolk will stop the whites from whisking up to a foam and you will have wasted the whole mixture.

Above, clockwise from left Vegetable shortening, soft margarine, hard block margarine, butter and oil.

Above, clockwise from left Raisins, currants, glacé and crystallized fruit and sultanas.

Above, from left to right Whole nutmegs, cinnamon sticks, ground ginger and cloves.

Fats

As well as giving flavour and texture to cakes, fats improve their keeping qualities. For cake-making (apart from mixtures that use the rubbed-in method), always use fats at room temperature to make mixing them into the other ingredients easier.

Butter and hard block margarine can be interchanged in a recipe, but butter will always give the best flavour to cakes, so it is well worth spending that little extra.

Soft tub margarine is suitable only for all-in-one sponge recipes where all the ingredients are quickly mixed together in one bowl. These cakes usually require an extra raising agent. Don't overbeat recipes using soft tub margarine, as the mixture will become wet and the cake will sink. Do not substitute this fat for butter or block margarine as it is a totally different kind of fat, and it will not produce the same results.

Vegetable shortenings are flavourless but can be used to produce very pale, light cakes.

Right, clockwise from left Whole hazelnuts, whole walnuts, blanched almonds and ground almonds.

Cooking oils can be used successfully in moist cakes such as carrot cake. As they do not hold air, the mixture cannot be creamed and these cakes have a dense texture.

Dried fruits

Sultanas (golden raisins), raisins and currants are usually sold pre-washed and cleaned, but it is still worth picking them over for pieces of stalk and grit. Dried fruit benefits from soaking in dark sherry, brandy or rum, which will make the fruits extra plump and succulent.

Glacé (candied) and crystallized fruits, such as cherries, ginger or angelica, need to be rinsed and dried

before use to wash away their sugary coating. If you do not do this, the sticky coating may cause the fruits to sink during baking.

Spices

Frequently used spices for baking include nutmeg, ground ginger, cinnamon, cloves and mixed (apple pie) spice, which all add warm and fragrant tones to cakes. Dried spices have a long shelf-life but will not keep indefinitely and will gradually lose aroma and flavour. Buy them in small quantities when you need them. Light and heat will affect the flavour of spices, so keep them out of the light. For a longer life, store them in a cool dry place.

If you add spices to hot mixtures, don't measure them into the mixture straight from the jar, as steam may get into the jar causing the spice to become damp and deteriorate.

Nuts

Because nuts are expensive and will deteriorate quickly, buy them in small quantities. If you buy a large pack of nuts that you are not going to use immediately, you can freeze them for up to six months.

Almonds are bought blanched, slivered, flaked (sliced), ground or whole. To remove the skins from shelled almonds, place the nuts in boiling water for 2–3 minutes. Drain and rub off the skins. Ground nuts have a fine, powdery texture.
Hazelnuts are bought whole, skinned, unskinned or ground.
Walnuts contain more oil than most other nuts and will quickly become rancid, so don't buy them in bulk. Walnut halves are more expensive, so if you need chopped walnuts, buy walnut pieces.

Chocolate

For a professional finish and fine flavour buy the best quality chocolate. Good chocolate is sleek and shiny and will snap easily. It also contains a higher percentage of real cocoa fat, which gives a superior flavour and texture. The amount of cocoa fat or solids will be noted on the wrapper of any chocolate. Those marked as 70 per cent or more cocoa solids will give the best results.

Above, clockwise from top left
Unsweetened cocoa powder, milk, white and plain chocolate.

Cocoa powder needs to be cooked so that its full flavour will be released. Blend it with boiling water to make it into a paste, then cool it before adding to a recipe.

Drinking chocolate contains milk powder and sugar. Don't substitute it for cocoa powder, as it will spoil the flavour of a cake.

White chocolate may be difficult to work with. Grate it finely, or, if melting it, keep the temperature low.

MELTING CHOCOLATE

Melting chocolate needs care and attention. To melt chocolate, break the bar into small pieces and put it in a heatproof bowl standing over a pan of warm water. Make sure the bowl containing the chocolate is dry and that steam cannot get into the bowl. Heat the water to a gentle simmer only and leave the bowl to stand for about five minutes. Do not let the water get too hot or the chocolate will reach too high a temperature and will lose its sheen.

TOASTING NUTS

The flavour of nuts is improved by toasting them for a few minutes before use. To do this, place them in a single layer on a baking tray lined with foil and grill (broil) them lightly.

GRINDING NUTS

If you don't have ground nuts available, place whole or flaked (sliced) nuts in a food processor and grind until they form a coarse powder. Do not over-grind or the powder will be oily rather than dry.

SKINNING HAZELNUTS

For the best flavour in cakes, choose whole nuts, then toast them quickly under a grill until the skins loosen. Rub the nuts in a dish towel to remove the skins. Chop or grind. Use immediately.

Basic equipment

For successful cake making you need an oven that will retain an accurate and even temperature. If you're new to baking, start off with some mixing bowls and utensils and a few pans. A 900g/2lb loaf tin, a muffin tin and a 20cm/8in cake pan are useful sizes to have.

Baking papers, paper cases and foil

For lining tins (pans) and baking sheets use baking parchment, which is non-stick, or greaseproof (waxed) paper. Paper cases can be purchased in many different and convenient sizes to fit round or square cake tins or cupcake and muffin tins. Waxed paper is a useful surface to pipe royal iced decorations on to, as they will peel away easily once dry. Kitchen foil is handy for wrapping rich fruit cakes or for protecting wrapped cakes in the freezer.

Baking sheets

Choose large, heavy-duty baking sheets that will not buckle at high temperatures. Non-stick sheets are useful, but avoid thin, cheaper bakeware, which might bend during baking and cause sloping cakes or burnt edges.

Below Paper cases can be purchased to fit an exact tin size, but you can make your own lining from sheets of baking parchment or greaseproof paper.

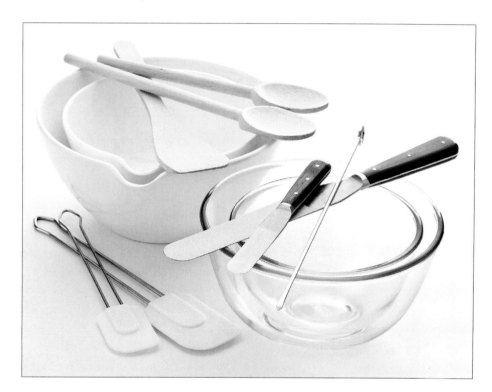

Above Mixing bowls, wooden spoons, palette knives, flexible scrapers and a skewer or cake tester are basic items of baking equipment.

Bowls

You'll need a set of different sizes of bowls for mixing and beating small and large amounts of cake batters, eggs, cream and other liquids.

Electric whisk

A hand-held electric whisk makes quick work of whisking cake batters and egg whites, and is an invaluable aid for cake-making.

Flexible scraper

A flexible scraper is perfect for getting the maximum amount of cake batter out of a bowl. Scrapers become softer with use.

Grater

A grater with a fine and a coarse side is useful for grating citrus rinds, chocolate and marzipan. You can also use a zester for citrus rinds.

Kitchen scales

Accurate kitchen scales are a vital piece of equipment for a baker. Old-fashioned scales with a pan and a set of weights are equally as good as a modern set with a digital display screen as long as they are accurate.

Measuring spoons and cups

Use a set of standard measuring spoons for accuracy of small quantities of ingredients. Sets of plastic or metal measures are sold specifically for this purpose. Remember that all spoon measures

*Above **Essential kitchen equipment
includes sieves, graters, scissors, pastry
brush and a large palette knife.***

should be level. Standard kitchen
tablespoons or teaspoons may be
inaccurate measures.

Metric and imperial are given in
the recipes. Follow one set of
measurements, as they are not
exactly equivalent.

Graded measuring cups are used
in many countries in place of
kitchen scales and are handy for
quick measuring. A measuring jug
(cup) is vital for liquids and it needs
to be graduated in small measures.

*Below **An electric mixer and whisk are
helpful and time-saving kitchen tools,
making light work of beating
cake batters.***

Oven

Each recipe usually begins with the
oven setting (unless some form of
preparation needs to be done in
advance). It is important to preheat
the oven to the correct temperature
before putting a cake in to bake.
Before you switch on the oven, it is
also essential to arrange the shelves
so that the tins (pans) will fit.

Fan-assisted ovens circulate hot
air around the oven and will heat up
very quickly. If you are using a fan
oven, you will need to reduce the
temperature stated in the recipe by
10 per cent; for example, if the
baking temperature is 180°C/350°F/
Gas 4, reduce it to 160°C/325°F/
Gas 3. If the oven is too hot, the
outside of a cake will burn before
the inside has had time to cook. If it
is too cool, cakes may sink or not
rise evenly. Try not to open the oven
door until at least halfway through
the baking time when the cake has

had time to rise and set, as a sudden
drop in temperature will stop the
cake rising and it will therefore sink.

Palette knife or spatula

These are ideal for many jobs
including loosening cakes from their
tins (pans), lifting cakes and
smoothing on icing and frostings.

Pastry brush

A pastry brush is necessary to brush
glazes over cakes and to brush
melted butter into tins. Brushes wear
out and start to shed bristles if used
regularly, so keep a spare one handy.

Scissors

These are essential for cutting lining
papers to size and snipping dried
fruits or nuts into chunks.

*Below **Measuring jug, kitchen scales,
measuring spoons and cups are
essential for accurate baking.***

Muffin tins are available in sets of six or 12 indentations and have deep-set muffin holes for larger individual cakes.

Fairy cake, bun or patty tins are similar to muffin tins but have shallower indentations for making smaller cakes. Line each indentation with a paper case.

Ring moulds and Kugelhopf tins are round metal moulds with a hole or funnel in the centre, and are specially designed for baking angel cakes and ring-shaped cakes. Grease these moulds well with melted butter, and put small strips of baking parchment in the base of plain ring moulds to aid the release of the cake.

Sieves (Strainers)

A large wire sieve is useful for sifting flour and dry ingredients, and a smaller nylon sieve can be kept just for icing (confectioners') sugar.

Skewer or cake tester

A thin metal skewer can be used to test if a cake is ready.

Spoons

Keep a large wooden spoon just for baking, for beating mixtures, butters and creaming. Don't use one that has been used for frying savoury things such as onions, as the flavours may taint the cake batter. Use a metal spoon for folding flour and beaten egg white into batter.

Tins (Pans)

Always use the size of tin stated in the recipe. If you use too large a tin, your cake may be too shallow when it is baked. Too small a tin may cause a peak in the mixture to form, which will then crack or sink in the middle.

Above A selection of tins (pans) in different sizes and shapes increases the range of baked goods you can make.

Choose good-quality rigid bakeware. When buying new tins, remember that top-quality tins will last longer and give better results. Non-stick coatings on some of the new ranges of bakeware need almost no greasing and cakes turn out beautifully, as do cakes cooked in the new heatproof flexible muffin and loaf moulds.

Sandwich tins and shallow round tins are designed to bake light sponges quickly.

Loaf tins in small and large sizes are ideal for teabreads and loaf cakes.

Deep round and square heavy-duty cake tins are ideal for baking rich fruit cakes.

Springform tins are round baking tins with a clipped side that can be loosened and removed easily from delicate bakes such as light sponges or cheesecakes. A loose-based tin makes a good substitute.

Wire racks

These cooling racks allow air to circulate around the hot baked cakes so that they will cool without becoming moist underneath.

ROUND OR SQUARE TINS AND COMPARABLE SIZING

If you use a tin (pan) that is a different size from the one stated in the recipe, the baking time, height, texture and appearance of the cake may be affected, as the quantity of mixture you have prepared will not be correct for that size of tin. Although you can use a square tin instead of a round tin, the sizes are not exactly equivalent, as there is a 2.5cm/1in size difference. A square tin will have a larger area than a round one; for example, a 20cm/8in round cake tin will take the same quantity of mixture as an 18cm/7in square tin.

Successful cake-making

Paying attention to the detail of a recipe will help to ensure a perfect cake. First, get all your equipment ready and prepare your cake tin. Take care with accurate measuring, and know how to test that the cake is cooked so that your hard work is rewarded with a delicious treat.

Assembling the ingredients

Ensure that you have all the necessary ingredients before baking.

Sifting flour makes a fine-textured product that is light and airy.

Accurate weighing and measuring

Recipes usually specify imperial, metric or cup weight. You must follow one set only and never use a combination, as they are not exact equivalents. If the measurements are muddled, it will affect the quality of the baked goods.

1 All spoon measurements must be level using a recognized set of metric or imperial spoon measures. Never estimate weights, as you will rarely achieve an accurate result.

2 As ingredients must be measured exactly, use good kitchen scales for weighing or graded measuring cups and scoops. These cups should be levelled for accurate measuring unless the recipe calls for a 'generous' cup.

Preparing tins (pans)

When recipes give instructions on how to prepare and line tins, don't be tempted to skip this, or you may ruin the baked cake. If using tins without a non-stick coating, give them a light greasing before use. Line the base of a tin to help the cake turn out easily.

1 Apply a thin film of melted butter with a pastry brush, or rub around the tin with kitchen paper and a little softened margarine.

Lining the sides of the tin

1 Cut a piece of baking parchment or greaseproof (waxed) paper 2.5cm/ 1in wider than the depth of the tin and long enough to fit around the circumference. Make a fold along one long edge of the strip, about 2.5cm/1in deep. Snip this folded edge at regular intervals with sharp scissors.

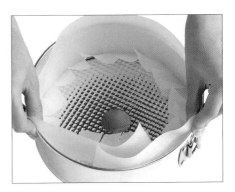

2 Line the sides of the tin using the strip, with the snipped edge at the base, lying flat. The baking parchment should adhere to the greased tin. Lightly grease any overlap of the edges so that it doesn't protrude into the cake batter. If your tin has a loose base this step will stop the baking batter from escaping and burning on the oven base.

Lining the base of a tin

1 Place the tin on a sheet of baking parchment and draw around it with a pencil. Cut out the shape.

2 Fit the rounds of paper in the base of the tin to cover the snipped edge.

Additional lining for a fruit cake

1 Tins for rich fruit cake batters should be double-lined. Cut a piece of baking parchment large enough to fold double and to stand 5cm/2in higher than the tin sides before continuing as for Lining the Sides of a Tin (above). A layer of brown paper wrapped around the outside will protect the cake.

Lining a baking tray

1 Cut a sheet of paper larger than the tray. Cut into each corner, then press in place.

Coating with flour

1 To coat with flour, tip a spoonful into the greased tin, then tip away the excess. This gives a golden edge.

Filling a cake tin (pan) with batter

1 Pour cake batter into the centre of the cake tin and spread it out to the edges. The batter should be spread evenly to ensure even baking. Rub off any drips from the cake tin because they will burn.

Checking to see if a cake is cooked

There are several clues to help determine whether a cake is ready. Has it baked for the suggested time? The baking times may need reviewing if you know that your oven temperature is inaccurate, if other items are being cooked at the same time, or if the oven door is opened in the baking process.

1 Cakes should be golden, risen and firm to the touch when pressed lightly in the centre. Lighter sponges and cakes should be a pale golden colour and the sides should shrink away slightly from the sides of the tin (pan).

2 To test a cake, insert a thin warmed skewer into the deepest part of the centre. If the cake is cooked, it should come out perfectly cleanly with no mixture sticking to it. If there is mixture on the skewer, bake the cake for a little longer and test again.

Releasing from the tin (pan) and cooling cakes

As freshly baked cakes are very fragile, they need time to stand in the tin to cool for a short time to firm them. Sponges and delicate cakes need 3–4 minutes standing time, but rich fruit cakes are very soft when freshly baked, so leave these in the tin for longer. To give a good shape to the edges, very rich fruit cakes such as wedding cakes should be left in the tins to go cold.

1 Loosen the cake sides by running a small metal spatula around the inside of the tin between the cake and tin, or lining paper and tin.

2 To turn the cake out on a wire rack, put a wire rack on top of the cake tin, then turn the whole thing over so that the cake is upside down. Peel away the lining papers while the cake is warm. Turn the cake back the right way up. Leave the cake to go completely cold before icing and storing.

Storing cakes

Make sure cakes are completely cold before storing, otherwise condensation will form in the tin and this can cause the cakes to go mouldy. Plastic food containers will help to keep cakes moist, so are ideal for storing richer sponges, but an airtight cake tin is necessary to keep fatless sponge-type cakes dry.

Cakes with fresh cream fillings and decorations need to be kept in the refrigerator and ideally, eaten on the day they are filled with cream.

Fatless sponges such as Swiss rolls (jelly rolls) will keep for only 1–2 days. Sponges with added fat will store for 3–5 days and richer cakes, such as creamed sponges, will keep for up to 1 week. Light fruit cakes will store for 2 weeks in a tin, but rich fruit cakes will keep for up to 3 months after cutting.

If you don't have a large cake container, invert a large mixing bowl over the cake on a plate or flat surface and the cake will stay fresh.

FEEDING A FRUIT CAKE
Fruit cakes fed with alcohol have a mellow flavour.

Prick the surface with a cocktail stick (toothpick) and brush with a little alcohol such as rum, brandy or sweet sherry.

Storing a rich fruit cake

Rich fruit cakes, such as wedding cakes, will mature in flavour and improve in texture if kept for 3 months before being eaten, especially if you feed them with alcohol two or three times during that 3 months. Store undecorated fruit cakes in their baking papers.

1 Wrap the original wrappings of the rich fruit cake with clean baking parchment and seal with tape.

2 Wrap in a double layer of foil and seal tightly, then store in a cool dry place.

Freezing cakes

Most cakes will freeze well, undecorated. Cool each cake completely, then wrap in strong freezer film or foil to exclude as much air as possible. Label and freeze. To use, completely unwrap and thaw at room temperature on racks, allowing plenty of time for larger cakes.

Different methods of making cakes

There are six basic ways to make cakes. Each method gives the cake a different texture and consistency. To get perfect results, it's important to know how the different types of mixture should be prepared and what to look out for.

Classic creaming method

Light cakes are made by the creaming method, which means that the butter and sugar are first beaten or 'creamed' together. A little care is needed to achieve a perfectly creamed mixture.

1 Use a large bowl, and either an electric whisk or a wooden spoon to beat the fat and sugar together until pale and fluffy. As the sugar dissolves it blends with the fat, lightening it and making it very soft.

2 Now add the eggs one by one, beating after each addition, to form a slackened batter. Eggs for baking are always best used at room temperature to prevent the mixture from 'splitting' or curdling, which will happen with cold eggs.

3 Adding a teaspoon of flour with each beaten egg will help to keep the mixture light and smooth and prevent the mixture from separating. A badly mixed and curdled batter will hold less air and be heavy, and can cause a sunken cake.

All-in-one method

This one-stage method is quick and easy, and it's perfect for those new to baking, as it does not involve any complicated techniques. It is an ideal method for making light sponges. Butter or tub margarine at room temperature must be used.

1 All the ingredients are placed in a large bowl and quickly beaten together for just a few minutes until smooth. Do not over-beat, as this will make the mixture too wet.

Rubbing-in method

This method is used for easy fruit cakes and small buns such as rock buns. In this method, the fat is lightly worked into the flour between cold fingers, in the same way as for making pastry. The fat should ideally be cold.

1 Rub the fat into the flour with your fingertips until the mixture resembles fine crumbs. This can be done by hand or using a food processor. Shake the bowl to allow the larger lumps of fat to rise to the surface, then rub in the larger lumps. Repeat until an even crumb is achieved.

2 Stir in enough liquid to give a soft mixture that will drop easily from a spoon.

Melting method

Cakes with a deliciously moist and sticky texture, such as gingerbread, are made by the melting method. These cakes use a high proportion of sugar and syrup and may contain heavier grains such as ground nuts or oats. These cakes benefit from storing for at least a day before cutting, to improve their moisture and stickiness.

1 Over a gentle heat and using a large pan, warm together the fat, sugar and syrup, until the sugar granules have dissolved and the mixture is liquid. Stir occasionally, but keep watching so that the sugar does not burn on the base of the pan.

2 Allow the mixture to cool a little before beating into the flour, eggs, spices and remaining ingredients to make a batter. Bicarbonate of soda (baking soda) is often used as a raising agent in this method, to help raise a heavy batter. These cakes rise but the texture is heavier.

Whisking method

Light and feathery sponges are made by the whisking method. These are not easy cakes for beginners, and require a little skill and care. The only raising agent for this method is the air that has been trapped in the mixture during preparation. As the air in the mixture expands in the heat of the oven, the cake rises. Fatless sponges such as a Swiss roll (jelly roll) are made by whisking.

1 A classic sponge is made by whisking eggs and caster (superfine) sugar together over a pan of hot water until the batter is thick enough to leave a trail when the whisk is lifted away from the bowl. When the mixture is pale, thick and airy, remove the bowl from the heat and continue to whisk until cool and doubled in volume.

2 Add the flour by sifting some over the surface and gently folding it in, using a large metal spoon, until all the flour is evenly blended.

3 Be gentle with the mixture; it is essential not to knock out the air bubbles when folding in the flour.

Making fruit cakes

Rich fruit cake recipes usually begin with the creaming method, then soaked dried fruits and nuts are folded in with the flour.

1 Cream the butter and sugar in a large bowl, add the eggs, a little flour to stop the eggs curdling, and in this instance, treacle (molasses).

2 Add the flour and any spices, then add the dried fruits last, stirring well to incorporate all the ingredients.

Fillings and toppings

Cakes are made extra special by adding a filling or topping, and there are many different coverings to suit a variety of uses. Use sugarpaste icing on celebration cakes, or frostings on gateaux, or decorate with simple frosted flowers.

Buttercream icing

This rich icing makes a good cake covering and filling, or can be used to adhere sugarpaste icing to cakes.

MAKES 350G/12OZ/2 CUPS

75g/3oz/6 tbsp unsalted
   butter, softened
225g/8oz/2 cups icing
   (confectioners') sugar, sifted
5ml/1 tsp vanilla extract
10ml/2 tsp milk

1 Place the butter, icing sugar and vanilla extract in a bowl and whisk or beat with a wooden spoon.

2 Add the milk and beat until soft, smooth and fluffy. Store, chilled, for up to 2 days in a covered container.

BUTTERCREAM VARIATIONS
• Coffee: Blend 10ml/2 tsp coffee essence with the milk and omit the vanilla extract.
• Citrus: Omit the vanilla extract and milk, add 30ml/2 tbsp orange or lemon juice and the finely grated zest of half the fruit.

Ganache

This rich icing makes a perfect topping or filling for a rich chocolate cake for a special occasion.

MAKES 350G/12OZ/2 CUPS

250ml/8fl oz/1 cup double
   (heavy) cream
225g/8oz plain (semisweet)
   chocolate, broken into pieces

Gently heat both ingredients in a pan, stirring until melted. Pour into a bowl, leave to cool, then spread over the the cake.

Vanilla frosting

Use this smooth and creamy frosting as a filling and topping.

MAKES 150G/5OZ/SCANT 1 CUP

150g/5oz/generous 1 cup icing
   (confectioners') sugar
25ml/5 tsp vegetable oil
15ml/1 tbsp milk
a few drops of vanilla extract

Sift the icing sugar into a bowl and beat in the oil, milk and vanilla extract until smooth and creamy.

Chocolate fudge frosting

Rich and tasty, this glossy frosting can be poured over a cake or spread as a filling and topping.

MAKES 350G/12OZ/2 CUPS

115g/4oz plain (semisweet)
   chocolate, broken into pieces
50g/2oz/½ cup unsalted butter
1 egg, beaten
175g/6oz/1½ cups icing
   (confectioners') sugar, sifted
2.5ml/½ tsp vanilla extract

1 Melt the chocolate and butter in a bowl set over a pan of hot water.

2 Remove from the heat and whisk in the egg, icing sugar and vanilla. Whisk until smooth. Use at once or leave to cool and thicken.

Glacé icing

Because it is made to a pourable consistency, this icing is used to drizzle over sponge cakes.

MAKES 225G/8OZ/1½ CUPS

225g/8oz/2 cups icing
    (confectioners') sugar
a few drops of vanilla extract
30–45ml/2–3 tbsp hot water
food colouring (optional)

1 Sift the icing sugar into a bowl and add flavouring. Gradually add enough water to mix to a consistency of thick cream.

2 Beat with a wooden spoon until the icing is thick enough to coat the back of the spoon. Add colouring, if you like, and use at once, as the icing will begin to form a skin. Liquid food colourings are ideal.

GLACÉ ICING VARIATIONS
• Citrus: Replace the water with freshly squeezed, strained orange or lemon juice.
• Chocolate: Sift 10ml/2 tsp unsweetened cocoa powder into the icing (confectioners') sugar.
• Coffee: Dissolve 5ml/1 tsp coffee granules in 15ml/1 tbsp of hot water, then cool, or add 5ml/1 tsp liquid coffee extract.

Making a paper piping (pastry) bag

Paper piping bags are useful for piping with or without a nozzle.

1 Cut out a 38 × 25cm/15 × 10in rectangle of baking parchment. Fold it diagonally in half to form two triangles. Cut along the fold line.

2 The long edge of the triangle forms the top opening edge of the piping bag. Roll one short side of the triangle into the centre to make a sharp-pointed cone, and hold in place at the centre. Fold the other end around the cone.

3 Hold all the points together at the back of the cone, keeping the pointed end sharp. Fold the outer layer firmly inside the top edge to lock in place. Keep the layers of the bag together. If they start to separate the bag will lose its strength and the icing forced through the tip may rip the bag. Snip a tiny hole at the tip. Part-fill with icing. Fold over the top.

Crystallized decorations

Flowers, berries, petals and leaves can all be crystallized and make a perfect addition to special cakes.

1 Wash herb sprigs, leaves or edible berries, under gently running water, then pat dry with kitchen paper. Leave to dry.

2 Separate petals from rosebuds, and brush small flowers such as violets or primroses using a clean paintbrush, but do not wash them.

3 Beat 1 egg white with 15ml/1 tbsp cold water until frothy.

4 Liberally paint the herbs, leaves, berries or petals with the egg white on all sides.

5 Sprinkle the painted items lightly with caster (superfine) sugar while still damp, and shake off any excess. Leave to dry on waxed paper in a warm place. Attach them to the cake with royal icing.

Apricot glaze

Use apricot glaze for sticking almond paste to a cake or for adding a shiny finish to toppings.

MAKES 450G/1LB/2 CUPS

450g/1lb/1 cup apricot jam
5ml/1 tsp lemon juice

1 Put the ingredients in a pan with 45ml/3 tbsp water. Heat gently, stir until melted. Boil fast for 1 minute.

2 Press through a fine sieve (strainer).

3 Pour into a clean jar and store in the refrigerator for up to 3 months.

Almond paste

Marzipan protects and seals the cake and helps to fill any imperfections. It makes a flat area for icing.

MAKES 450G/1LB/2 CUPS

115g/4oz/1 cup sifted icing (confectioners') sugar
115g/4oz/generous ½ cup caster (superfine) sugar
225g/8oz/2 cups ground almonds
1 egg
5ml/1 tsp lemon juice
15ml/1 tbsp brandy

1 Stir the sugars and ground almonds together.

2 Whisk the egg, lemon juice and brandy together and mix into the dry ingredients.

3 Knead the almond paste until it is smooth. Pat into shape. Wrap the paste in clear film (plastic wrap) and store in the refrigerator for a maximum of 3 days.

To use almond paste

1 Knead the paste on a surface lightly dusted with icing (confectioners') sugar until soft. If the paste has been refrigerated, bring it back to room temperature first.

2 Place the cake upside down on a cake board so that the top is level.

3 Measure the circumference of the cake using a piece of string.

4 Brush the cake all over with apricot glaze. Fill in the gaps around the base with a rope of almond paste. Fill any holes or surface dips with small pieces of paste.

5 Roll out the almond paste to a square or circle large enough to cover the top of the cake. Make sure the paste is evenly rolled. Cut out the circle or square, then press it on top of the cake.

6 Roll a sausage of almond paste the length of the string, then use a rolling pin to roll it deep enough to cover the sides of the cake. Trim the edges. Roll it into a coil.

7 Roll the coiled strip around the side of the cake and press it on with the palms of your hands. Trim if necessary, and leave to dry out for at least 24 hours.

Royal icing

Use royal icing to cover Christmas or wedding cakes to form a snowy-white surface.

MAKES 500G/1¼LB

2 medium egg whites
500g/1¼lb/5 cups icing
(confectioners') sugar, sifted
10ml/2 tsp lemon juice

1 Put the egg whites into a clean, grease-free bowl and whisk lightly with a fork to break up the whites until foamy.

2 Sift in half the icing sugar with the lemon juice, and beat well with a wooden spoon for 10 minutes, or until smooth.

3 Gradually sift in the remaining icing sugar and beat again until thick, smooth and brilliant white. Alternatively, use a hand-held electric mixer set on a slow speed to make the mixing easier.

4 Keep the royal icing covered with a damp cloth until you are ready to use it, or store in the refrigerator in a tightly lidded plastic container until needed. If making royal icing ahead of time for use later, beat it again before use to expel any air bubbles that may have formed in the mixture.

5 To cover a cake, spread the icing over the top and sides of the cake using a palette knife or metal spatula, then smooth down over the sides or flick into points with a knife to make a snowy effect. Leave the icing to dry and become firm for 3 days.

COOK'S TIP
For a softer royal icing that will not set too hard, beat 5ml/1 tsp of glycerine into the mixture. Glycerine is sold bottled in liquid form in pharmacies and larger supermarkets.

Sugarpaste icing

This soft icing is also sold as roll-out icing, ready-to-roll icing or fondant icing. If you are covering a particularly large cake or a tiered cake, you will need to make the sugarpaste in batches. It is suitable for covering a Madeira cake, or a fruit cake that has first been covered in almond paste, *see page 24–25*.

MAKES 350G/12OZ/2 CUPS

1 egg white
15ml/1 tbsp liquid glucose
350g/12oz/3 cups icing
   (confectioners') sugar, sifted,
   plus extra for dusting
paste food colouring, if required

1 Place the egg white and liquid glucose in a large mixing bowl and stir together with a fork, breaking up the egg white.

2 Add the icing sugar gradually, mixing in with a flat-bladed knife until the mixture binds together, forming a ball.

COOK'S TIP
Always use special paste colours for sugarpaste. Don't use liquid food colour, as this will make the sugarpaste go soft and sticky and be difficult to roll out.

3 Turn the sugarpaste out on to a clean surface dusted with icing sugar and knead for 5 minutes, or until soft but firm enough to roll out. If it is too soft, knead in a little more icing sugar until the paste is pliable.

Colouring sugarpaste

1 Colour the paste gradually and knead well to colour evenly.

Working with sugarpaste

1 Roll out the sugarpaste to a circle or square large enough to cover the top and sides of the cake.

2 If you are covering almond paste, brush it with a little cool boiled water, Kirsch or vodka.

3 If you are covering a sponge cake, apply a layer of buttercream icing to the cake surface. The sugarpaste will adhere to the buttercream.

4 Roll the sugarpaste around the rolling pin to hold it. Place the sugarpaste over the cake and sides; avoid pleating the edges.

5 Smooth down over the top and sides, pushing out any air bubbles with your palms. Trim any excess icing away from the base using a metal spatula or sharp knife and smooth the join at the base. Leave to dry out for 24 hours. Work carefully to avoid marking the paste.

DECORATING TIP
Leave sugarpaste-covered cakes to dry out for 24 hours before adding decorations, as this provides a firmer finished surface to work on and one less likely to mark.

Adapting recipes for special diets

Although there are fewer recipes that are suitable to make for people with special diets, it's still possible to adapt some to make gluten-free cakes for people who have an intolerance. Healthier cakes with a lower fat content can be made for anyone who is limiting fats in their diet.

Gluten-free baking

Having an intolerance to gluten does not mean that you have to forego the pleasures of home baking. Gluten is the protein found in wheat that gives the elasticity to cakes and bread, making them light and springy. Gluten is also present in barley, rye and oats. Leaving out wheat flour means that gluten-free cakes will not have the same characteristics as cakes baked with ordinary flours. Gluten-free flours are available, and although these are a little more difficult to work with than regular flours, you will find some recipes can be adapted by following the manufacturer's instructions. A product that aids gluten-free baking is xanthan gum, which is sold in health-food shops. This gum replaces the elastic qualities of gluten lacking in gluten-free flours, and when used in baking will make the cake less crumbly.

Below Sunflower oil is an unsaturated fat. It is useful for making low-fat cakes.

Above clockwise from top left Gluten-free ingredients include ground almonds, cornmeal, xanthan gum and rice flour.

You will find that practice is needed to adapt your favourite recipes for gluten-free flours, but scones, soda breads and banana tea breads are all successful. Replacing wheat flour in a recipe with ground almonds, cornmeal, rice flour, soya flour or a mixture of these flours plus ground almonds can produce light and delicious results.

Lower-fat cakes

Some cakes and bakes are rich in fat and are calorie-laden. Most cakes are based on a mixture of butter, sugar, eggs and flour, with the butter forming a base to help bind and retain moisture in the mixture. It is possible to produce delicious cakes without fat. Meringues, angel cake and a classic fatless sponge, with a filling of fresh fruits instead of lashings of cream, will help cut down your fat intake considerably. You will also find recipes in this

Above Dates, prunes, figs, bananas and sunflower oil provide flavour and moisture to low-fat baking.

book that use oil instead of butter; unsaturated oils such as sunflower are generally healthier than solid fats, and baked goods made with them will appeal to all the family. Choosing recipes that contain less fat and a high percentage of healthy ingredients such as puréed prunes, dates, figs or mashed bananas will also help cut down on your intake of saturated fats. These cakes bake to a deliciously moist texture, usually keep a little longer than others and freeze well.

Low-sugar cakes

Baking for diabetics or those following a low-sugar diet can be a challenge. Diabetics do not need to avoid sugar altogether, but to moderate their intake. Choose recipes with a lower quantity of sugar in them in preference to high-sugar bakes. Sugar substitutes are mostly unsuitable for baking cakes.

Problem solving

If you accurately measure ingredients and follow the recipe steps carefully, your cakes should work out well each time, but if your cake does not turn out as expected, refer to the following problems and their solutions in turn to find out what might have happened.

Why do cakes stick to the tin (pan)?

• You will not be able to turn a cake out of a tin that was not greased sufficiently into all the corners or properly lined with paper.
• Poor-quality tins tend to produce bad results and can buckle in the heat, causing a misshapen cake.
• If the cake has been left in the tin for too long it may have dried to it.

Why does a cake sink?

• Too much raising agent such as baking powder or bicarbonate of soda (baking soda) may have been used in proportion to the amount of flour and other ingredients. It is important to weigh out and measure all the ingredients correctly.

• If the oven is too cool, the cake will be under-baked and sink.
• A mixture that is too wet. This can be caused by over-beating when using soft tub margarine, or by adding too much liquid.
• If the mixture was cooked in a tin that is too small, it will not cook through properly. The use of the correct size of tin is important.
• Opening or slamming the oven door during the baking time.
• If the cake is underbaked, particularly in the centre, and the batter there is still damp and heavy, the cake will sink.

What causes a close and heavy texture?

• Too little raising agent, or adding too much fat, egg or flour.
• A mixture that is too dry or too wet.
• If the cake is not whisked or beaten sufficiently to incorporate air, the texture will be coarse.
• Too much sugar in the batter.
• Baking in an oven that is too cool will also affect the texture.
• Fat and sugar not beaten enough before the other ingredients added.

What causes a cake with a dry texture?

• Cakes with a dry texture tend to be crumbly when cut and stale rapidly. This can be caused if the cake is baked too slowly or contains too much raising agent.
• The mixture was not rubbed in or beaten sufficiently.
• The cake was overbaked, making it dry.

Why do small fairy cakes spread?

• Small cakes spread out if the mixture is too wet or if there is too much mixture in each paper case; for best results half-fill the cases.
• Too much or too little raising agent may have been added.

What causes a dark, hard outer crust?

- Too hot an oven or over-baking in a fan-assisted oven at a high temperature. If you are using a fan-assisted oven you will usually need to turn the temperature down by 10 degrees, or follow your instruction booklet.
- Rich fruit cakes taking several hours to bake should be protected by a double lining inside the tin (pan) and by wrapping around the outside of the tin with a layer of brown paper or newspaper.

Why do cakes fail to rise?

- Insufficient raising agent or over-beating a mixture, which knocks out the air.
- If a mixture is too stiff and does not contain enough liquid or is baked in too cool an oven.
- If too large a cake tin was used.
- If the batter was left to stand for a while before baking it will not rise.

Why do large air bubbles and tunnels form in the centre of the cake?

- An uneven texture is caused by under-mixing when adding the flour or liquid.
- If the mixture is too dry it will tend to contain pockets of air instead of the air being distributed throughout the mixture.
- If the flour and raising agent are not sieved (sifted) into the mixture or properly incorporated.

What causes a crack or peak to appear in the top of a cake?

- If the tin is too small and it therefore contains too much mixture, the batter will rise up and the top will form a peak.
- Baking in an oven that is too hot, or baking the cake too near the top of the oven, where it is hottest.
- The mixture is too wet or too dry.
- Too little liquid in the batter.

Why does the fruit sink in a sponge cake?

- All vine fruits must be dry when added to the mixture. Glacé (candied) cherries must be washed of their syrup, dried and tossed in flour to prevent them sinking.
- If the mixture is too wet or if it contains too much raising agent.
- Using too cool an oven or opening the oven door too soon before the end of the baking time.

OTHER PROBLEMS
- **The cake sloped or was uneven** Check that the oven shelves are level. Centre the cake in the oven. Check the oven temperature with a thermometer to ensure it is correct. The batter was not mixed thoroughly.
- **The cake was lumpy** The ingredients were unevenly mixed.
- **The batter ran out of the pan into the oven base** If a loose-base tin or springform tin was used, ensure it was adequately lined. The tin was too small for the volume of batter. Check the oven shelves are level.
- **The cake went soggy after being stored** The cake was underbaked. It wasn't cold before it was stored or wrapped. It was stored in a warm place.

Classic cakes

Many cakes are 'classics' and every family has their favourite. This appealing collection includes all of the traditional recipes that have stood the test of time. You will find recipes here for Victoria Sponge, Madeira Cake and Frosted Walnut Layer Cake. There is a Simple Chocolate Cake, light-as-air sponges such as Angel Food Cake, and a delicate Lemon Drizzle Cake. Some of these bakes are super-quick to make, such as the Easy All-in-one Sponge. If you are a novice baker, try a simple recipe such as Carrot Cake with Cream Cheese Icing to impress your friends and family. You will find this chapter contains recipes that you will return to, and they are sure to become your own favourites for years to come.

Left: Cherry Cake and Lemon Roulade with Lemon-curd Cream.

Madeira cake

This fine-textured cake is a good choice for a birthday or celebration cake, as it is firm but light, which makes it the perfect base for decorating. It is ideal to serve with hot drinks, either as it is or split and sandwiched with buttercream. Store for up to one week in an airtight container.

SERVES 8–10

175g/6oz/¾ cup butter, softened,
  plus extra for greasing
175g/6oz/scant 1 cup caster
  (superfine) sugar
3 eggs
15ml/1 tbsp lemon juice
225g/8oz/2 cups plain
  (all-purpose) flour
7.5ml/1½ tsp baking powder

1 Preheat the oven to 160°C/325°F/ Gas 3. Grease and line an 18cm/7in round deep cake tin (pan) with baking parchment.

2 In a large bowl, beat the butter and sugar together until light and fluffy, then beat in the eggs one at a time, beating well after each addition. Stir in the lemon juice.

3 Sift in the flour and baking powder and stir to combine.

4 Spoon the mixture into the prepared tin and smooth the top level with the back of the spoon.

5 Bake in the centre of the oven for 1¼–1½ hours, until golden, or until a skewer inserted into the centre comes out clean.

6 Leave the cake to cool in the tin for 45 minutes, then turn out on to a wire rack to go cold. Remove the lining paper.

Energy 453kcal/1894kJ; Protein 6.1g; Carbohydrate 51.4g, of which sugars 30g; Fat 26.3g, of which saturates 15.5g; Cholesterol 155mg; Calcium 74mg; Fibre 0.9g; Sodium 208mg.

Easy all-in-one sponge

This strawberry and 'cream' cake is so quick and easy to make. You'll find this simple topping handy for other cakes too, as you can make it from store-cupboard ingredients. Store for up to three days in an airtight container. Freeze the cakes, undecorated, for up to two months.

SERVES 12

175g/6oz/1½ cups self-raising
  (self-rising) flour
5ml/1 tsp baking powder
175g/6oz/¾ cup soft tub
  margarine, plus extra for greasing
175g/6oz/scant 1 cup caster
  (superfine) sugar
3 eggs
15ml/1 tbsp milk
5ml/1 tsp vanilla extract

For the filling and topping
150g/5oz white chocolate chips
200g/7oz/scant 1 cup cream cheese
25g/1oz/¼ cup icing
  (confectioners') sugar
30ml/2 tbsp strawberry jam
12 strawberries

1 Preheat the oven to 180°C/350°F/ Gas 4. Grease and line two 20cm/8in round shallow cake tins (pans) with baking parchment.

2 Sift the flour and baking powder into a large bowl, then add all the remaining cake ingredients.

3 Beat until smooth, then divide between the tins and smooth level.

4 Bake for 20 minutes, or until the cakes spring back when pressed. Allow to stand for 5 minutes, then turn out on to a wire rack to go cold. Remove the lining papers.

5 To make the filling and topping, melt the chocolate chips in a heatproof bowl over a pan of gently simmering water. Remove from the heat and cool slightly, then beat in the cream cheese and icing sugar.

6 Spread the top of one sponge with jam. Slice 4 strawberries, then arrange them over the jam.

7 Spread one-third of the filling over the base of the other cake.

8 Put the cakes together. Spread the remaining topping over the cake top. Decorate with strawberries.

Energy 395kcal/1648kJ; Protein 4.7g; Carbohydrate 39.6g, of which sugars 28.5g; Fat 25.3g, of which saturates 15.2g; Cholesterol 94mg; Calcium 90mg; Fibre 0.5g; Sodium 173mg.

Fresh fruit Genoese sponge

Genoese is the original fatless sponge, which can be used for luxury gateaux and Swiss rolls. It has a soft and light texture, but because it is made without fat it should be eaten soon after making, as it does not store well. Decorate with cream and fresh fruit for an indulgent cake.

SERVES 8–10

butter, for greasing
4 eggs
115g/4oz/generous ½ cup caster (superfine) sugar
175g/6oz/1½ cups plain (all-purpose) flour, sifted

For the filling and topping
90ml/6 tbsp orange-flavoured liqueur such as Cointreau
600ml/1 pint/2½ cups double (heavy) cream
60ml/4 tbsp vanilla sugar
450g/1lb/4 cups fresh soft fruit, such as raspberries, strawberries, redcurrants and blueberries
65g/2½oz/½ cup shelled pistachio nuts, finely chopped
60ml/4 tbsp apricot jam, warmed and sieved (strained)

1 Preheat the oven to 180°C/350°F/ Gas 4. Grease and line a 21cm/ 8½in round deep cake tin (pan) with baking parchment.

2 Put the eggs and sugar in a large bowl and beat with an electric whisk for about 10 minutes, or until the mixture is thick and pale.

3 Sift the pre-sifted flour into the bowl with the egg and sugar mixture, then fold together gently.

4 Transfer the batter to the prepared tin. Bake in the centre of the oven for 30–35 minutes, or until a skewer inserted into the centre of the cake comes out clean.

5 Leave the cake in the tin for 5 minutes, then turn out on to a wire rack to go cold. Peel off the lining paper.

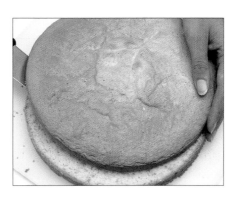

6 Cut the cake in half horizontally to make two layers. Put the bottom layer on to a serving plate.

7 Sprinkle the orange-flavoured liqueur, if using, over the cut side of each cake.

8 To make the filling and topping, put the double cream and vanilla sugar in a large bowl and beat together with an electric whisk until the mixture holds its shape.

9 Spread two-thirds of the cream over the bottom layer of the cake and top with half of the soft fruit.

10 Carefully put the second layer of the cake on top of the first layer and spread the remaining cream over the top.

11 Arrange the rest of the fresh fruit on the top of the cake and sprinkle with the chopped pistachio nuts.

12 Lightly glaze the top layer of fruit by brushing over the warmed apricot jam.

Energy 815kcal/3411kJ; Protein 8.5g; Carbohydrate 99.6g, of which sugars 85.9g; Fat 43g, of which saturates 21.8g; Cholesterol 158mg; Calcium 128mg; Fibre 2g; Sodium 132mg.

Victoria sponge

This light cake was named in honour of Queen Victoria of England. Often referred to as a Victoria sandwich, the mixture is based on equal quantities of fat, sugar and flour. It is usually sandwiched with a layer of jam. Store this cake for up to three days in an airtight container.

4 Sift the flour over the top in two batches and, using a metal spoon, fold in lightly using a figure-of-eight motion until the mixture is smooth.

5 Divide the batter between the prepared tins and smooth out to the edges so that the mixture is level. Bake for 20 minutes, or until golden and firm to the touch in the centre of the cake.

6 Leave the cakes to cool in the tins for a few minutes, then turn out on to a wire rack to go cold. Remove the lining paper.

SERVES 6–8

175g/6oz/¾ cup butter, softened, plus extra for greasing
3 large eggs
a few drops of vanilla extract
175g/6oz/scant 1 cup caster (superfine) sugar
175g/6oz/1½ cups self-raising (self-rising) flour
about 60ml/4 tbsp jam
icing (confectioners') sugar, for dusting

1 Preheat the oven to 180°C/350°F/ Gas 4. Grease and line two 20cm/8in round shallow cake tins (pans) with baking parchment.

2 In a small bowl, lightly beat the eggs with the vanilla extract.

3 In a large bowl, beat the butter with the sugar until the mixture is pale, light and fluffy, then beat in the eggs in small quantities, beating well after each addition.

7 Sandwich the cakes together with jam.

8 Sift a little icing sugar over the top before serving.

Energy 368kcal/1543kJ; Protein 4.6g; Carbohydrate 44.7g, of which sugars 28.5g; Fat 20.3g, of which saturates 12g; Cholesterol 118mg; Calcium 104mg; Fibre 0.7g; Sodium 241mg.

Pound cake

The original pound cake, enjoyed both in the US and Britain for many years, was made using 450g/1lb of each ingredient and having as many as eight eggs to raise it. This recipe is for a smaller variation and is served warm with a delicious, fresh fruit sauce. Keep for up to three days.

SERVES 6–8

175g/6oz/¾ cup butter, softened, plus extra for greasing
175g/6oz/¾ cup caster (superfine) sugar, plus extra for sprinkling
175g/6oz/1½ cups plain (all-purpose) flour
10ml/2 tsp baking powder
3 eggs
grated rind of 1 orange
15ml/1 tbsp orange juice

For the sauce
450g/1lb/4 cups fresh raspberries or strawberries
25g/1oz/2 tbsp caster (superfine) sugar
15ml/1 tbsp lemon juice

1 To make the sauce, reserve a few fruits for decoration. Process the remaining fruit until smooth in a food processor. Add the sugar and lemon juice, and process to combine. Strain and chill the sauce.

2 Preheat the oven to 180°C/350°F/ Gas 4. Grease a 20cm/8in round ring tin (pan). Sprinkle the base and sides lightly with sugar.

3 Sift the flour with the baking powder into a bowl.

4 In another bowl, beat the butter until creamy. Add the remaining sugar and beat until light and fluffy. Add the eggs, one at a time, beating well after each addition, then beat in the orange rind and juice.

5 Gently fold in the flour mixture in batches, then spoon the batter into the prepared tin and tap gently to release any air bubbles. Bake for 35–40 minutes, or until the top of the cake is golden and springs back when pressed with the fingers.

6 Allow the cake to cool in the tin for 10 minutes, then turn it out on to a wire rack and leave to cool for a further 30 minutes. Serve warm slices with a little of the fruit sauce. Decorate with the reserved fruit.

Energy 366kcal/1533kJ; Protein 5.4g; Carbohydrate 42.7g, of which sugars 26.1g; Fat 20.5g, of which saturates 12.1g; Cholesterol 118mg; Calcium 71mg; Fibre 2.1g; Sodium 163mg.

Cherry cake

Both dried and glacé cherries are used in this elegant cake, partnered with the delicate flavour of almonds and decorated with a drizzle of icing. It is a combination that is perfect for a summer tea party. Store in an airtight container for up to five days. Freeze, undecorated, for two months.

SERVES 10

175g/6oz/¾ cup unsalted butter, softened, plus extra for greasing
175g/6oz/scant 1 cup caster (superfine) sugar
3 eggs, beaten
150g/5oz/1¼ cups self-raising (self-rising) flour
50g/2oz/½ cup plain (all-purpose) flour
75g/3oz/¾ cup ground almonds
75g/3oz/scant ½ cup glacé (candied) cherries, washed, dried and halved, plus extra to decorate
25g/1oz dried cherries
a few drops of almond extract

For the decoration
115g/4oz/1 cup icing (confectioners') sugar, sifted
5ml/1 tsp lemon juice
50g/2oz/½ cup flaked (sliced) almonds, toasted
10 natural glacé (candied) cherries

1 Preheat the oven to 160°C/325°F/ Gas 3. Grease and line a 20cm/8in round deep cake tin (pan).

2 In a bowl, beat the butter with the sugar until light and fluffy, using an electric whisk, if possible. Add the eggs a little at a time, including 5ml/1 tsp of flour with each addition.

3 Sift in the flours, the ground almonds and cherries. Stir well.

4 Add the flour and cherry mixture to the butter and sugar and fold together with the almond extract until smooth. Spoon into the cake tin and smooth level.

5 Bake for 45–50 minutes, or until a skewer inserted into the centre comes out clean. Cool slightly, then turn on to a wire rack to go cold. Remove the lining paper.

6 In a bowl, mix the icing sugar with the lemon juice, and 10–15ml/ 2–3 tsp water, to make a soft icing. Drizzle half over the cake top. Sprinkle the almonds into the centre. Place the cherries around the edge. Drizzle over the remaining icing.

Energy 367kcal/1535kJ; Protein 5g; Carbohydrate 43.7g, of which sugars 26.6g; Fat 20.4g, of which saturates 12g; Cholesterol 118mg; Calcium 75mg; Fibre 0.9g; Sodium 309mg.

Chocolate-orange marble cake

Relive your memories of childhood and make this magical cake with its clever marbled pattern.
Two cake batters are swirled together to give the marbled effect, and, because one is flavoured
with orange and the other with chocolate, the overall taste is wonderful too.

SERVES 10

225g/8oz/1 cup butter, softened,
  plus extra for greasing
225g/8oz/1 generous cup caster
  (superfine) sugar
4 eggs, beaten
225g/8oz/2 cups self-raising
  (self-rising) flour
30ml/2 tbsp unsweetened
  cocoa powder
15ml/1 tbsp milk
grated rind from 1 large orange
15ml/1 tbsp orange juice

For the frosting
115g/4oz plain (semisweet) or milk
  chocolate, melted and cooled
115g/4oz/½ cup unsalted butter
225g/8oz/2 cups icing
  (confectioners') sugar, sifted

1 Preheat the oven to 180°C/350°F/
Gas 4. Grease and line a 20cm/8in
round deep cake tin (pan) with
baking parchment.

2 In a large bowl, beat the butter and
sugar together until pale and fluffy.

3 Beat in the eggs a little at a time.
Fold the flour into the mixture. Put
half of the batter into another bowl.

4 Sift the cocoa into one bowl of
batter and mix well with the milk.

5 Put the rind and orange juice into
the other bowl and mix well.

6 Spoon alternate tablespoonfuls of
each mixture into the cake tin. Swirl
a knife through the mixture once,
then smooth the top level.

7 Bake for 45 minutes, or until the
centre springs back when pressed.
Leave to cool. Remove the papers.

8 In another bowl, whisk the butter.
Beat in the icing sugar. Stir in the
chocolate. Spread over the cake.

COOK'S TIP
The cake keeps for up to 5 days
in a sealed container.

Energy 505kcal/2109kJ; Protein 6.5g; Carbohydrate 48.1g, of which sugars 36.6g; Fat 32.9g, of which saturates 18.8g; Cholesterol 119mg; Calcium 98mg; Fibre 1.5g; Sodium 322mg.

Lady Baltimore cake

This recipe was published in the 19th-century novel *Lady Baltimore* by Owen Wister. The cake usually contains the same basic ingredients: pecan nuts, figs and raisins in a fluffy white frosting. Make it for a special tea-time treat – it looks quite stunning. Store it for up to three days.

SERVES 10–12

250ml/8fl oz/1 cup vegetable oil, plus extra for greasing
275g/10oz/2½ cups plain (all-purpose) flour
12.5ml/2½tsp baking powder
4 eggs
350g/12oz/1¾ cups caster (superfine) sugar
grated rind of 1 large orange
250ml/8fl oz/1 cup fresh orange juice

For the frosting
2 egg whites
350g/12oz/1¾ cups caster (superfine) sugar
1.25ml/¼ tsp cream of tartar
5ml/1 tsp vanilla extract
50g/2oz/½ cup pecan nuts, finely chopped
85g/3oz/generous ½ cup raisins, chopped
3 ready-to-eat dried figs, finely chopped
18 pecan halves, to decorate

1 Preheat the oven to 180°C/350°F/ Gas 4. Grease and line two 23cm/ 9in round shallow cake tins (pans) with baking parchment.

2 In a bowl, sift together the flour and baking powder. Set aside.

3 Beat the eggs and sugar in another large bowl, using an electric whisk, until thick and pale. Beat in the orange rind and juice, then add the vegetable oil and mix well.

4 On a low speed, beat in the flour mixture in three batches.

5 Divide the cake batter between the tins. Bake for 30 minutes, or until a skewer inserted in to the centre comes out clean.

6 Leave to stand for 15 minutes, then run a knife around the inside of the tins, and transfer the cakes to a rack to go cold. Remove the lining.

7 To make the filling and topping, put the egg whites, sugar, 75ml/ 5 tbsp cold water and the cream of tartar in the top of a double boiler, or in a large heatproof bowl set over a pan of boiling water. Beat the mixture, using an electric whisk, until glossy and thick.

8 Remove the pan from the heat, add the vanilla extract and continue beating until thick.

9 Fold in the nuts, raisins and figs.

10 Spread a layer of the frosting on top of one cake. Sandwich with the second cake.

11 Spread the cake top and sides with the remainder of the frosting. Arrange the pecan halves on top.

Energy 529kcal/2229kJ; Protein 5.9g; Carbohydrate 90.2g, of which sugars 74.3g; Fat 18.6g, of which saturates 2.2g; Cholesterol 63mg; Calcium 107mg; Fibre 1.9g; Sodium 51mg.

Angel food cake

Similar to a whisked sponge cake, the texture of this American classic is springy but slightly sticky, and the colour is snowy white. The cream of tartar helps to aerate the egg whites, and the addition of sugar creates a light meringue mixture. This will keep refrigerated, for up to five days.

SERVES 20

65g/2½oz/9 tbsp plain
  (all-purpose) flour
15ml/1 tbsp cornflour (cornstarch)
225g/8oz/generous 1 cup caster
  (superfine) sugar
10 egg whites
5ml/1 tsp cream of tartar
7.5ml/1½ tsp vanilla extract

For the frosting
2 egg whites
115g/4oz/generous ½ cup caster
  (superfine) sugar
10ml/2 tsp golden (light corn)
  syrup
2.5ml/½ tsp vanilla extract
rind of 1 orange, to decorate

1 Preheat the oven to 180°C/350°F/ Gas 4.

2 In a large bowl, sift together the flour, cornflour and 50g/2oz/¼ cup of the sugar three times, so that the texture is very, very light.

3 Put the egg whites and the cream of tartar into a clean, grease-free bowl and whisk until they form stiff peaks.

4 Gradually whisk in the remaining sugar, 15ml/1 tbsp at a time, until the mixture becomes thick and glossy.

5 Using a metal spoon, gently fold the sifted flour and the vanilla extract into the whisked egg whites until combined. Transfer the mixture to a 25cm/10in non-stick ring mould and smooth out the batter so that it is level.

6 Bake for 35–40 minutes, or until risen and golden. Remove from the oven, invert the cake in its mould on to a wire rack. Leave to go cold.

7 To make the frosting, put the egg whites into a clean, grease-free bowl. Whisk until stiff and dry, then set aside.

8 Heat the sugar and 60ml/4 tbsp water in a small pan, stirring constantly until the sugar dissolves.

9 Increase the heat and boil until the temperature reaches 115°C/240°F on a sugar thermometer. As soon as this temperature is reached, remove the pan from the heat.

10 Pour the syrup into the egg whites, whisking constantly, until the mixture is thick and glossy.

11 Beat in the golden syrup and vanilla, beating for 5 minutes.

12 Lift the mould off the cake and put the cake on a serving plate.

13 Quickly spread the frosting over the cake. Sprinkle with orange rind.

Energy 117kcal/500kJ; Protein 3.1g; Carbohydrate 27.7g, of which sugars 21.4g; Fat 0.1g, of which saturates 0g; Cholesterol 0mg; Calcium 24mg; Fibre 0.3g; Sodium 49mg.

Boston cream pie

Created by chef M. Sanzian at the Parker House Hotel in Boston, in the 1850s, this famous 'pie' is actually a cake. It is unusual, because sandwiched between the two cake layers is a rich custard. With its chocolate glaze it is really very appealing. Keep, refrigerated, for up to three days.

SERVES 8

butter, for greasing
225g/8oz/2 cups plain
  (all-purpose) four
15ml/1 tbsp baking powder
pinch of salt
115g/4oz/½ cup butter, softened,
  plus extra for greasing
200g/7oz/1 cup caster
  (superfine) sugar
2 eggs
5ml/1 tsp vanilla extract
6fl oz/175ml/¾ cup milk

For the filling
8fl oz/250ml/1 cup milk
3 egg yolks
90g/3½oz/½ cup caster
  (superfine) sugar
25g/1oz/¼ cup plain
  (all-purpose) flour
15ml/1 tbsp butter
5ml/1 tsp vanilla extract

For the chocolate glaze
25g/1oz dark (bittersweet)
  chocolate
15g/½oz/1 tbsp butter
50g/2oz/½ cup icing
  (confectioners') sugar, plus extra
  for dusting
2.5ml/½ tsp vanilla extract
15ml/1 tbsp hot water

1 Preheat the oven to 190°C/375°F/ Gas 5. Grease and line two 20cm/ 8in round shallow cake tins (pans) with baking parchment.

2 Sift the flour with the baking powder and salt into a large bowl.

3 In a large bowl, beat the butter and sugar together until light and fluffy. Beat in the eggs one at a time, beating well after each addition. Stir in the vanilla extract.

4 Add the milk and the dry ingredients, alternating the batches and mixing only enough to blend.

5 Divide the cake batter between the prepared tins and spread it out evenly.

6 Bake for 25 minutes, or until a skewer inserted into the centre comes out clean. Allow to stand in the tins for 5 minutes before turning out on to a wire rack to cool completely. Remove the lining.

7 To make the filling, heat the milk to boiling point in a small pan, and remove from the heat.

8 In a heatproof bowl, beat the egg yolks until smooth. Gradually add the sugar and continue beating until pale yellow, then beat in the flour.

9 While beating, pour the hot milk into the egg yolk mixture.

10 When all the milk has been added, put the bowl over a pan of boiling water. Heat, stirring constantly, until thickened. Cook for 2 minutes more, then remove from the heat.

11 Stir in the butter and vanilla extract. Leave to cool.

12 Slice off the domed top of each cake to create a flat surface, if necessary. Put one cake on a serving plate and spread on the filling in a thick layer. Set the other cake on top, cut side down. Smooth the edge of the filling layer so that it is flush with the sides of the cake layers.

13 To make the chocolate glaze, melt the chocolate and butter in a heatproof bowl set over a pan of gently simmering water. Stir well.

14 When smooth, remove from the heat and beat in the icing sugar using a wooden spoon. Add the vanilla extract, then beat in a little hot water to give a spreadable consistency. Spread evenly over the top of the cake. When it is set, dust the top with icing sugar.

Energy 499kcal/2100kJ; Protein 6g; Carbohydrate 77.1g, of which sugars 53.1g; Fat 20.3g, of which saturates 12.1g; Cholesterol 146mg; Calcium 112mg; Fibre 1g; Sodium 297mg.

Frosted walnut layer cake

Walnuts go very well in rich cakes, especially when combined with a sweet filling. This moist and nutty cake is layered with vanilla buttercream and then topped with swirls of light and fluffy frosting. It is ideal for a special party. Keep the cake for five days in an airtight container.

SERVES 12

225g/8oz/1 cup butter, softened,
  plus extra for greasing
225g/8oz/2 cups self-raising
  (self-rising) flour
5ml/1 tsp baking powder
225g/8oz/1 cup soft light
  brown sugar
75g/3oz/¾ cup walnuts,
  finely chopped
4 eggs
15ml/1 tbsp treacle (molasses)

For the buttercream
75g/3oz/6 tbsp unsalted butter
5ml/1 tsp vanilla extract
175g/6oz/1½ cups icing
  (confectioners') sugar

For the meringue frosting
2 large (US extra large) egg whites
350g/12oz/1¾ cups golden caster
  (superfine) sugar
pinch of salt
pinch of cream of tartar
15ml/1 tbsp warm water
whole walnut halves, to decorate

1 Preheat the oven to 160°C/325°F/ Gas 3. Grease and line two 20cm/8in round shallow cake tins (pans) with baking parchment.

2 Sift the flour and baking powder into a large bowl, then add all the remaining ingredients.

3 Beat together for 2 minutes, or until smooth, then divide between the tins and spread level.

4 Bake for 25 minutes, or until golden and springy to the touch in the centre.

5 Allow to stand for 5 minutes, then turn out on to a wire rack to go cold. Remove the lining papers. Cut each cake in half horizontally using a long-bladed sharp knife.

6 To make the buttercream, in a large bowl, beat the butter, vanilla extract and icing sugar together until light and fluffy.

7 Spread a third thinly over one sponge half and place a sponge layer on top, then continue layering the sponges with the buttercream. Put the cake on to a serving plate.

8 To make the frosting, put the egg whites in a large heatproof bowl and add the caster sugar, salt, cream of tartar and water. Put the bowl over a pan of hot water and whisk with an electric mixer for 7 minutes, or until the mixture is thick and stands in peaks.

9 Immediately, use a metal spatula to swirl the frosting over the top and sides of the cake.

10 Arrange the walnut halves on top and leave to set for 10 minutes before serving.

Energy 563kcal/2349kJ; Protein 8.5g; Carbohydrate 50.6g, of which sugars 39.2g; Fat 35.3g, of which saturates 10.1g; Cholesterol 108mg; Calcium 114mg; Fibre 1.5g; Sodium 177mg.

Simple chocolate cake

Make this easy, everyday chocolate cake and fill it with chocolate buttercream for a sweet afternoon treat that will be popular with all the family. Use a good quality chocolate with more than 70 per cent cocoa solids for the best flavour. Store this cake for up to three days.

SERVES 6–8

150g/5oz/10 tbsp unsalted butter, softened, plus extra for greasing
115g/4oz plain (semisweet) chocolate, broken into pieces
45ml/3 tbsp milk
150g/5oz/generous ½ cup light muscovado (brown) sugar
3 eggs
200g/7oz/1¾ cups self-raising (self-rising) flour
15ml/1 tbsp unsweetened cocoa powder

For the buttercream

75g/3oz/6 tbsp unsalted butter, softened
175g/6oz/1½ cups icing (confectioners') sugar, plus extra for dusting
15ml/1 tbsp unsweetened cocoa powder, plus extra for dusting
2.5ml/½ tsp vanilla extract

1 Preheat the oven to 180°C/350°F/Gas 4. Grease and line two 18cm/7in round shallow cake tins (pans).

2 Melt the chocolate with the milk in a heatproof bowl set over a pan of simmering water. Cool.

3 In a bowl, beat the butter with the sugar until fluffy, then beat in the eggs. Stir in the chocolate mixture.

4 Sift the flour and cocoa over the mixture and fold in until evenly mixed. Spoon into the tins and smooth level. Bake for 35–40 minutes, or until risen and firm. Turn out on to wire racks to cool. Remove the lining papers.

5 To make the buttercream, put all the ingredients into a large bowl. Beat well to a smooth, spreadable consistency. Sandwich the cake layers together with the buttercream. Dust with cocoa and icing sugar.

Energy 427kcal/1776kJ; Protein 6.1g; Carbohydrate 29.2g, of which sugars 9.8g; Fat 32.6g, of which saturates 19.6g; Cholesterol 139mg; Calcium 65mg; Fibre 1.4g; Sodium 238mg.

Mississippi mud cake

This rich chocolate cake is a variation of Mississippi mud pie, a gooey dessert baked in a pie shell. The cake tastes good served, as you would serve the pie, with a scoop of vanilla ice cream or a dollop of whipped cream – or even both. This cake will keep refrigerated for two days.

SERVES 8–10

225g/8oz/1 cup butter, plus extra
    for greasing
unsweetened cocoa powder,
    for dusting
150g/5oz plain (semisweet)
    chocolate, broken into pieces
300ml/½ pint/1¼ cups strong,
    brewed coffee
50ml/2fl oz/¼ cup bourbon
400g/14oz/2 cups caster
    (superfine) sugar
225g/8oz/2 cups plain
    (all-purpose) flour
5ml/1 tsp baking powder
2 eggs
7.5ml/1½ tsp vanilla extract

1 Preheat the oven to 140°C/275°F/ Gas 1. Grease a 25cm/10in round deep cake tin (pan), then dust it lightly with cocoa powder.

2 Put the chocolate in a heatproof bowl with the coffee, bourbon and butter. Set the bowl over a pan of gently simmering water. Stir the mixture with a wooden spoon until melted and smooth. Remove the bowl from the heat and set aside to cool slightly.

3 Using an electric whisk on low speed, gradually beat the sugar into the chocolate. Continue beating until the sugar dissolves.

4 Increase the speed to medium and add the flour and baking powder. Mix well, then beat in the eggs and vanilla extract.

5 Pour the batter into the tin. Bake for 1 hour 20 minutes, or until a skewer inserted into the centre comes out clean. Leave to cool in the tin for 15 minutes, then turn out on to a wire rack to go cold.

6 Place on a serving plate and dust the cake with cocoa powder.

Energy 534kcal/2227kJ; Protein 6.3g; Carbohydrate 49.5g, of which sugars 38.5g; Fat 35.2g, of which saturates 19.6g; Cholesterol 87mg; Calcium 110mg; Fibre 2.1g; Sodium 142mg.

Lemon roulade with lemon-curd cream

This feather-light roulade is flavoured with almonds and filled with a rich lemon-curd cream.
It makes a marvellous dessert or a tea-time treat. Use best-quality or home-made lemon curd for
that perfect touch. Eat this cake fresh for the best taste. It will store chilled for 1–2 days.

SERVES 8

butter, for greasing
4 eggs, separated
115g/4oz/generous ½ cup caster
   (superfine) sugar
finely grated rind of 2 lemons,
   plus extra to decorate
5ml/1 tsp vanilla extract
40g/1½oz/⅓ cup plain
   (all-purpose) flour
25g/1oz/¼ cup ground almonds

For the lemon-curd cream
300ml/½ pint/1¼ cups double
   (heavy) cream
60ml/4 tbsp lemon curd
45ml/3 tbsp icing (confectioners')
   sugar, for dusting

1 Preheat the oven to 190°C/375°F/
Gas 5. Grease and line a 33 × 23cm/
13 × 9in Swiss roll tin (jelly roll
pan) with baking parchment.

2 In a large bowl, beat the egg yolks
with half the sugar until foamy. Beat
in the lemon rind and vanilla extract.

3 Sift the flour over the egg mixture
and lightly fold in with the ground
almonds, using a metal spoon.

4 Put the egg whites into a clean,
grease-free bowl and whisk until
they form stiff, glossy peaks.

5 Gradually whisk in the remaining
sugar to form a stiff meringue.

6 Stir half the meringue mixture into
the egg yolk mixture to slacken it.
When combined, fold in the
remainder of the meringue mixture.

7 Pour the batter into the prepared
tin and smooth level.

8 Bake for 10 minutes, or until
risen and spongy to the touch.

9 Put the tin on a wire rack and
cover loosely with a sheet of baking
parchment and a damp dish towel.
Leave to cool.

10 To make the lemon curd-cream,
whip the cream until it holds its
shape, then fold in the lemon cream.

11 Sift the icing sugar over a piece of
baking parchment. Turn the sponge
out on to it. Peel off the lining paper
and spread over the filling.

12 Using the paper, roll up the
sponge from one long side. Sprinkle
with lemon rind.

Energy 337kcal/1401kJ; Protein 5g; Carbohydrate 24.5g, of which sugars 18.9g; Fat 25.1g, of which saturates 13.6g; Cholesterol 148mg; Calcium 55mg; Fibre 0.4g; Sodium 50mg.

Lemon drizzle cake

Wonderfully moist and lemony, this cake is a favourite at coffee mornings and for afternoon tea. A lemon and sugar syrup is poured over the cooked cake and allowed to soak through, so that the whole cake is sweet and tangy. It will store in an airtight container for up to five days.

SERVES 6–8

225g/8oz/1 cup unsalted butter,
    softened, plus extra for greasing
finely grated rind of 2 lemons
175g/6oz/scant 1 cup caster
    (superfine) sugar, plus 5ml/1 tsp
4 eggs
225g/8oz/2 cups self-raising
    (self-rising) flour
5ml/1 tsp baking powder
shredded rind of 1 lemon,
    to decorate

For the syrup
juice of 1 lemon
150g/5oz/¾ cup caster
    (superfine) sugar

1 Preheat the oven to 160°C/325°F/Gas 3. Grease and line the base and sides of an 18–20cm/7–8in round deep cake tin (pan) with baking parchment.

2 Mix the lemon rind and sugar together in a bowl.

3 In a large bowl, beat the butter with the lemon and sugar mixture until light and fluffy, then beat in the eggs one at a time.

4 Sift the flour and baking powder into the mixture in three batches and beat well.

5 Turn the batter into the prepared tin and smooth the top level. Bake for 1½ hours, or until golden brown and springy to the touch.

6 To make the syrup, slowly heat the juice with the sugar until dissolved.

7 Prick the cake top with a skewer and pour over the syrup. Sprinkle over the shredded lemon rind and 5ml/1 tsp sugar, then leave to cool. Remove the lining paper.

Energy 659kcal/2765kJ; Protein 8g; Carbohydrate 84.1g, of which sugars 56.2g; Fat 34.8g, of which saturates 21.4g; Cholesterol 213mg; Calcium 184mg; Fibre 1.2g; Sodium 466mg.

Almond and raspberry-filled roll

This light and airy whisked sponge cake is rolled up with a gorgeous filling of fresh raspberries and cream, making it a perfect treat with tea in the garden in summer. It is also excellent filled with other soft fruits, such as small or sliced strawberries, or blackcurrants. Eat fresh.

SERVES 8

butter, for greasing
4 eggs
115g/4oz/generous ½ cup caster
   (superfine) sugar, plus extra
   for dusting
150g/5oz/1¼ cups plain
   (all-purpose) flour, sifted
25g/1oz/¼ cup ground almonds

For the filling
250ml/8fl oz/1 cup double
   (heavy) cream
275g/10oz/1⅔ cups fresh
   raspberries
toasted flaked (sliced) almonds,
   to decorate

1 Preheat the oven to 200°C/400°F/ Gas 6. Grease and line a 33 × 23cm/ 13 × 9in Swiss roll tin (jelly roll pan) with baking parchment.

2 Put the eggs and sugar in a large bowl and beat with an electric whisk for about 10 minutes, or until the mixture is thick and pale.

3 Sift the flour over the mixture and gently fold in with the ground almonds, using a metal spoon.

4 Spoon the batter into the tin and smooth level. Bake for 10–12 minutes, or until the sponge is well risen and springy to the touch.

5 Dust a sheet of baking parchment liberally with caster sugar. Turn out the cake on to the paper, and leave to cool with the tin still in place.

6 Lift the tin off the cooled cake and carefully peel away the lining paper.

7 To make the filling, whip the cream until it holds its shape. Fold in 250g/8oz/1¼ cups of the raspberries, and spread over the cooled cake, leaving a border.

8 Carefully roll up the cake from a narrow end, using the paper to lift the sponge.

9 Dust with caster sugar. Serve decorated with the remaining raspberries and the toasted flaked almonds.

Energy 271kcal/1127kJ; Protein 4.7g; Carbohydrate 16.7g, of which sugars 11.9g; Fat 21.1g, of which saturates 11.2g; Cholesterol 114mg; Calcium 56mg; Fibre 1.2g; Sodium 35mg.

Old-fashioned treacle cake

Just a little treacle gives this cake a rich colour and a deep flavour. Mixed fruit and warm spices make it a traditional tea-time cake. The cake is made using what is known as the rubbing-in method, where the fat is rubbed into the flour rather than beaten with the sugar.

SERVES 8–10

75g/3oz/6 tbsp butter, diced, plus
  extra for greasing
250g/9oz/2¼ cups self-raising
  (self-rising) flour
2.5ml/½ tsp mixed (apple pie)
  spice
25g/1oz/2 tbsp caster (superfine)
  sugar
150g/5oz/scant 1 cup mixed
  dried fruit
1 egg
15ml/1 tbsp treacle (molasses)
about 100ml/3½fl oz/
  scant ½ cup milk

1 Preheat the oven to 180°C/350°F/ Gas 4. Grease and line a 20–23cm/ 8–9in round deep tin (pan).

2 Sift the flour and spice into a large bowl.

3 Add the butter and rub in until the mixture resembles fine breadcrumbs. Stir in the sugar and mixed dried fruit.

4 Beat the egg in a jug (pitcher), then stir in the treacle using a small whisk, followed by the milk.

5 Stir the liquid into the flour and fruit mixture to make a fairly stiff but moist consistency, adding a little extra milk, if necessary.

6 Spoon the cake batter into the prepared tin and smooth the top level. Bake for 1 hour, or until the cake is firm to the touch and a skewer inserted into the centre comes out clean.

7 Leave to cool in the tin for 5 minutes, then turn out on to a wire rack to go cold. Remove the lining paper.

> **COOK'S TIP**
> Keep for up to 5 days in an airtight container, or wrap tightly in foil.

Energy 208kcal/880kJ; Protein 3.7g; Carbohydrate 34g, of which sugars 15.2g; Fat 7.2g, of which saturates 4.2g; Cholesterol 35.6mg; Calcium 72mg; Fibre 1.1g; Sodium 67mg.

Lemon-and-lime cake

Here's a quick all-in-one moist citrus cake that has a lime syrup poured over the baked lemon sponge. It's a perfect recipe for busy cooks, and the tangy topping transforms it without the need for icing. Keep this cake for up to three days in an airtight container.

SERVES 8

225g/8oz/1 cup butter, softened,
   plus extra for greasing
225g/8oz/2 cups self-raising
   (self-rising) flour
5ml/1 tsp baking powder
225g/8oz/generous 1 cup caster
   (superfine) sugar
4 eggs, beaten
grated rind of 2 lemons
30ml/2 tbsp lemon juice

For the topping
finely pared rind of 1 lime
juice of 2 limes
150g/5oz/¾ cup caster
   (superfine) sugar

1 Preheat the oven to 160°C/325°F/ Gas 3. Grease and line a 20cm/8in round deep cake tin (pan) with baking parchment.

2 Sift the flour and baking powder into a large bowl.

3 Add the sugar, butter and eggs, then beat together for 2 minutes until the mixture is smooth and fluffy. Use an electric mixer for speed, if you like.

4 Beat in the lemon rind and juice. Turn the mixture into the prepared tin, smooth the top and make a shallow indentation in the centre.

5 Bake for 1¼–1½ hours, or until the cake is golden on top, and a skewer inserted into the centre comes out clean.

6 Meanwhile, make the topping by mixing all the ingredients together in a bowl.

7 As soon as the cake is baked, pour the topping over the surface. Leave to stand on a wire rack and allow the cake to cool in the tin. Remove the lining paper when cold.

Energy 527kcal/2209kJ; Protein 6.2g; Carbohydrate 71g, of which sugars 49.6g; Fat 26.3g, of which saturates 15.5g; Cholesterol 155mg; Calcium 84mg; Fibre 0.9g; Sodium 209mg.

Carrot cake with cream cheese icing

As well as keeping this well-known cake moist, grated carrot also adds its own sweetness. Here, this cake is topped with a zesty orange and cream cheese icing, which goes perfectly with the nutty flavour of the cake. This cake will keep, refrigerated, for up to three days.

SERVES 10

120ml/4fl oz/½ cup sunflower oil,
  plus extra for greasing
90g/3½oz/scant 1 cup wholemeal
  (whole-wheat) flour
150g/5oz/1¼ cups plain
  (all-purpose) flour
10ml/2 tsp baking powder
5ml/1 tsp bicarbonate of soda
  (baking soda)
5ml/1 tsp ground cinnamon
2.5ml/½ tsp ground allspice
250g/9oz/1¼ cups soft light
  brown sugar
3 carrots, peeled and
  coarsely grated
115g/4oz/1 cup chopped walnuts
3 large eggs
juice of 1 orange
shreds of pared orange rind,
  to decorate

For the icing
50g/2oz/¼ cup butter, softened
200g/7oz/scant 1 cup cream
  cheese, softened
grated rind of 1 orange
200g/7oz/1¾ cups icing
  (confectioners') sugar
5ml/1 tsp vanilla extract

1 Preheat the oven to 180°C/350°F/ Gas 4. Grease and line a 23cm/9in round deep cake tin (pan) with baking parchment.

2 Sift the flours, baking powder, bicarbonate of soda, cinnamon and allspice into a bowl, then add the bran from the sieve (strainer).

3 Add the brown sugar, carrots and walnuts. Make a well in the centre.

4 In another bowl, beat together the eggs and orange juice. Add the egg mixture with the remaining oil to the dry ingredients. Mix well.

5 Spoon the batter into the prepared tin and level the top. Bake for about 1 hour, or until risen and springy to the touch.

6 Leave the cake to set in the tin on a wire rack for 10 minutes, then slide a knife between the cake and the tin to loosen it. Turn the cake out on to a rack and remove the lining paper. Leave to go cold, then place on a serving plate.

7 To make the icing, beat the butter, cream cheese and grated orange rind in a large bowl.

8 Sift the icing sugar, then gradually add to the bowl with the vanilla extract, beating well after each addition, until the mixture is creamy.

9 Spread the icing on top of the cake. Sprinkle the shreds of orange rind over the top of the iced cake to decorate.

Energy 397kcal/1664kJ; Protein 7.6g; Carbohydrate 49.2g, of which sugars 29.5g; Fat 20.3g, of which saturates 8.5g; Cholesterol 88mg; Calcium 75mg; Fibre 1.8g; Sodium 99mg.

Spice, nut and seed cakes

The simplest of bakes can be transformed by the addition of spices, as the volatile oils in the spices give their characteristic flavour and aroma. You may be familiar with ground cinnamon, allspice and ginger as the basic spices used in baking, but it is also fun to experiment with new flavours, so – a taste of the exotic in Cardamom Cake. Baking with seeds emphasizes their aromatic qualities, as found in Caraway Seed Cake, with its warm hues, a hint of lemon and delicious buttery flavour. Ginger adds heat and piquancy to baking. Its rich, sweet flavour blends beautifully in Pineapple and Ginger Upside-down Cake. It is always worth keeping a few oranges and lemons in your kitchen, as well as a lime, to add extra zest to your baking. Citrus fans will find plenty of zest packed into Date and Walnut Spice Cake, as well as tangy Rich Lemon Poppy Seed Cake.

Left: Pear and Cardamom Spice Cake and Lavender Cake.

Cardamom cake

Warm-flavoured cardamom is a favourite spice among all the Scandinavian countries and it is used in a variety of cakes, buns and other dishes. Here is a traditional tea- or coffee-time treat that tastes good without being too rich. Keep this for up to five days in an airtight container.

SERVES 10

250g/9oz/generous 1 cup butter,
  softened, plus extra for greasing
375g/13oz/3¼ cups plain
  (all-purpose) flour
45ml/3 tbsp baking powder
10 cardamom pods, seeds removed
  and finely crushed
250g/9oz/1¼ cups caster
  (superfine) sugar
3 large (US extra large) eggs,
  lightly beaten
150ml/¼ pint/⅔ cup milk
45ml/3 tbsp raisins
45ml/3 tbsp candied peel
15ml/1 tbsp flaked
  (sliced) almonds

1 Preheat the oven to 190°C/
375°F/Gas 5. Grease and line a
1kg/2¼lb loaf tin (pan) with
baking parchment.

2 Sift the flour, baking powder and
crushed cardamom seeds together.

3 In a large bowl, cream together the
butter and sugar until light and
fluffy. Beat in the eggs one at a time,
adding a teaspoon of the flour with
each egg. Fold in the remaining flour.

4 Add the milk, a little at a time,
folding in well after each addition.

5 Add the raisins, candied peel and
almonds, and fold in well. Turn the
mixture into the tin and smooth
the top level.

6 Bake for 50 minutes, or until risen
and firm to the touch. Turn out and
cool on a wire rack. Remove the
lining paper.

Energy 389kcal/1619kJ; Protein 4.6g; Carbohydrate 34.9g, of which sugars 17.7g; Fat 26.6g, of which saturates 14.8g; Cholesterol 97mg; Calcium 61mg; Fibre 2g; Sodium 201mg.

Caraway seed cake

Just a few caraway seeds give this cake a delicately warm and spicy flavour that blends well with the tang of the citrus peel. It's a simple and traditional tea-time cake, ideal with a cup of tea on a chilly afternoon. This cake will keep for up to two days in an airtight container.

SERVES 8

175g/6oz/¾ cup butter, softened,
  plus extra for greasing
175g/6oz/scant 1 cup caster
  (superfine) sugar
3 eggs
225g/8oz/2 cups plain
  (all-purpose) flour
5ml/1 tsp baking powder
10ml/2 tsp caraway seeds
50g/2oz/⅓ cup finely chopped
  mixed (candied) peel
milk

1 Preheat the oven to 180°C/ 350°F/Gas 4. Grease and line a 20cm/8in round deep cake tin (pan) with baking parchment.

2 In a bowl, beat the butter and sugar until fluffy, then beat in the eggs one at a time. Sift the flour with the baking powder into the bowl. Add the caraway seeds. Beat well.

3 Using a metal spoon, fold in the remaining ingredients.

4 Spoon the batter into the prepared tin and smooth the top level. Bake for 1–1¼ hours, or until a skewer comes out clean when inserted.

5 Cool for 15 minutes in the tin, then turn out on to a wire rack to go cold. Remove the lining paper.

Energy 281kcal/1181kJ; Protein 4.6g; Carbohydrate 36.9g, of which sugars 15.5g; Fat 13.8g, of which saturates 8g; Cholesterol 87mg; Calcium 58mg; Fibre 0.8g; Sodium 109mg.

Lavender cake

The delicate flavour and fragrance of lavender makes a delightful addition to cooking and is most suitable for sweet baking. Make this scented moist cake for tea on a summer's day using fresh lavender, or dried culinary lavender. This cake will keep for up to three days in an airtight container.

2 In a large bowl, cream the butter and sugar together until light and fluffy. Add the eggs one at a time, beating thoroughly between each addition, until a skewer comes out clean when inserted.

3 Sift in the flour, then fold in with the lavender, vanilla and milk.

4 Spoon the mixture into the tin and smooth the top level. Bake for 1 hour, until golden.

5 Leave to cool for 5 minutes before turning out on to a wire rack to go cold.

SERVES 8

175g/6oz/¾ cup unsalted butter, softened, plus extra for greasing
175g/6oz/scant 1 cup caster (superfine) sugar
3 eggs
175g/6oz/1½ cups self-raising (self-rising) flour
15ml/1 tbsp fresh lavender florets or dried culinary lavender, roughly chopped (see Tip)
2.5ml/½ tsp vanilla extract
30ml/2 tbsp milk

For the topping
50g/2oz/½ cup icing (confectioners') sugar, sifted
fresh lavender florets, to decorate

1 Preheat the oven to 180°C/350°F/Gas 4. Grease and flour a 20cm/8in round deep cake tin (pan).

COOK'S TIP
Dried lavender is stronger in flavour than fresh florets, so use half the amount.

6 To make the topping, mix the icing sugar with a few drops of water until smooth. Pour over the cake. Decorate with lavender florets.

Energy 375kcal/1572kJ; Protein 4.7g; Carbohydrate 46.2g, of which sugars 30g; Fat 20.4g, of which saturates 12.1g; Cholesterol 118mg; Calcium 111mg; Fibre 0.7g; Sodium 241mg.

Spice cake

Cardamom, cloves and allspice join the more usual cake spices to give this cake a heady blend that smells so good as you take it out of the oven. The flavour will improve after a few days, so make the cake in advance and wrap well. This will keep for up to five days in an airtight container.

SERVES 20

butter, for greasing
breadcrumbs, for sprinkling
500g/1¼lb/5 cups plain
  (all-purpose) flour
20ml/4 tsp baking powder
pinch of salt
350g/12oz/1½ cups light
  muscovado (brown) sugar
10ml/2 tsp ground cinnamon
1.5ml/¼ tsp ground allspice
1.5ml/¼ tsp ground cloves
2.5ml/½ tsp freshly grated nutmeg
1.5ml/¼ tsp ground cardamom
400–450ml/14–15fl oz/
  1⅔–2 cups milk

1 Preheat the oven to 150°C/300°F/ Gas 2. Grease a 20–23cm/8–9in round deep cake tin (pan) and sprinkle with breadcrumbs. Remove the excess crumbs.

2 Sift the flour, baking powder and salt into a large bowl. Stir in the sugar, cinnamon, allspice, cloves, nutmeg and cardamom.

3 Gradually stir the milk into the mixture, then whisk until smooth and with a pourable consistency.

4 Pour the mixture into the prepared tin and bake for 1½ hours, or until a skewer inserted into the centre comes out clean. Leave to stand in the tin for 5 minutes.

5 Turn out on to a wire rack to go cold. Wrap the cake in foil and store for at least 3 days before eating to allow the flavour of the spices to develop fully.

Energy 166kcal/708kJ; Protein 3.2g; Carbohydrate 39.2g, of which sugars 19.6g; Fat 0.7g, of which saturates 0.3g; Cholesterol 1.2mg; Calcium 80mg; Fibre 0.7g; Sodium 227mg.

Coffee and mint cream cake

Ground almonds give this buttery coffee-flavoured sponge a moist texture and delicate flavour. It is sandwiched together with a generous filling of mint buttercream, which contrasts wonderfully with the coffee. Keep this cake for up to three days in a cool place.

2 Put the butter, sugar, flour, almonds, eggs and infused ground coffee in a large bowl. Beat well for 1 minute until blended.

3 Divide the mixture evenly between the tins and smooth the top level. Bake for 25 minutes, or until well risen and firm to the touch. Leave in the tins for 5 minutes, then turn out on to a wire rack to go cold.

4 To make the filling, cream the butter, icing sugar, peppermint extract and milk together in a bowl until light and fluffy.

5 Remove the lining paper from the sponges and sandwich together with the filling. Generously dust the top with icing sugar. Top with the fresh mint leaves just before serving.

SERVES 8

175g/6oz/³⁄₄ cup unsalted butter, softened, plus extra for greasing
15ml/1 tbsp ground coffee infused (steeped) in 25ml/1½ tbsp near-boiling water for 4 minutes, then strained and cooled
175g/6oz/scant 1 cup caster (superfine) sugar
225g/8oz/2 cups self-raising (self-rising) flour, sifted
50g/2oz/½ cup ground almonds
3 eggs
small sprigs of fresh mint, to decorate

For the filling
50g/2oz/¼ cup unsalted butter
115g/4oz/1 cup icing (confectioners') sugar, sifted, plus extra for dusting
2 drops of peppermint extract plus 15ml/1 tbsp milk

1 Preheat the oven to 180°C/350°F/ Gas 4. Grease and line two 18cm/ 7in round shallow cake tins (pans).

COOK'S TIP
Freeze, unfilled, for 2 months.

Energy 508kcal/2127kJ; Protein 6.5g; Carbohydrate 59.6g, of which sugars 38.5g; Fat 28.8g, of which saturates 16.1g; Cholesterol 136mg; Calcium 148mg; Fibre 1.3g; Sodium 341mg.

Coconut and coffee cake

Some flavours work particularly well together and make natural partners, such as coconut and coffee, and the combination is at its best here. Ground coffee has a good strong flavour that is perfect for this cake. It will keep for up to five days in an airtight container.

SERVES 9

75g/3oz/6 tbsp butter, plus extra
   for greasing
25g/1oz/2 tbsp caster (superfine)
   sugar
175g/6oz/¾ cup golden (light
   corn) syrup
40g/1½oz/½ cup desiccated (dry
   unsweetened shredded) coconut
175g/6oz/1½ cups plain
   (all-purpose) flour
2.5ml/½ tsp bicarbonate of soda
   (baking soda)
2 eggs, lightly beaten
45ml/3 tbsp ground coffee infused
   (steeped) in 75ml/5 tbsp
   near-boiling milk for 4 minutes,
   then strained

For the icing
115g/4oz/½ cup butter, softened
225g/8oz/2 cups icing
   (confectioners') sugar, sifted
25g/1oz/⅓ cup shredded or flaked
   coconut, toasted

1 Preheat the oven to 160°C/325°F/ Gas 3. Grease and line a 20cm/8in square deep cake tin (pan) with baking parchment.

2 Heat the caster sugar, golden syrup, butter and desiccated coconut in a pan, stirring with a wooden spoon, until completely melted.

3 Sift the flour and bicarbonate of soda into the butter mixture. Add the eggs and 45ml/3 tbsp of the coffee-flavoured milk. Stir well to combine.

4 Spoon the mixture into the prepared tin and smooth it level.

5 Bake for 40–50 minutes, or until well risen and firm.

6 Allow the cake to cool in the tin for 10 minutes. Turn out on to a wire rack to go cold. Remove the lining papers.

7 To make the icing, beat the softened butter until smooth, then gradually beat in the icing sugar and remaining coffee-flavoured milk to give a soft consistency.

8 Spread over the top of the cake with a flat-bladed knife and decorate with toasted coconut. Cut into 5cm/2in squares to serve.

COOK'S TIP
This will freeze, undecorated, for 2 months.

Energy 418kcal/1756kJ; Protein 3.7g; Carbohydrate 59.7g, of which sugars 44.9g; Fat 20g, of which saturates 13g; Cholesterol 90mg; Calcium 57mg; Fibre 1g; Sodium 225mg.

Coffee and walnut roll

There's something about coffee and walnuts together in a cake that gives it such a delicious taste. Here they appear together in a light and fluffy sponge enclosing a smooth and creamy filling that is luxuriously flavoured with Cointreau. Eat this roll fresh for the best flavour.

SERVES 8

butter, for greasing
3 eggs
75g/3oz/6 tbsp caster (superfine) sugar, plus extra for dusting
75g/3oz/¾ cup self-raising (self-rising) flour
10ml/2 tsp ground coffee infused (steeped) in 15ml/1 tbsp near-boiling water for 4 minutes, then strained
50g/2oz/½ cup toasted walnuts, finely chopped

For the filling
115g/4oz/generous ½ cup caster (superfine) sugar, plus extra for dusting
50ml/2fl oz/¼ cup cold water
2 egg yolks
115g/4oz/½ cup unsalted butter, softened
15ml/1 tbsp Cointreau or orange liqueur

1 Preheat the oven to 200°C/400°F/ Gas 6. Grease and line a 33 × 23cm/13 × 9in Swiss roll tin (jelly roll pan) with baking parchment.

2 Whisk the eggs and sugar together in a large bowl until pale and thick.

3 Sift the flour over the egg and sugar mixture and fold in with the coffee and walnuts.

4 Pour into the tin and bake for 10–12 minutes, until golden.

5 Turn out on to a piece of baking parchment sprinkled with caster sugar, peel off the lining paper and cool for about 2 minutes. Trim the edges.

COOK'S TIP
Try this decorated with swirls of piped whipped cream and walnuts, if you like.

6 Roll up from one of the short ends, using the baking parchment. Leave to cool, still rolled up.

7 To make the filling, put the sugar in a pan with the water over a low heat until dissolved. Boil rapidly until the syrup reaches 105°/220°F on a sugar thermometer.

8 Pour the syrup over the egg yolks, whisking all the time, until thick and mousse-like. Gradually add the butter, then whisk in the orange liqueur. Leave to cool and thicken.

9 Unroll the sponge and spread with filling. Re-roll and place on a serving plate, seam-side down.

10 Dust with extra caster sugar and chill until ready to serve.

Energy 357kcal/1489kJ; Protein 4.1g; Carbohydrate 31.9g, of which sugars 28.7g; Fat 24.6g, of which saturates 11.9g; Cholesterol 125mg; Calcium 43mg; Fibre 0.4g; Sodium 153mg.

Pear and cardamom spice cake

Fresh pears and cardamom, a classic combination of flavours, are used together in this moist fruit and nut cake that has added crunch from the poppy seeds. It makes a delicious and mouthwatering tea-time treat. This cake keeps in an airtight container for up to five days.

SERVES 8–12

115g/4oz/½ cup butter, plus extra
  for greasing
115g/4oz/generous ½ cup caster
  (superfine) sugar
2 eggs, beaten
225g/8oz/2 cups plain
  (all-purpose) flour
15ml/1 tbsp baking powder
30ml/2 tbsp milk
crushed seeds from 2 cardamom
  pods (beans)
50g/2oz/½ cup walnuts, chopped
15ml/1 tbsp poppy seeds
500g/1¼lb dessert pears, peeled,
  cored and thinly sliced
3 walnut halves
45ml/3 tbsp clear honey

1 Preheat the oven to 180°C/350°F/
Gas 4. Grease and line a 20cm/
8in round deep cake tin (pan) with
baking parchment.

2 In a bowl, beat the butter and
sugar together until pale and light.
Beat in the eggs a little at a time.

3 Sift the flour and baking powder
together over the butter and sugar
mixture, then fold in with the milk.

4 Stir in the cardamom seeds,
chopped nuts and poppy seeds.
Reserve one-third of the pear slices,
and chop the remainder. Fold
the chopped pears into the
creamed mixture.

5 Transfer the batter to the prepared
tin and smooth the top, making a
small dip in the centre.

6 Put the walnut halves in the centre
and fan the reserved pear slices
around them, overlapping each
slice and covering the batter.

7 Bake for 1¼–1½ hours, or until
a skewer inserted in the centre
comes out clean.

8 Leave the cake to cool in the tin
for 20 minutes, turn out and then
transfer to a wire rack. Remove the
lining paper.

9 While the cake is warm, use a soft
pastry brush and glaze the cake top
with a generous quantity of clear
honey. Leave to go cold.

Energy 231kcal/970kJ; Protein 3.7g; Carbohydrate 29g, of which sugars 14.7g; Fat 12g, of which saturates 5.5g; Cholesterol 52.3mg; Calcium 49mg; Fibre 1.6g; Sodium 73.5mg.

Pineapple and ginger upside-down cake

This light and moist cake has a sticky ginger glaze over stem ginger and pineapple pieces, which are arranged in the cake tin before the cake batter is added. It is superb served warm as a dessert with home-made custard or thick cream. This cake will keep refrigerated, for two days.

SERVES 8

20g/¾oz/1½ tbsp butter, plus extra
   for greasing
2 pieces preserved stem ginger,
   chopped, plus 60ml/4 tbsp syrup
450g/1lb can pineapple pieces in
   natural juice, drained
250g/9oz/2¼ cups wholemeal
   (whole-wheat) self-raising
   (self-rising) flour
15ml/1 tbsp baking powder
5ml/1 tsp ground ginger
5ml/1 tsp ground cinnamon
115g/4oz/½ cup soft light
   brown sugar
250ml/8fl oz/1 cup milk
45ml/3 tbsp sunflower oil
1 banana, peeled

1 Preheat the oven to 180°C/235°F/ Gas 4. Grease and line a 20cm/8in round deep cake tin (pan).

2 Melt the butter in a small pan over a gentle heat, then stir in the ginger syrup. Turn up the heat until the liquid thickens.

3 Pour the mixture into the prepared tin and smooth out to the sides.

4 Arrange the stem ginger, and one-third of the pineapple pieces, in the syrup in the tin. Set aside.

5 Sift together the flour, baking powder and spices into a large bowl, then stir in the sugar.

6 In a food processor or blender, blend together the milk, oil, the remaining pineapple and the banana until almost smooth, then add this mixture to the flour. Stir until thoroughly combined.

7 Spoon the mixture over the pineapple and ginger pieces in the tin and smooth level.

8 Bake for 45 minutes, or until a skewer inserted into the centre of the cake comes out clean. Leave to cool slightly, then place a serving plate over the tin and turn upside down. Remove the lining.

Energy 358kcal/1508kJ; Protein 4.6g; Carbohydrate 55.2g, of which sugars 47.1g; Fat 14.8g, of which saturates 8.3g; Cholesterol 126mg; Calcium 63mg; Fibre 1g; Sodium 126mg.

Rich lemon poppy-seed cake

The classic combination of poppy seeds and lemon is used for this light cake. Luxurious lemon curd adds richness to both the cake and the creamy filling, making it very moreish. Eat this cake fresh for best flavour, or freeze without filling, wrapped in foil for up to two months.

4 Put the egg whites into a clean, grease-free bowl and whisk until they form soft peaks. Carefully fold them into the cake mixture until just combined.

5 Divide the cake mixture between the prepared tins. Bake for 40–45 minutes, or until golden and a skewer inserted into the centre of the cakes comes out clean.

6 Leave to cool in the tins for 5 minutes, then turn out on to wire racks to go cold. Remove the lining.

SERVES 10–12

350g/12oz/1½ cups unsalted
  butter, plus extra for greasing
350g/12oz/1¾ cups golden caster
  (superfine) sugar
45ml/3 tbsp poppy seeds
20ml/4 tsp finely grated lemon rind
60ml/4 heaped tbsp lemon curd
6 eggs, separated
120ml/4fl oz/½ cup milk
350g/12oz/3 cups self-raising
  (self-rising) flour
icing (confectioners') sugar,
  for dusting

For the filling
150g/5oz/½ lemon curd
150ml/¼ pint/⅔ cup mascarpone

1 Preheat the oven to 180°C/350°F/ Gas 4. Grease and line two 23cm/ 9in round shallow cake tins (pans) with baking parchment.

2 Beat together the butter and sugar until light and fluffy. Add the poppy seeds, lemon rind, lemon curd and egg yolks. Beat well, then add the milk and mix well.

3 Sift the flour over the mixture and gently fold in until combined.

7 To finish, spread one cake with lemon curd and spoon the mascarpone evenly over the top. Put the second cake on top, press down gently, then dust with icing sugar before serving.

Energy 805kcal/3374kJ; Protein 10.7g; Carbohydrate 99.6g, of which sugars 60.9g; Fat 43.3g, of which saturates 25.3g; Cholesterol 246mg; Calcium 242mg; Fibre 1.4g; Sodium 509mg.

Apple and cinnamon cake

Dates and grated apples bring lots of fruitiness and moisture to this spicy cake mix. It also includes gram flour (made from ground chickpeas) and coconut milk, giving it an Asian touch. It is a good cake to add to packed lunches. Keep this for up to five days in an airtight container.

SERVES 8–10

115g/4oz/½ cup butter, plus extra
    for greasing
200g/7oz/generous 1 cup dried,
    stoned (pitted) dates
1–2 tart eating apples or 1 cooking
    apple, about 225g/8oz
12.5ml/2½ tsp mixed (apple pie)
    spice
pinch of salt
150g/5oz/1¼ cups wholemeal
    (whole-wheat) flour
115g/4oz/ 1 cup gram flour
10ml/2 tsp baking powder
75g/3oz/generous ½ cup raisins
2 eggs, beaten
175ml/6fl oz/¾ cup unsweetened
    coconut milk

1 Preheat the oven to 180°C/350°F/ Gas 4. Grease and line a 20cm/8in deep square cake tin (pan) with baking parchment.

2 Combine the butter and dates in a food processor.

3 Peel, core and grate the apple and add to the butter and date mixture with the mixed spice and salt. Process until thoroughly blended.

4 Spoon the apple and date mixture into a bowl. In batches, sift and fold in the flours and baking powder, alternating with the raisins, beaten eggs and coconut milk. Transfer to the prepared tin and smooth the top level.

5 Bake for 30–40 minutes, or until dark golden and firm to the touch, and a skewer inserted into the centre comes out clean. Allow the cake to cool in the tin for 15 minutes before turning out on to a wire rack to go completely cold. Remove the lining.

Energy 587kcal/2472kJ; Protein 5.5g; Carbohydrate 92g, of which sugars 69.7g; Fat 24.5g, of which saturates 10.6g; Cholesterol 40mg; Calcium 95mg; Fibre 2.5g; Sodium 129mg.

Pecan cake

Ground pecan nuts give this light cake a mellow flavour, which is further enriched with butter and honey drizzled over the cake once cooked. Serve with a dollop of whipped cream to make an unusual dessert. Keep refrigerated for up to three days.

6 Fold the beaten whites into the butter mixture, then gently fold in the flour and nut mixture.

7 Spoon the batter into the prepared tin and bake for 30 minutes, or until a skewer inserted in the centre comes out clean.

SERVES 8

115g/4oz/½ cup butter, softened, plus extra for greasing
115g/4oz/1 cup pecan nuts
75g/3oz/¾ cup plain (all-purpose) flour
115g/4oz/½ cup soft light brown sugar
5ml/1 tsp vanilla extract
4 large (US extra large) eggs, separated
pinch of salt
12 whole pecan nuts, to decorate
whipped cream, to serve

For drizzling
50g/2oz/¼ cup butter
120ml/4fl oz/scant ½ cup clear (runny) honey

1 Preheat the oven to 180°C/350°F/Gas 4. Grease and line a 20cm/8in round shallow cake tin (pan) with baking parchment.

2 Toast the pecan nuts in a dry frying pan for 5 minutes, shaking frequently.

3 Grind the nuts finely in a blender or food processor. Stir in the flour.

4 In a mixing bowl, beat the butter and sugar together until light and fluffy, then beat in the vanilla extract and egg yolks.

5 Put the egg whites and salt into a clean, grease-free bowl and whisk until they form soft peaks.

8 Allow the cake to cool in the tin for 5 minutes, then turn out on to a wire rack to go cold. Remove the lining paper. Arrange the pecan nuts on top of the cake. Transfer to a serving plate.

9 Melt the butter for drizzling in a small pan, add the honey and bring to the boil, stirring. Lower the heat and simmer for 3 minutes. Pour over the cake. Serve with whipped cream.

Energy 428kcal/1785kJ; Protein 6.2g; Carbohydrate 34.7g, of which sugars 27.4g; Fat 30.5g, of which saturates 12.5g; Cholesterol 158mg; Calcium 51mg; Fibre 1g; Sodium 170mg.

Almond cake

Toasted almonds are the main ingredient in this light cake, giving it a nutty flavour and an excellent texture. It is best served warm, and a scoop of vanilla or good-quality chocolate ice cream would also go well with it. Eat this fresh, or keep it for one day in an airtight container.

SERVES 4–6

25g/1oz/2 tbsp butter, plus extra
   for greasing
225/8oz/2 cups blanched
   whole almonds
75g/3oz/¾ cup icing (confectioners')
   sugar, plus extra for dusting
3 eggs
2.5ml/½ tsp almond extract
25g/1oz/¼ cup plain
   (all-purpose) flour
3 egg whites
15ml/1 tbsp caster (superfine)
   sugar

4 Add the whole eggs and the remaining icing sugar to the bowl. With an electric whisk, beat until the mixture forms a trail when the beaters are lifted away.

5 In a small pan, melt the butter, then mix into the nut and egg mixture with the almond extract.

6 Sift over the flour and fold in.

7 Whisk the egg whites into a clean, grease-free bowl until they form soft peaks. Add the sugar. Beat until stiff.

8 Fold the egg whites into the batter. Spoon into the cake tin. Bake for 15–20 minutes, until golden. Turn out of the tin. Remove the papers.

9 Decorate with the toasted almonds and dust with icing sugar.

1 Preheat the oven to 160°C/325°F/ Gas 3. Grease and line a 23cm/9in round shallow cake tin (pan) with baking parchment.

2 Spread the almonds in an even layer in a baking tray and bake for 10 minutes. Allow the almonds to cool. Set aside a few of the almonds for decoration. Chop the rest, then grind them with half of the icing sugar in a food processor. Transfer to a large bowl.

3 Increase the oven temperature to 200°C/400°F/Gas 6.

Energy 376kcal/1568kJ; Protein 13g; Carbohydrate 21.5g, of which sugars 17.3g; Fat 27.2g, of which saturates 4.6g; Cholesterol 104mg; Calcium 120mg; Fibre 2.9g; Sodium 97mg.

Walnut cake

Brandy, orange and cinnamon warmed in a sugar syrup are poured over this baked walnut cake, making it superbly moist and full of complementary flavours. This technique is an excellent way to add flavour and moisture to a cake. Keep this cake, refrigerated, for three days.

SERVES 10–12

150g/5oz/10 tbsp unsalted butter,
  plus extra for greasing
115g/4oz/generous ½ cup caster
  (superfine) sugar
4 eggs, separated
60ml/4 tbsp brandy
2.5ml/½ tsp ground cinnamon
300g/11oz/2¾ cups walnuts
150g/5oz/1¼ cups self-raising
  (self-rising) flour
5ml/1 tsp baking powder
pinch of salt

For the syrup
250g/9oz/1¼ cups caster
  (superfine) sugar
30ml/2 tbsp brandy
2 or 3 strips of pared orange rind
2 cinnamon sticks

1 Preheat the oven to 190°C/375°F/ Gas 5. Grease and line a 35 × 23cm/ 14 × 9in shallow cake tin (pan).

2 In a bowl, beat the butter and sugar together until light and fluffy. Beat in the egg yolks one at a time. Stir in the brandy and cinnamon.

3 Coarsely chop the walnuts, using a food processor, and stir them in.

4 Sift the flour with the baking powder and set aside.

5 Put the egg whites and salt into a clean, grease-free bowl and whisk until they form stiff peaks.

6 Fold the egg whites into the butter and sugar mixture, alternating with tablespoons of flour.

7 Spread the batter evenly in the prepared tin. Bake for about 40 minutes, or until the top is golden and a skewer inserted into the centre comes out clean. Set on a wire rack in the tin.

8 To make the syrup, mix the sugar and 300ml/½ pint/1¼ cups water in a small pan. Heat gently, stirring, until the sugar has dissolved. Bring to the boil, lower the heat and add the brandy, orange rind and cinnamon sticks. Simmer for 10 minutes.

9 Remove the lining. Slice the cake into diamonds while still hot and strain the syrup over it. Let it stand for 10–20 minutes, then turn out on to a wire rack to go cold.

Energy 563kcal/2349kJ; Protein 8.5g; Carbohydrate 50.6g, of which sugars 39.2g; Fat 35.3g, of which saturates 10.1g; Cholesterol 108mg; Calcium 114mg; Fibre 1.5g; Sodium 177mg.

Pine nut and almond cake

This unusual recipe uses olive oil, toasted semolina and nuts to give the cake a rich flavour and a dense, grainy texture. It is also incredibly moist because it is soaked in a cinnamon and sugar syrup. Unlike traditional cakes it is not baked in the oven, but heated in a pan. Eat fresh.

SERVES 6–8

500g/1¼lb/2¾ cups caster
   (superfine) sugar
1 cinnamon stick
250ml/8fl oz/1 cup olive oil
350g/12oz/2 cups coarse semolina
50g/2oz/½ cup blanched almonds
30ml/2 tbsp pine nuts
5ml/1 tsp ground cinnamon

1 Put the sugar in a heavy pan with 1 litre/1¾ pints/4 cups cold water and the cinnamon stick. Bring to the boil, stirring until the sugar dissolves, then boil without stirring for 4 minutes to make a syrup.

2 Meanwhile, heat the oil in a separate, heavy pan. When it is almost smoking, add the semolina gradually and stir constantly until it turns light brown.

3 Lower the heat, add the almonds and pine nuts, and brown together for 2–3 minutes, stirring constantly.

4 Take the semolina mixture off the heat and set aside. Remove the cinnamon stick from the hot syrup using a slotted spoon and discard it.

5 Carefully add the hot syrup to the semolina mixture, stirring all the time. The mixture will hiss and spit at this point, so stand well away from it.

6 Return the pan to a gentle heat and stir until the syrup has been absorbed and the mixture is smooth.

7 Remove the pan from the heat, cover it with a clean dish towel and leave it to stand for 10 minutes so that any remaining moisture is absorbed.

8 Spoon the mixture into a 20–23cm/ 8–9in round non-stick cake tin (pan), and set it aside. When cold, unmould it on to a platter and dust it all over with the cinnamon.

Energy 643kcal/2706kJ; Protein 6.8g; Carbohydrate 99.8g, of which sugars 65.7g; Fat 26.8g, of which saturates 3.3g; Cholesterol 0mg; Calcium 56mg; Fibre 1.5g; Sodium 10mg.

Poppy seed cake

This plain and simple cake is flavoured with lemon and vanilla and is packed with black poppy seeds – a popular ingredient for speciality breads. As well as giving the cake a good crunch, poppy seeds add a nutty and distinctive taste. Serve it with cream, and keep for up to three days.

3 Sift and fold the flour and baking powder into the egg and poppy seed mixture, in three batches, alternating with the milk.

4 Add the cooled, melted butter and the sunflower oil, and stir in.

5 Pour the mixture into the tin and bake for 40 minutes, or until firm. Cool in the tin for 15 minutes, then invert on to a wire rack. Leave until cold, dust with icing sugar and serve with cream.

SERVES 8

130g/4½oz/generous ½ cup unsalted butter, melted, plus extra for greasing
2 eggs
225g/8oz/generous 1 cup caster (superfine) sugar
5–10ml/1–2 tsp vanilla extract
200g/7oz/scant 1½ cups poppy seeds, ground
15ml/1 tbsp grated lemon rind
130g/4½oz/generous 1 cup self-raising (self-rising) flour
5ml/1 tsp baking powder
120ml/4fl oz/½ cup milk
30ml/2 tbsp sunflower oil
icing (confectioners') sugar, sifted, for dusting
whipped cream, to serve

1 Preheat the oven to 180°C/350°F/ Gas 4. Grease a 23cm/9in round deep cake tin (pan).

2 In a large bowl, beat together the eggs, sugar and vanilla extract, using an electric whisk, for 4–5 minutes, or by hand until pale and fluffy. Stir in the poppy seeds and the lemon rind.

COOK'S TIP
Culinary poppy seeds have a distinctive nutty taste. To enhance the aroma and flavour, lightly toast them first.

Energy 485kcal/2023kJ; Protein 8.3g; Carbohydrate 42.7g, of which sugars 30.5g; Fat 32.4g, of which saturates 11.4g; Cholesterol 83mg; Calcium 267mg; Fibre 2.5g; Sodium 188mg.

Date and walnut spice cake

This deliciously moist and rich spiced cake is topped with a sticky honey and orange glaze.
Serve it as a dessert with a generous spoonful of natural yogurt, or crème fraîche, flavoured with
grated orange rind. Keep this cake, refrigerated, for up to three days.

SERVES 8

115g/4oz/½ cup unsalted butter,
   plus extra for greasing
175g/6oz/¾ cup soft dark
   brown sugar
2 eggs
175g/6oz/1½ cups self-raising
   (self-rising) flour, plus extra
   for dusting
5ml/1 tsp bicarbonate of soda
   (baking soda)
2.5ml/½ tsp freshly grated nutmeg
5ml/1 tsp mixed spice
pinch of salt
175ml/6fl oz/¾ cup buttermilk
50g/2oz/⅓ cup ready-to-eat stoned
   (pitted) dates, chopped
25g/1oz/¼ cup walnuts, chopped

For the topping
60ml/4 tbsp clear honey
45ml/3 tbsp fresh orange juice
15ml/1 tbsp coarsely grated
   orange rind

1 Preheat the oven to 180°C/350°F/
Gas 4. Grease and lightly flour a
23cm/9in round deep cake tin (pan).

2 In a bowl, beat the butter and
sugar until light and fluffy, then beat
in the eggs one at a time.

3 Sift together the flour, bicarbonate
of soda, spices and salt into a bowl.

4 Add the flour mixture to the egg
and sugar mixture, alternating with
the buttermilk, and stir well to
combine. Add the dates and
walnuts, and mix in.

5 Spoon the batter into the prepared
cake tin and smooth the top level.

6 Bake for 50 minutes, or until a
skewer inserted into the centre
comes out clean. Leave to cool for
5 minutes. Turn out on to a wire
rack to go cold.

7 To make the topping, heat the
honey, orange juice and rind in a
pan. Bring to the boil. Boil rapidly,
without stirring, for 3 minutes, or
until syrupy.

8 Prick holes in the top of the cake
and pour over the hot syrup.

Energy 350kcal/1472kJ; Protein 5.1g; Carbohydrate 50.3g, of which sugars 34.1g; Fat 15.7g, of which saturates 8.1g; Cholesterol 79mg; Calcium 131mg; Fibre 1g; Sodium 196mg.

Chocolate cakes

Most people love chocolate, and this luxurious ingredient makes cakes rich and delectable. The flavour of chocolate varies according to the brand but, as a general rule, the higher the cocoa content, the better the quality. However, it is more important to find a chocolate that you enjoy. Melted block chocolate has many uses in baking, such as for toppings, frostings and sauces. Cocoa powder, with its concentrated flavour, will add a deep chocolate richness to cakes, icings and buttercreams.

It is amazing how many ingredients work well with chocolate, and what a variety of combinations you can make by adding nuts, fruit, orange, ginger, mint, coffee, cinnamon and spirits such as rum and brandy. Who could resist juicy dark cherries with chocolate in Black Forest Gateau? Or try a sophisticated Chocolate Orange Marquise – ideal for a dessert. You may be surprised by the Chocolate and Beetroot Layer Cake and the Chocolate Potato Cake, but just try a slice to experience their sweet, rich notes and moist textures.

Left: Black Forest Gateau and Sachertorte.

Chocolate sandwich cake

A light chocolate sponge cake has lots of appeal, especially when filled and topped with a rich, chocolatey frosting. It also works as a celebration cake, topped with small squares of fudge and white chocolate buttons, or flaked chocolate. Keep it for up to three days in an airtight container.

SERVES 10–12

130g/4½oz/generous ½ cup
   butter, softened, plus extra
   for greasing
250g/9oz/1¼ cups caster
   (superfine) sugar
3 eggs, beaten
225g/8oz/2 cups plain
   (all-purpose) flour
5ml/1 tsp bicarbonate of soda
   (baking soda)
50g/2oz/½ cup unsweetened
   cocoa power
250ml/8fl oz/1 cup buttermilk

For the chocolate buttercream
50g/2oz dark (bittersweet)
   chocolate
175g/6oz/1½ cups icing
   (confectioners') sugar, sifted
115g/4oz/½ cup unsalted
   butter, softened
few drops of vanilla extract

1 Preheat the oven to 180°C/350°F/ Gas 4. Grease and line two 20cm/8in round shallow cake tins (pans) with baking parchment.

2 In a mixing bowl, cream the butter and sugar until light and fluffy.

3 Gradually beat in the eggs. Sift the flour, bicarbonate of soda and cocoa over in batches and beat well to combine. Add the buttermilk and mix well.

4 Spoon into the prepared tins and bake for 30–35 minutes, or until firm to the touch.

5 Let stand for 5 minutes, then turn out of the tins, peel off the papers and leave on a wire rack to go cold.

6 To make the buttercream, melt the chocolate in a heatproof bowl set over a pan of gently simmering water. Stir occasionally. Allow to cool slightly.

7 In another bowl, beat the icing sugar with the butter until soft and creamy. Mix in the melted chocolate.

8 Use half of the buttercream to sandwich the cakes together, and spread the remainder on the top of the cake. Store refrigerated to keep the buttercream firm.

Energy 430kcal/1790kJ; Protein 7.8g; Carbohydrate 29.5g, of which sugars 28.8g; Fat 32.1g, of which saturates 13.6g; Cholesterol 96mg; Calcium 92mg; Fibre 1.9g; Sodium 125mg.

Chocolate, almond and coffee cake

This easy all-in-one cake recipe is a favourite because it is so quick to make. Add a lovely coffee buttercream for the filling and topping, and the chocolate cake is transformed into something extra special. Keep this cake for up to three days, refrigerated, in an airtight container.

SERVES 8

175g/6oz/¾ cup butter, softened, plus extra for greasing
175g/6oz/1½ cups self-raising (self-rising) flour
25ml/1½ tbsp unsweetened cocoa powder
pinch of salt
175g/6oz/¾ cup soft dark brown sugar
50g/2oz/½ cup ground almonds
3 large (US extra large) eggs, lightly beaten

For the coffee buttercream
175g/6oz/¾ cup unsalted butter
350g/12oz/3 cups icing (confectioners') sugar, sifted
30ml/2 tbsp coffee extract
whole hazelnuts or pecan nuts, to decorate (optional)

1 Preheat the oven to 180°C/350°F/Gas 4. Grease and line two 18cm/7in round shallow cake tins (pans).

2 Sift the flour, cocoa and salt into a large bowl.

3 In another bowl, cream the butter with the sugar until light and fluffy.

4 Add the ground almonds, eggs, flour and cocoa, and beat well. Divide the batter between the tins.

5 Bake for 25–30 minutes. Turn out on a wire rack to go cold. Remove the paper lining.

6 To make the buttercream, beat the butter, then gradually beat in the icing sugar and coffee extract.

7 Put one quarter of the buttercream into a small piping (pastry) bag fitted with a star nozzle.

8 Sandwich the cakes together with some of the buttercream. Cover the top and sides with the rest.

9 Pipe rosettes around the top of the cake and decorate with whole hazelnuts or pecan nuts, if you like.

Energy 737kcal/3085kJ; Protein 7g; Carbohydrate 86.4g, of which sugars 69.6g; Fat 43g, of which saturates 24g; Cholesterol 1.4mg; Calcium 1.06mg; Fibre 12.2g; Sodium 3.28mg.

Frosted chocolate fudge cake

Rich and dreamy, this chocolate cake has added depth of flavour from muscovado sugar and thick yogurt. The chocolate fudge frosting also contains yogurt, giving it a creamy consistency. It couldn't be easier to make, or more delicious to eat. Keep, refrigerated, for up to three days.

SERVES 8

175g/6oz/¾ cup unsalted butter, softened, plus extra for greasing
115g/4oz plain (semisweet) chocolate, broken into pieces
200g/7oz/scant 1 cup light muscovado (brown) sugar
5ml/1 tsp vanilla extract
3 eggs, beaten
150ml/¼ pint/⅔ cup Greek (US strained plain) yogurt
150g/5oz/1¼ cups self-raising (self-rising) flour

For the frosting and chocolate curls
2255g/8oz plain (semisweet) chocolate, broken into pieces
50g/2oz/¼ cup unsalted butter
90ml/6 tbsp Greek (US strained plain) yogurt
350g/12oz/3 cups icing (confectioners') sugar, plus extra for dusting

1 Preheat the oven to 190°C/375°F/ Gas 5. Grease and line two 20cm/ 8in round shallow cake tins (pans) with baking parchment.

2 Melt the chocolate in a heatproof bowl over a pan of simmering water.

3 Meanwhile, in a large bowl, beat the butter with the sugar until light and fluffy.

4 Beat in the vanilla extract, then gradually beat in the egg in small quantities, beating well after each addition.

5 Stir in the melted chocolate and yogurt. Sift the flour over the mixture, then fold in gently with a large metal spoon.

6 Divide the mixture between the tins. Bake for 25–30 minutes, or until the cakes are firm to the touch.

7 Leave to stand for 5 minutes, then turn out on to a wire rack to go cold. Remove the lining papers.

8 To make the chocolate curls, melt 115g/4oz of the chocolate in a heatproof bowl set over a pan of gently simmering water.

9 Spread the melted chocolate out on to a clean, cold hard surface, preferably marble, and allow to set.

10 Meanwhile, to make the frosting, melt the rest of the chocolate and all the butter in a medium pan over a gentle heat.

11 Stir in the yogurt and icing sugar. Mix with a rubber spatula until smooth, then beat until the frosting begins to cool and thicken slightly.

12 Use a third of the mixture to sandwich the cakes together. Working quickly, spread the rest of the frosting over the top and sides.

13 To make the curls, using a long, sharp knife, scrape along the surface of the set chocolate to make thin curled shavings.

14 Position the shavings on the cake and then dust with icing sugar.

Energy 753kcal/3160kJ; Protein 8g; Carbohydrate 105.4g, of which sugars 90.9g; Fat 36.6g, of which saturates 21.7g; Cholesterol 133mg; Calcium 133mg; Fibre 1.3g; Sodium 224mg.

Devilish chocolate roulade

This decadent roulade can be made a day ahead and then filled and rolled before serving. It has a rich brandy, chocolate and mascarpone filling and is decorated with chocolate-dipped strawberries to make it extra special. Once filled, keep it, refrigerated, for up to two days.

SERVES 6–8

butter, for greasing
175g/6oz plain (semisweet)
  chocolate, broken into pieces
4 eggs, separated
115g/4oz/generous ½ cup caster
  (superfine) sugar
unsweetened cocoa powder,
  for dusting

For the filling
225g/8oz plain (semisweet)
  chocolate, broken into pieces
45ml/3 tbsp brandy
2 eggs, separated
250g/9oz/generous 1 cup
  mascarpone
chocolate-dipped strawberries

1 Preheat the oven to 180°C/350°F/ Gas 4. Grease and line a 33 × 23cm/ 13 × 9in Swiss roll tin (jelly roll pan) with baking parchment.

2 Melt the chocolate in a heatproof bowl over a pan of gently simmering water, then remove from the heat.

3 Whisk the egg yolks and sugar in a bowl until pale and thick, then stir in the melted chocolate.

4 Put the egg whites into a clean, grease-free bowl and whisk until they form soft peaks, then fold lightly and evenly into the egg and chocolate mixture.

5 Pour the mixture into the prepared tin and smooth level. Bake for 15–20 minutes, or until well risen and firm to the touch.

6 Dust a sheet of baking parchment with cocoa. Turn the sponge out on to the paper, cover with a clean dish towel and leave to cool.

7 To make the filling, melt the chocolate with the brandy in a heatproof bowl set over a pan of gently simmering water. Remove from the heat.

8 Beat the egg yolks together, then beat into the warm chocolate mixture until smooth.

9 Put the egg whites into a clean, grease-free bowl and whisk until they form soft peaks. Fold them lightly and evenly into the filling in three batches until the mixture is light and smooth. Cool completely.

10 Uncover the roulade, remove the lining paper and spread with most of the mascarpone.

11 Spread the chocolate mixture over the top, then roll up from a long side to enclose the filling.

12 Transfer to a serving plate, top with mascarpone, fresh chocolate-dipped strawberries, and dust with cocoa powder.

CHOCOLATE-DIPPED STRAWBERRIES
Dip the lower half of each strawberry into some good quality melted chocolate. Leave to set on a baking sheet lined with baking parchment.

Energy 486kcal/2022kJ; Protein 10.2g; Carbohydrate 32.8g, of which sugars 32.4g; Fat 34.5g, of which saturates 19.9g; Cholesterol 189mg; Calcium 41mg; Fibre 1.3g; Sodium 143mg.

Black Forest gateau

Perhaps the most famous chocolate cake of all, this Kirsch-flavoured gateau is layered with fresh cream containing chopped black cherries, and is decorated with chocolate curls. It is the perfect gateau for a special-occasion party. This will keep, refrigerated, for up to three days.

SERVES 10–12

75g/3oz/6 tbsp butter, melted,
 plus extra for greasing
5 eggs
175g/6oz/scant 1 cup caster
 (superfine) sugar
50g/2oz/½ cup plain (all-purpose)
 flour, sifted
50g/2oz/½ cup unsweetened cocoa
 powder, sifted

For the filling and topping
75–90ml/5–6 tbsp Kirsch
600ml/1 pint/2½ cups double
 (heavy) cream
425g/15oz can black cherries,
 drained, pitted and chopped

For the decoration
225g/8oz plain (semisweet)
 chocolate, to make chocolate
 curls, *see page 84*
15–20 fresh cherries, preferably
 with stems
sifted icing (confectioners')
 sugar (optional)

1 Preheat the oven to 180°C/350°F/ Gas 4. Grease and line two 20cm/ 8in round deep cake tins (pans) with baking parchment.

2 Put the eggs and sugar in a large bowl and beat with an electric whisk for about 10 minutes, or until the mixture is thick and pale and leaves a trail when the beaters are lifted.

3 Sift together the flour and cocoa powder, then sift again into the whisked mixture. Fold in gently using a metal spoon and a figure-of-eight motion.

4 Slowly trickle in the cooled melted butter and fold in gently.

5 Divide the batter between the tins and smooth level. Bake for 30 minutes, until springy to the touch.

6 Leave in the tin for 5 minutes, then turn out on to a wire rack to cool. Peel off the lining paper.

7 Cut each cake in half horizontally. Sprinkle the four layers evenly with the Kirsch.

8 In a large bowl, whip the cream until it holds soft peaks.

9 Transfer two-thirds of the cream to another bowl and stir in the chopped cherries.

10 Place a layer of cake on a serving plate and spread over one-third of the filling. Top with another portion of cake and continue layering, finishing with the cake top.

11 Use the remaining whipped cream to cover the top and sides of the gateau. Decorate with chocolate curls, cherries and a dusting of icing sugar.

Energy 448kcal/1864kJ; Protein 4.8g; Carbohydrate 26.4g, of which sugars 22.7g; Fat 35.2g, of which saturates 21.1g; Cholesterol 161mg; Calcium 61.8mg; Fibre 0.8g; Sodium 121mg.

Death by chocolate

One of the richest chocolate cakes ever, this amazing confection has layers of jam and brandy-flavoured chocolate filling between layers of light cake. It is covered with chocolate ganache – a rich chocolate-truffle topping. Serve this in thin slices, and store, refrigerated, for up to three days.

SERVES 16–20

115g/4oz/½ cup unsalted butter, plus extra for greasing
225g/8oz plain (semisweet) chocolate, broken into pieces
150ml/¼ pint/⅔ cup milk
225g/8oz/1 cup light muscovado (brown) sugar
10ml/2 tsp vanilla extract
2 eggs, separated
150ml/¼ pint/⅔ cup sour cream
225g/8oz/2 cups self-raising (self-rising) flour
5ml/1 tsp baking powder

For the filling
60ml/4 tbsp seedless raspberry jam
60ml/4 tbsp brandy
400g/14oz plain (semisweet) chocolate, broken into pieces
200g/7oz/scant 1 cup unsalted butter
plain and white chocolate curls, *see page 84*, and chocolate-dipped physalis, to decorate

For the ganache
250ml/8fl oz/1 cup double (heavy) cream
225g/8oz plain (semisweet) chocolate, broken into pieces

1 Preheat the oven to 180°C/350°F/Gas 4. Grease and line a 23cm/9in round deep cake tin (pan) with baking parchment.

2 Put the chocolate, butter and milk in a pan. Stir over a very low heat until the chocolate melts. Remove from the heat.

3 Beat in the sugar and vanilla.

4 Beat the egg yolks and cream in a bowl, then beat into the chocolate mixture. Sift the flour and baking powder over the mixture and fold in.

5 Spoon into the cake tin and bake for 45–55 minutes. Turn on to a wire rack to go cold. Remove the lining papers. Slice into three even layers.

6 To make the filling, warm the jam with 15ml/1 tbsp of the brandy in a small pan. Brush over one side of two cake layers, then leave to set.

7 Put the remaining brandy in the pan with the chocolate and butter. Melt gently over a low heat, stirring until smooth. Cool until the filling is just beginning to thicken.

8 Spread one layer of the cake with half of the chocolate filling. Top with a second layer of cake, jam side up, and the remaining filling. Top with the final cake and leave to set.

9 To make the ganache, heat the cream and chocolate together in a pan over a low heat, stirring until the chocolate melts. Pour into a bowl, leave to cool, then whisk until the mixture begins to hold its shape.

10 Spread the cake top and sides with ganache.

11 Decorate with chocolate curls and chocolate-dipped physalis. Store, chilled, until ready to serve.

CHOCOLATE-DIPPED PHYSALIS
Melt chocolate in a heatproof bowl over a pan of gently simmering water. Peel back the papery leaves from the physalis. Holding the leaves, dip each physalis into the chocolate. Leave to set on a baking sheet lined with baking parchment.

Energy 432kcal/1809kJ; Protein 4.7g; Carbohydrate 49.9g, of which sugars 38.4g; Fat 24.7g, of which saturates 14.9g; Cholesterol 57mg; Calcium 99mg; Fibre 1.4g; Sodium 120mg.

Chocolate gooey cake

For perfect results it is essential to undercook this cake so that it is soft in the middle, so it is unsuitable for children and the elderly. It is made with almonds instead of flour, and so has a superb nutty flavour and is also gluten-free. Serve as a dessert with whipped cream. Eat fresh.

SERVES 8

115g/4oz/½ cup unsalted butter,
   diced, plus extra for greasing
115g/4oz dark (bittersweet)
   chocolate, broken into pieces
2 eggs, separated
175g/6oz/1½ cups ground almonds
5ml/1 tsp vanilla sugar
whipped double (heavy) cream,
   to serve

1 Preheat the oven to 180°C/350°F/Gas 4. Grease and line a 20cm/8in round shallow cake tin (pan).

2 Put the chocolate into a pan. Add 5ml/1 tsp water and heat very gently until the chocolate has melted, stirring occasionally. Remove from the heat.

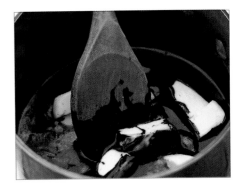

3 Add the butter to the chocolate and stir until melted.

4 Add the egg yolks, ground almonds and vanilla sugar, and stir together. Turn the mixture into a large bowl.

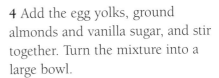

5 Put the egg whites into a clean, grease-free bowl and whisk until they form stiff peaks, then fold in batches into the chocolate mixture.

6 Put the mixture into the prepared tin and bake for 15–17 minutes, or until just set. The mixture should still be soft in the centre. Remove the lining paper.

7 Leave to cool in the tin, then carefully turn out on to a serving plate. Serve with whipped cream.

Energy 311kcal/1288kJ; Protein 6.8g; Carbohydrate 10g, of which sugars 9.3g; Fat 27.4g, of which saturates 9.9g; Cholesterol 75mg; Calcium 66.2mg; Fibre 1.9g; Sodium 97mg.

Devil's food cake

Originating in the US and dating back to 1905, this cake is always made using cocoa powder rather than melted chocolate. The chocolate cake is layered and covered with a fine white frosting flavoured with orange. It tastes very good indeed, and will keep for four days.

SERVES 10–12

175g/6oz/¾ cup butter, at room
  temperature, plus extra
  for greasing
50g/2oz/½ cup unsweetened
  cocoa powder
350g/12oz/scant 2 cups soft dark
  brown sugar
3 eggs
275g/10oz/1½ cups plain
  (all-purpose) flour
7.5ml/1½ tsp bicarbonate of soda
  (baking soda)
1.5ml/¼ tsp baking powder
120ml/4fl oz/½ cup sour cream
shreds of orange rind, to decorate

For the frosting
300g/11oz/1½ cups caster
  (superfine) sugar
2 egg whites
60ml/4 tbsp orange juice
  concentrate
15ml/1 tbsp lemon juice
grated rind of 1 orange

1 Preheat the oven to 180°C/350°F/ Gas 4. Grease and line two 23cm/9in round shallow cake tins (pans) with baking parchment.

2 In a bowl, mix the cocoa powder with 175ml/6fl oz/¾ cup boiling water until smooth. Leave to cool.

3 Beat the butter and sugar until light and fluffy, then beat in the eggs one at a time.

4 When the cocoa mixture is luke-warm, add it to the butter mixture.

5 Sift the flour, bicarbonate of soda and baking powder into the cocoa mixture in three batches, alternating with the soured cream.

6 Pour into the tins and bake for 30–35 minutes, or until the cake pulls away from the sides.

7 Leave to cool in the tins for 15 minutes, then turn out to cool on a wire rack to go cold. Remove the lining papers.

8 To make the frosting, put all the ingredients into a heatproof bowl set over a pan of gently simmering water. With an electric whisk, beat until the mixture holds soft peaks. Remove from the heat and continue beating until thick enough to spread.

9 Quickly sandwich the cake layers with frosting, then spread over the top and sides. Decorate with orange rind shreds.

Energy 455kcal/1916kJ; Protein 5.7g; Carbohydrate 75.5g, of which sugars 57.6g; Fat 16.6g, of which saturates 9.6g; Cholesterol 84.6mg; Calcium 86.5mg; Fibre 1.2g; Sodium 165mg.

Chocolate drizzle party cake

Make this moist chocolate and hazelnut cake to celebrate almost any family occasion.
The decoration couldn't be simpler, but it looks effective. The cake is easy to make, children and
adults love it, and it can even be served with fresh summer fruits or a scoop of ice cream.

SERVES 10

115g/4oz/½ cup butter, softened,
  plus extra for greasing
175g/6oz/scant 1 cup natural caster
  (superfine) sugar
4 large (US extra large) eggs,
  separated
175g/6oz/1½ cups self-raising
  (self-rising) flour, sifted
115g/4oz plain (semisweet)
  chocolate, grated
90ml/6 tbsp milk
115g/4oz/1 cup ground hazelnuts

For the filling and topping
60ml/4 tbsp chocolate and
  hazelnut spread, warmed
200g/7oz milk chocolate
150g/5oz white chocolate
edible gold or silver balls
Materials: wired silver ribbon

1 Preheat the oven to 220°C/
425°F/Gas 7. Grease and line a
20cm/8in deep round cake tin (pan)
with baking parchment.

2 Beat the butter and sugar
together until light and fluffy, then
whisk in the egg yolks gradually,
adding 5ml/1 tsp flour with each
addition to prevent the mixture
from curdling.

COOK'S TIP
The cake keeps for 4 days in an
airtight container. Freeze the
base, undecorated and wrapped
in foil, for up to 2 months.

3 Fold in the grated chocolate, milk
and ground hazelnuts until smooth.

4 Whisk the egg whites in a clean,
grease-free bowl until they form soft
peaks. Fold them into the mixture,
alternating with the remaining flour.

5 Spoon into the tin and smooth
level. Reduce the oven temperature
to 170C/350F/Gas 3. Bake in the
centre of the oven for about 1 hour
10 minutes, or until the centre
springs back when pressed.

6 Cool in the tin for 5 minutes, then
turn out to cool on a wire rack and
peel away the lining paper.

7 Cut the cake in half, and cover
one half with warmed chocolate
spread.

8 Sandwich the other half on top
and put them on to a serving plate.

9 Melt the chocolates in two
separate heatproof bowls set over
pans of gently simmering water,
then spoon into two separate small
paper piping (pastry) bags.
Alternatively, melt in two heatproof
bowls in the microwave oven.

10 Snip off the end of each bag and
drizzle each chocolate over the top
and side of the cake in a
random pattern.

11 Sprinkle the edible gold or
silver balls over the top and leave
to set for 1 hour. Finish with a large
wired bow in the centre of the cake,
or add candles if made for a
birthday celebration.

Energy 430kcal/1790kJ; Protein 7.8g; Carbohydrate 29.5g, of which sugars 28.8g; Fat 32.1g, of which saturates 13.6g; Cholesterol 96mg; Calcium 92mg; Fibre 1.9g; Sodium 125mg.

Chocolate, cherry and polenta cake

Almonds and polenta give this richly flavoured chocolate cake a nutty and dense texture, which is lightened with whisked egg whites. Crisp glacé cherries and a hint of orange make a delicious contrast. This cake will keep for up to three days in an airtight container.

3 Melt the chocolate in a heatproof bowl over a pan of simmering water.

4 Whisk the egg yolks with the sugar in a bowl until thick and pale.

5 Beat in the chocolate. Fold in the polenta, almonds, flour and orange.

6 Put the egg whites into a clean, grease-free bowl and whisk until they form stiff peaks.

7 Stir 15ml/1 tbsp of the whites into the chocolate mixture, then fold in the rest. Finally, fold in the cherries.

SERVES 8

50g/2oz/½ cup quick-cook polenta
butter, for greasing
200g/7oz plain (semisweet)
  chocolate, broken into pieces
5 eggs, separated
175g/6oz/scant 1 cup caster
  (superfine) sugar
115g/4oz/1 cup ground almonds
60ml/4 tbsp plain
  (all-purpose) flour
finely grated rind of 1 orange
115g/4oz/½ cup glacé (candied)
  cherries, halved
icing (confectioners') sugar,
  for dusting

1 Put the polenta in a bowl and add 120ml/4fl oz/½ cup boiling water, cover and leave for 30 minutes.

2 Preheat the oven to 190°C/375°F/ Gas 5. Grease and line a 20cm/8in round deep cake tin (pan).

8 Turn the mixture into the prepared tin and bake for 45–55 minutes, or until firm to the touch. Turn out and cool on a wire rack. Remove the lining paper. Dust with icing sugar.

Energy 420kcal/1764kJ; Protein 9.6g; Carbohydrate 56.4g, of which sugars 45.5g; Fat 18.8g, of which saturates 5.8; Cholesterol 120mg; Calcium 89mg; Fibre 2.2g; Sodium 53mg.

Chocolate and prune cake

Ready-to-eat prunes add moisture and a depth of flavour that complements chocolate in this cake. The rich mixture also includes gram flour, made from chickpeas, which has no gluten and is higher in carbohydrates than ordinary flour. Keep for up to five days in an airtight container.

SERVES 8–10

150g/5oz/10 tbsp butter, plus extra for greasing
300g/11oz dark (bittersweet) chocolate
150g/5oz/1¼ cups gram flour
10ml/2 tsp baking powder
200g/7oz/generous 1 cup ready-to-eat stoned (pitted) prunes, quartered
3 eggs, beaten
120ml/4fl oz/½ cup coconut milk

1 Preheat the oven to 180°C/350°F/ Gas 4. Grease and line a 20cm/8in round deep cake tin (pan) with baking parchment.

2 Melt the chocolate in a heatproof bowl set over a pan of gently simmering water. Remove from the heat to cool.

3 Sift the flour and baking powder into a bowl.

4 Place the butter and prunes in a food processor fitted with a flat blade. Process until light and fluffy, then scrape into a large bowl.

5 Gradually fold the melted chocolate and eggs into the prunes, alternating with the flour mixture.

6 Beat in the coconut milk, then spoon into the prepared tin and smooth the top level.

7 Bake for 20–30 minutes, or until the cake is firm to the touch and a skewer inserted into the centre comes out clean. Remove the lining.

8 Leave to cool on a wire rack before serving.

Energy 317kcal/1329kJ; Protein 6.5g; Carbohydrate 37.7g, of which sugars 26g; Fat 16.6g, of which saturates 7.3g; Cholesterol 60mg; Calcium 54mg; Fibre 2.4g; Sodium 127mg.

Chocolate and beetroot layer cake

Vegetables, like fruit, can add moisture to a cake, and although beetroot might seem like an unusual choice, it is actually wonderful for giving a cake depth of colour and a good consistency. Top with ganache to make a chocolate-lover's delight. Keep refrigerated, for up to three days.

SERVES 10–12

115g/4oz/½ cup unsalted butter, softened, plus extra for greasing
unsweetened cocoa powder, for dusting
225g/8oz can cooked whole beetroot, drained and juice reserved
425g/15oz/scant 2 cups soft light brown sugar
3 eggs
15ml/1 tbsp vanilla extract
75g/3oz dark (bittersweet) chocolate, melted and cooled
225g/8oz/2 cups plain (all-purpose) flour
10ml/2 tsp baking powder
pinch of salt
120ml/4fl oz/½ cup buttermilk
chocolate curls (optional), *see page 84*

For the ganache
475ml/16fl oz/2 cups whipping cream or double (heavy) cream
500g/1¼ lb dark (bittersweet) chocolate, broken into pieces
15ml/1 tbsp vanilla extract

1 Preheat the oven to 160°C/325°F/ Gas 3. Grease two 23cm/9in round shallow cake tins (pans) and dust the base and sides with cocoa.

2 Grate the beetroot and add to the reserved juice. Set aside.

3 Using an electric whisk, beat the butter, sugar, eggs and vanilla extract in a large bowl until pale. Reduce the speed and beat in the cooled melted chocolate.

4 With the whisk on low speed, gradually beat the flour, baking powder and salt into the chocolate mixture, alternating with the buttermilk.

5 Add the beetroot and juice, then beat for 1 minute.

6 Divide between the prepared tins. Bake for 30–35 minutes, or until a skewer inserted in the centre of each cake comes out clean.

7 Cool for 10 minutes in the tins, then turn out on to a wire rack to go cold. Remove the lining papers.

8 To make the ganache, heat the cream in a pan over medium heat, until it just begins to boil, stirring occasionally.

9 Remove from the heat and stir in the chocolate, stirring constantly until melted and smooth. Stir in the vanilla extract, then pour the mixture into a bowl.

10 Allow to cool, then chill, stirring every 10 minutes for about 1 hour, until the mixture thickens to a spreadable consistency.

11 To assemble the cake, put one layer on a serving plate and spread with one-third of the ganache. Put the second layer on top and spread the remaining ganache over the top and sides of the cake.

12 Decorate with the chocolate curls, if you like. Allow to set for 20–30 minutes, then chill until ready to serve. Any leftover cake can be frozen for up to 3 months.

Energy 699kcal/2925kJ; Protein 7.4g; Carbohydrate 85.1g, of which sugars 70.3g; Fat 38.9g, of which saturates 23.5g; Cholesterol 113mg; Calcium 109mg; Fibre 2.1g; Sodium 108mg.

Chocolate potato cake

This very rich chocolate cake owes its moist texture to the addition of smooth mashed potato.
Topped with chocolate fudge icing, the cake makes a superb dessert with a little whipped cream.
Use a good-quality dark chocolate for the best results. This will keep for up to four days, chilled.

SERVES 10–12

225g/8oz/1 cup butter, plus extra
 for greasing
200g/7oz/1 cup caster
 (superfine) sugar
4 eggs, separated
175g/6oz dark (bittersweet)
 chocolate, finely grated
75g/3oz/¾ cup ground almonds
165g/5½oz/1½ cups
 mashed potato
225g/8oz/2 cup self-raising
 (self-rising) flour
5ml/1 tsp cinnamon
45ml/3 tbsp milk
chocolate curls, to decorate,
 see page 84
whipped cream, to serve

For the icing
115g/4oz dark (bittersweet)
 chocolate, broken into pieces
25g/1oz/2 tbsp butter, diced

1 Preheat the oven to 180°C/350°F/
Gas 4. Grease and line a 23cm/9in
round deep cake tin (pan) with
baking parchment.

2 In a large bowl, cream together
the sugar and butter until fluffy.

3 Beat the egg yolks into the
creamed mixture.

4 Stir the chocolate into the creamed
mixture with the ground almonds.

5 Pass the mashed potato through a
sieve (strainer) or ricer, and stir it
into the creamed chocolate mixture.

6 Sift the flour and cinnamon and
fold into the mixture with the milk.

7 Put the egg whites into a clean,
grease-free bowl and whisk until stiff
peaks form. Fold into the batter.

8 Turn into the prepared tin. Bake for
1¼ hours, or until a skewer inserted
into the cake comes out clean.

9 Allow the cake to cool in the tin
for 5 minutes. Turn out on to a wire
rack to go cold. Peel off the paper.

10 To make the icing, melt the
chocolate in a heatproof bowl over
a pan of gently simmering water.
Add the butter and stir until the
mixture is smooth and glossy.

11 Smooth the icing over the cake.
Decorate with white and dark
chocolate shavings. Allow to set.
Serve with whipped cream.

Energy 575kcal/2403kJ; Protein 8.7g; Carbohydrate 59g, of which sugars 39g; Fat 35.5g, of which saturates 18.8g; Cholesterol 146mg; Calcium 141mg; Fibre 2.1g; Sodium 273mg.

Chocolate orange marquise

This fabulous cake has very little flour, but is rich with butter, eggs and chocolate, and flavoured with orange rind and juice. Enjoy this special cake with coffee, or with cream as a dessert. Store chilled in an airtight container for up to three days.

SERVES 6–8

225g/8oz/1 cup unsalted butter, diced, at room temperature, plus extra for greasing
200g/7oz/1 cup caster (superfine) sugar
60ml/4 tbsp freshly squeezed orange juice
350g/12oz plain (semisweet) chocolate, broken into pieces
5 eggs
finely grated rind of 1 orange
45ml/3 tbsp plain (all-purpose) flour
icing (confectioners') sugar, to decorate
finely pared strips of orange rind, to decorate

1 Preheat the oven to 180°C/350°F/ Gas 4. Grease and line a 23cm/9in round deep cake tin (pan) with baking parchment.

2 Put 115g/4oz/generous ½ cup of the caster sugar in a heavy pan with the fresh orange juice. Place over a low heat until all the sugar has dissolved. Stir constantly so that the sugar does not catch and burn. Do not allow to boil.

3 Remove from the heat and stir in the chocolate until melted, then add the butter, stirring, until melted and evenly mixed. Cool.

4 Put the eggs with the remaining sugar in a large bowl and whisk until pale and very thick. Add the orange rind.

5 Using a metal spoon, fold the chocolate mixture lightly and evenly into the egg mixture using a metal spoon and a figure-of-eight motion. Sift the flour over and fold in evenly.

COOK'S TIP
Make the marquise ahead of time and freeze for up to 3 months in a freezerproof box.

6 Scrape the mixture into the prepared tin. Put the tin into a roasting pan, then pour hot water into the roasting pan to reach halfway up the outside of the cake tin.

7 Bake for 1 hour, or until the cake is firm to the touch. Carefully remove the cake tin from the roasting pan and cool for 15–20 minutes.

8 Invert the cake on a baking sheet. Lift away the tin and lining paper. Place a serving plate over the cake, then turn the baking sheet and plate over as one so that the cake is transferred to the plate.

9 Dust with icing sugar, decorate with strips of pared orange rind and serve slightly warm or cold.

Energy 553kcal/2309kJ; Protein 3.1g; Carbohydrate 59.1g, of which sugars 54.4g; Fat 35.5g, of which saturates 22g; Cholesterol 63mg; Calcium 41mg; Fibre 1.3g; Sodium 176mg.

Sachertorte

This glorious gateau has a pedigree going back to 1832, when it was created by Franz Sacher, a chef of the royal household in Vienna. It is rich and dark, with a flavour that contrasts with the apricot glaze – and it's topped with a rich, glossy icing. Keep, refrigerated, for up to three days.

SERVES 10–12

150g/5oz/10 tbsp unsalted butter,
  plus extra for greasing
115g/4oz/generous ½ cup caster
  (superfine) sugar
8 eggs, separated
225g/8oz dark (bittersweet)
  chocolate, melted and cooled
115g/4oz/1 cup plain
  (all-purpose) flour

For the glaze
225g/8oz/1 cup apricot jam
15ml/1 tbsp lemon juice

For the icing
225g/8oz dark (bittersweet)
  chocolate, broken into pieces
200g/7oz/1 cup caster
  (superfine) sugar
15ml/1 tbsp golden
  (light corn) syrup
250ml/8fl oz/1 cup double
  (heavy) cream
5ml/1 tsp vanilla extract
chocolate curls, to decorate,
  see page 84

1 Preheat the oven to 180°C/350°F/ Gas 4. Grease and line a 23cm/9in round deep cake tin (pan).

2 In a bowl, beat the butter with the sugar until pale and fluffy, then add the egg yolks, one at a time, beating well after each addition.

3 Beat in the melted chocolate, then sift the flour over the mixture and fold it in evenly with a large metal spoon.

4 Put the egg whites into a clean, grease-free bowl and whisk until they form stiff peaks.

5 Stir about a quarter of the whites into the chocolate mixture to lighten it, then fold in the remaining whites.

6 Tip the mixture into the prepared tin and smooth the top level. Bake for 50–55 minutes, or until firm.

7 Leave to stand in the tin for 5 minutes, then turn out on to a wire rack to go cold. Remove the lining paper. Slice in half across the middle to make two even layers.

8 To make the glaze, heat the apricot jam with the lemon juice in a small pan until melted, then strain through a sieve (strainer) into a bowl.

9 Brush the top and sides of each layer with the apricot glaze, then sandwich them together. Put the cake on a wire rack.

10 To make the icing, put the chocolate, sugar, golden syrup, cream and vanilla extract in a pan. Heat gently, stirring constantly, until the mixture is thick and smooth.

11 Simmer gently for 3–4 minutes, without stirring, until the mixture registers 95°C/200°F on a sugar thermometer.

12 Pour the icing quickly over the cake, spreading to cover the top and sides completely.

13 Leave to set, then decorate with chocolate curls.

Energy 625kcal/2618kJ; Protein 7.6g; Carbohydrate 73.1g, of which sugars 65.5g; Fat 35.8g, of which saturates 20.8g; Cholesterol 184mg; Calcium 73mg; Fibre 1.2g; Sodium 143mg.

Individual cakes

Miniature cakes are attractive and fun to make, and are always popular. They are visually appealing and make a focal point at parties. Muffins and cupcakes have good keeping qualities and are ideal to prepare ahead, so you can bake them the day before and store them in an airtight tin. You can also freeze them undecorated (although you will need to replace the paper cases). Fun cakes for children to help decorate include Novelty Party Cupcakes and the scary Hallowe'en Horrors. Make up a selection of little cakes for a coffee morning or a tea party and include some light and delicate cakes such as Simple Coconut Cakes and French Madeleines, which will make a beautiful display alongside richer cakes such as Rich Chocolate Ruffles. Some plainer bakes, such as Rock Buns and Buttermilk Scones, are best freshly made and eaten on the same day. Bake a tray for a brunch party and serve them warm from the oven – you'll find they will soon disappear.

Left: Marshmallow Daisy Cakes, Snowballs and Buttermilk Scones.

Fondant fancies

A classic fondant coating is light and shiny, and ideal to finish these delicate little cakes. These fancies are extra special, so serve them for a classic celebration such as a christening. They will keep for two days in an airtight container. Freeze the undecorated base for up to three months.

MAKES 28

50g/2oz/½ cup unsalted butter
  oil, for greasing
3 large (US extra large) eggs
100g/3¾oz/generous ½ cup caster
  (superfine) sugar
100g/3¾oz/scant 1 cup plain
  (all-purpose) flour
15ml/1 tbsp cornflour (cornstarch)
pinch of salt

For the icing and decoration
500g/1lb/5 cups fondant icing
  sugar, sifted
food colourings

1 Melt the butter in a small pan over a gentle heat and allow to cool.

2 Preheat the oven to 180°C/ 350°F/Gas 4. Oil and line a 28 × 18cm/11 × 7in baking tin with baking parchment.

3 In a large bowl, whisk the eggs and sugar together, using an electric mixer, until pale, thick and creamy, and the mixture leaves a trail when the beaters are lifted away.

4 Sift the flour, cornflour and salt over the surface and pour the melted butter around the sides of the bowl. Gently fold together, taking care not to knock out the air, then pour into the lined tin.

5 Bake for 20 minutes, or until light golden and just firm to the touch.

6 Cool in the tin for 5 minutes, then turn out, peel away the lining paper and leave on a wire rack until cold.

7 Stamp out rounds using a 3.5cm/ 1½in pastry (cookie) cutter, fancy shapes or small squares, and put on a wire rack standing over a tray.

8 Put the sifted fondant icing sugar into a bowl and add enough cold water to give a coating consistency. Divide the icing among several bowls and colour it delicately with a few drops of food colouring. Keep each bowl covered with a damp cloth until needed.

9 Working quickly, spoon the icing over each cake and smooth down to cover the tops and sides. Put in paper cases to serve.

Energy 259kcal/1094kJ; Protein 2.7g; Carbohydrate 49.7g, of which sugars 41.4g; Fat 6.9g, of which saturates 4g; Cholesterol 40mg; Calcium 50mg; Fibre 0.3g; Sodium 66mg.

Marshmallow daisy cakes

These lemony cakes are as fresh as a daisy; they are quick and very simple to make and bake. The marshmallow flowers take moments to create – all you need is a pair of scissors. They are sure to be a hit, especially with children, and will keep for two days in an airtight container.

MAKES 12

115g/4oz/1 cup self-raising
   (self-rising) flour
5ml/1 tsp baking powder
115g/4oz/generous ½ cup caster
   (superfine) sugar
115g/4oz/½ cup soft tub margarine
2 large (US extra large)
   eggs, beaten
15ml/1 tbsp lemon juice
finely grated rind of 1 lemon

For the decoration
½ quantity buttercream, *see
   page 22*
12 pink and white marshmallows
caster (superfine) sugar, for dusting
small sweets (candies)

1 Preheat the oven to 180°C/350°F/
Gas 4. Line a 12-cup muffin tin
(pan) with paper cases.

2 Sift the flour, baking powder and
sugar into a large bowl, then add the
remaining ingredients. Beat until
light and creamy, then place heaped
spoonfuls into the paper cases.

3 Bake for about 20 minutes, or
until golden and firm to the touch.

4 Allow to cool for 2 minutes, then
turn out on to a wire rack to go cold.

5 When cold, spread the top of each
cake with a little buttercream.

6 Use kitchen scissors to cut each
marshmallow in half horizontally.

7 Dip the cut marshmallow edges in
caster sugar to prevent sticking.
Repeat, cutting the marshmallows in
half again, and dipping the cut edge
in caster sugar.

8 Press the tips of four halves
together to form four petals of a
flower. Arrange them on top of a
cupcake and press a small sweet
into the centre.

COOK'S TIP
Freeze undecorated. You may
have to replace the paper cases,
as these tend to peel away.

Energy 115kcal/483kJ; Protein 1.3g; Carbohydrate 16.5g, of which sugars 12.1g; Fat 5.4g, of which saturates 3.2g; Cholesterol 31mg; Calcium 18mg; Fibre 0.2g; Sodium 43mg.

Rock buns

These old-fashioned favourites are perfect fun in the kitchen and provide a great introduction to baking, as the mixture can be formed into little balls – great for hands-on kids' cooking. As rock cakes are not a rich mixture, they are best eaten on the day they are baked.

4 Stir the sugar, fruit and grated rind into the dry mixture.

5 In a small bowl, beat the egg with the milk and add to the cake batter. Mix with a fork until the mixture leaves the sides of the bowl clean and is stiff but not sticky. If it is too dry add a little more milk, one teaspoon at a time.

6 Divide the mixture into 12 balls and put on to the baking tray, spacing well apart.

7 Flick the tops with a fork to roughen, then sprinkle each lightly with demerara sugar.

8 Bake for 15 minutes, or until firm and golden. Remove from the sheet and cool on a wire rack.

MAKES 12

65g/2½oz/generous ½ cup butter, diced, plus extra for greasing
225g/8oz/2 cups plain (all-purpose) flour
1.5ml/¼ tsp mixed (apple pie) spice
pinch of salt
10ml/2 tsp baking powder
65g/2½oz/generous ¼ cup golden caster (superfine) sugar
115g/4oz/⅔ cup mixed dried fruit
finely grated rind of ½ lemon or small orange
1 egg
about 30ml/2 tbsp milk
30ml/2 tbsp demerara (raw) sugar

1 Preheat the oven to 200°C/400°F/ Gas 6. Grease a large baking sheet.

2 Sift the flour, spice, baking powder and salt into a bowl. Add the butter.

3 Rub the butter into the flour until the mixture resembles crumbs.

Energy 206kcal/866kJ; Protein 2.7g; Carbohydrate 31.3g, of which sugars 17g; Fat 8.7g, of which saturates 5.2g; Cholesterol 36mg; Calcium 45mg; Fibre 0.8g; Sodium 71mg.

Simple coconut cakes

Made with just three ingredients stirred up in a pan, these little cakes are so easy to make that children will love to get involved with baking them. They are quick and simple to make, and are also fat-free – they taste good too! Keep them for three days in an airtight container.

MAKES 14

225g/8oz/2⅔ cups desiccated (dry unsweetened shredded) coconut
275g/10oz/scant 1½ cups caster (superfine) sugar
5 egg whites

1 Preheat the oven to 180°C/350°F/ Gas 4. Line a muffin tin (pan) with paper cases.

2 Put the desiccated coconut, sugar and egg whites in a large, heavy pan. Stir over a low heat with a wooden spoon for about 5 minutes, or until the mixture is warmed through.

COOK'S TIP
These cakes cannot be frozen.

3 Spoon a heaped tablespoonful of the mixture into each paper case.

4 Bake for 15 minutes, or until the cakes are pale golden. Allow to cool on a wire rack.

VARIATION
For coffee and hazelnut macaroons, in a bowl mix together 115g/4oz/1 cup ground hazelnuts with 225g/8oz/ generous 1 cup caster (superfine) sugar, 15ml/1 tbsp ground rice, 10ml/2 tsp ground coffee and 2 egg whites to form a stiff paste. Spoon heaped tablespoons of the mixture into paper cases and bake for 15–20 minutes until pale golden. Leave to cool.

Energy 190kcal/793kJ; Protein 1.5g; Carbohydrate 16g, of which sugars 16g; Fat 13.9g, of which saturates 10.6g; Cholesterol 25mg; Calcium 17mg; Fibre 2g; Sodium 12mg.

Buttermilk scones

Plain scones filled with jam and cream make a delicious addition to afternoon tea. Baking them with buttermilk instead of plain milk gives them additional flavour. Serve with a good bought or home-made jam and clotted cream to make them a little special. They are best eaten fresh.

MAKES 12

75g/3oz/6 tbsp butter, diced, plus
   extra for greasing
350g/12oz/3 cups self-raising
   (self-rising) flour, plus extra
   for dusting
115g/4oz/generous ½ cup caster
   (superfine) sugar
175ml/6fl oz/¾ cup buttermilk or
   natural (plain) low-fat yogurt
raspberry jam, to serve
clotted cream, to serve

1 Preheat the oven to 200°C/
400°F/Gas 6 and lightly grease a
baking sheet.

2 Sift the flour into a large bowl and
add the diced butter.

3 Rub together with your fingertips
until the mixture resembles fine
breadcrumbs. Stir in the sugar and
mix, then make a well in the centre.

4 Add the buttermilk or yogurt.
Stir in lightly with a flat-bladed
knife until the mixture forms a
soft dough.

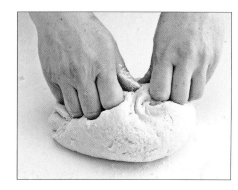

5 Turn the dough out on to a lightly
floured surface and knead lightly.

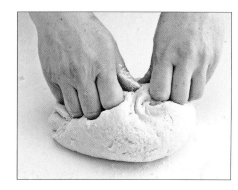

6 Roll out to a 2.5cm/1in thickness.
Stamp out rounds using a 5cm/2in
round pastry (cookie) cutter, then
gather up the trimmings, re-knead
and stamp out more rounds.

7 Put the rounds on the baking
sheet and bake for 12–14 minutes,
or until risen and light golden.

8 Allow to cool on a wire rack and
serve split open with jam and cream.
Home-made scones are best eaten
fresh on the day of baking.

Energy 74kcal/311kJ; Protein 1.7g; Carbohydrate 10.9g, of which sugars 0.7g; Fat 3g, of which saturates 1.8g; Cholesterol 8mg; Calcium 34mg; Fibre 0.4g; Sodium 26mg.

Madeleines

These small shell-shaped sponge cakes are light as a feather and traditionally served with a cup of tea. In France on Christmas Eve, however, you'll find them coloured a delicate pink and accompanied by a glass of champagne. Eat these fresh on the day they are made. Do not freeze.

MAKES 15

50g/2oz/¼ cup unsalted butter, melted, plus extra melted butter for greasing
2 eggs
50g/2oz/¼ cup vanilla caster (superfine) sugar
50g/2oz/½ cup plain (all-purpose) flour, plus extra for dusting
a few drops of orange flower water
pink food colouring (optional)
icing (confectioners') sugar, for dusting

1 Preheat the oven to 200°C/400°F/ Gas 6. Lightly grease a scalloped madeleine mould with a little melted butter, making sure all the indentations are greased well, so the cakes are released easily. Dust with a little flour, shake the tin, then tap out any excess.

2 Put the eggs and sugar in a heatproof bowl set over a pan of hot water. Whisk until very thick and mousse-like, and the mixture leaves a thick ribbon trail when the beaters are lifted away. Remove from the heat and continue whisking for 2 minutes.

3 Sift half the flour over the surface and fold in gently with a large metal spoon, then repeat with the remaining flour.

4 Gently fold in the cooled melted butter and the orange flower water.

5 Divide the mixture in half, if you like, and colour half a delicate pink with a few drops of food colour.

6 Spoon into the moulds to just level with the top. Smooth level and bake for 10 minutes, or until firm and pale golden.

7 Cool in the tin for a few minutes, then turn out to cool on a wire rack.

8 Re-grease and flour the tins, then use up the remaining batter.

9 Serve with the shell sides upward, dusted with icing sugar.

Energy 130kcal/547kJ; Protein 2.4g; Carbohydrate 17.3g, of which sugars 6.8g; Fat 6.2g, of which saturates 3.5g; Cholesterol 45mg; Calcium 28mg; Fibre 0.4g; Sodium 50mg.

Novelty party cupcakes

One of the easiest ways to keep children happy is to let them bake and decorate their own party cakes. You can use sweets or bought decorations – or even make your own from sugarpaste. This simple all-in-one batter can be mixed together in a food processor, if you like. Eat fresh.

MAKES 12

115g/4oz/1 cup self-raising (self-rising) flour
5ml/1 tsp baking powder
115g/4oz/generous ½ cup caster (superfine) sugar
115g/4oz/1 cup soft tub margarine
2 large (US extra large) eggs
5ml/1 tsp vanilla extract

For the decoration
1 quantity glacé icing, *see page 24*
food colourings
small coloured sweets (candies), jellies or piped decorations

COOK'S TIP
Freeze the cakes undecorated for up to 1 month. You may need to replace the paper cases when the cakes have thawed as these can peel away from the cakes.

1 Preheat the oven to 160°C/325°F/ Gas 3. Line a 12-cup muffin tin (pan) with cupcake cases.

2 Sift the flour and baking powder into a bowl, or food processor, and add all the remaining ingredients.

3 Beat with an electric mixer, or process until smooth, then divide among the paper cases.

4 Bake for 20 minutes, or until firm to the touch. Cool on a wire rack.

5 To decorate, colour the glacé icing in batches and spoon a little over each cake. Decorate with sweets while the icing is wet. Leave to set.

Energy 228kcal/957kJ; Protein 2.5g; Carbohydrate 27.9g, of which sugars 20.5g; Fat 12.7g, of which saturates 7.9g; Cholesterol 74mg; Calcium 32mg; Fibre 0.3g; Sodium 121mg.

Cinnamon meringues

These meringues have a hint of cinnamon and almond, which gives them a delicate flavour. They have a slightly chewy texture that goes particularly well with luscious summer fruits and amaretto-flavoured cream. Eat fresh, or store, undecorated, in an airtight container for two weeks.

MAKES 10

4 egg whites
1.25ml/¼ tsp cream of tartar
225g/8oz/generous 1 cup caster
  (superfine) sugar
2.5ml/½ tsp ground cinnamon
a few drops of almond extract
40g/1½oz/generous ⅓ cup
  ground almonds

For the filling
300ml/½ pint/1¼ cups double
  (heavy) cream
15ml/1 tbsp amaretto liqueur
  (optional)
350g/12oz/3 cups fresh redcurrants
  and raspberries
tiny sprigs of fresh mint

1 Preheat the oven to 110°C/225°F/ Gas ¼. Line two baking sheets with baking parchment.

2 Rinse out a clean mixing bowl with boiling water, then dry with kitchen paper to make sure it is totally grease-free.

3 Put the egg whites into the bowl and whisk until they form stiff peaks. Add the cream of tartar. Gradually whisk in the sugar with the cinnamon and almond extract in small batches until the mixture is thick and stiff. Fold in the almonds.

> **COOK'S TIP**
> These cakes are not suitable for freezing.

4 Spoon 20 rough dessertspoonfuls on to the baking sheets, then bake for 2 hours, or until crisp and dry, swapping over the position of the baking sheets halfway through. Cool, then peel off from the papers.

5 Whip the cream until soft peaks form. Fold in the liqueur, if using, then fill a piping (pastry) bag. Pipe cream on to 10 meringue bases. Arrange the fruits, mint and meringue lid and serve immediately.

Energy 193kcal/821kJ; Protein 2.7g; Carbohydrate 40g, of which sugars 40g; Fat 1.6g, of which saturates 0.1g; Cholesterol 0mg; Calcium 31mg; Fibre 1.4g; Sodium 26mg.

Snowballs

These snowy muffins prove that variations on this simple theme appear to be endless. They have the tastiest topping ever, white chocolate mixed with coconut liqueur and cream, then sprinkled with coconut strands. They make an irresistible winter's treat. Keep for up to two days.

4 Divide the batter evenly among the paper cases.

5 Bake for 18–20 minutes, or until risen, golden and firm to the touch. Leave in the tin for 2 minutes, then turn out to cool on a wire rack.

6 To make the topping, put the chocolate and liqueur in a bowl. Put the cream in a pan and bring to the boil, then pour it over the chocolate and liqueur. Stir until smooth, then cool and chill for 30 minutes.

7 Whisk with an electric mixer for a few minutes, or until light and fluffy.

8 Spread the icing over the top of each muffin, then sprinkle coconut strands liberally over the icing to cover completely.

MAKES 12

175g/6oz/12 tbsp caster
   (superfine) sugar
2.5ml/½ tsp baking powder
200g/7oz/1¾ cups self-raising
   (self-rising) flour
15ml/2 tbsp desiccated (dry
   unsweetened shredded) coconut
175g/6oz/¾ cup soft tub margarine
3 eggs, beaten
15ml/1 tbsp milk

For the topping
175g/6oz white chocolate, chopped
15ml/1 tbsp coconut liqueur
75ml/5 tbsp double (heavy) cream
175g/6oz/2 cups large shredded
   coconut strands or curls

1 Preheat the oven to 180°C/350°F/ Gas 4. Line a 12-cup deep muffin tin (pan) with paper cases.

2 Sift the sugar, baking powder, flour and coconut into a large bowl.

3 Add the margarine, eggs and milk and beat until smooth and creamy.

Energy 481kcal/2005kJ; Protein 5.9g; Carbohydrate 39.6g, of which sugars 35.2g; Fat 34.3g, of which saturates 23.9g; Cholesterol 12mg; Calcium 137mg; Fibre 3g; Sodium 167mg.

Rich chocolate ruffles

These glossy chocolate cakes are a class act, decorated with ruffles of chocolate and glinting with gold leaf. Each one is contained in a gold foil case to make them perfect individual cakes for a special occasion. The attractive ruffle is a useful technique for using on other cakes.

MAKES 12

65g/2½oz/9 tbsp self-raising (self-rising) flour
25g/1oz/¼ cup unsweetened cocoa powder
75g/3oz/⅓ cup soft dark brown sugar
75g/3oz/6 tbsp butter, softened
3 eggs
30ml/2 tbsp milk

For the ruffles
125g/4oz plain (semisweet) chocolate, grated
37.5ml/2½ tbsp liquid glucose (clear corn syrup)

For the topping
100ml/3½fl oz/scant ½ cup double (heavy) cream
15ml/1 tbsp liquid glucose (clear corn syrup)
200g/7oz dark (bittersweet) chocolate, melted
scraps of edible gold leaf (optional)

1 Preheat the oven to 190°C/375°F/ Gas 5. Line a 12-cup muffin tray with gold foil cases.

2 Sift the flour and cocoa into a bowl, add the sugar, butter, eggs and milk, and beat for about 2 minutes, or until smooth.

3 Divide the batter among the cases and bake for 15 minutes, or until just firm to the touch in the centre.

4 Remove from the tray and leave to cool on a wire rack.

5 To make the ruffles, melt the chocolate in a heatproof bowl set over a pan of warm water. Remove from the heat. Beat in the glucose until a paste forms that comes away from the sides of the bowl. Chill in a plastic bag for 1 hour.

6 Break off pieces and knead until pliable. Roll out between sheets of non-stick paper until 5mm/¼in thick. Mould into delicate fans.

7 To make the topping, bring the cream to the boil in a pan.

8 Remove from the heat, add the liquid glucose and the melted chocolate, and stir.

9 Spoon the mixture over the top of each cake, top with a chocolate ruffle and tiny scraps of gold leaf, if you like, then leave to set. Eat fresh for the best taste.

Energy 392kcal/1641kJ; Protein 5g; Carbohydrate 42.2g, of which sugars 30.5g; Fat 23.8g, of which saturates 14.8g; Cholesterol 111mg; Calcium 110mg; Fibre 0.7g; Sodium 235mg.

Sugar sparkle cupcakes

These delicate rose-flavoured cakes are pretty in pink and perfect for a girls-only party.
Make the cakes ahead, if you like, and have fun decorating them with sugar sprinkles, sugar
flowers or shapes in your choice of colours. Keep for up to two days in an airtight container.

MAKES 12

115g/4oz/1 cup self-raising
  (self-rising) flour
115g/4oz/generous ½ cup caster
  (superfine) sugar
115g/4oz/½ cup unsalted
  butter, softened
2 eggs
15ml/1 tbsp rose water
15ml/1 tbsp milk
pink food colouring, optional

For the topping and decoration
225g/8oz/2 cups icing
  (confectioners') sugar, sifted
15ml/1 tbsp rose water
pink sugar sprinkles, or sugar
  flowers or shapes

1 Preheat the oven to 190°C/375°F/
Gas 5. Line a 12-cup muffin tin
(pan) with paper cases.

2 Put the flour, sugar, butter and
eggs into a large bowl with the rose
water and beat until smooth. Add
the milk and a few drops of pink
food colouring.

3 Divide among the paper cases.

4 Bake for 15–20 minutes, or until
the cakes are risen and golden,
and are just firm to the touch.
Remove them from the tray and put
on a wire rack to cool.

5 To make the topping, sift the icing
sugar into a bowl. Add the rose
water with a few drops of pink
food colouring and 5ml/1 tsp cold
water, or enough to mix to a
spreadable icing.

6 Spoon a little icing over the top of
each cake, then top with sugar
sprinkles, flowers or shapes.

COOK'S TIP
Freeze, undecorated, for up to
3 months.

Energy 249kcal/1041kJ; Protein 2.4g; Carbohydrate 27g, of which sugars 20.4g; Fat 16.5g, of which saturates 9.5g; Cholesterol 76mg; Calcium 35mg; Fibre 0.3g; Sodium 89mg.

Autumn passionettes

Moist and moreish, these sweet carrot and apple bakes are guaranteed to be a winner with children and adults alike. They are perfect for autumn snacks, with their warming mixed spice flavouring and walnut topping. These cakes will keep for up to four days in an airtight container.

MAKES 24

150g/5oz/scant ¾ cup
  butter, melted
200g/7oz/1 cup soft light
  brown sugar
115g/4oz/1 cup carrots, peeled
  and finely grated
50g/2oz/1 cup dessert apples,
  peeled and finely grated
pinch of salt
1–2 tsp/5–10ml mixed (apple
  pie) spice
2 eggs
200g/7oz/1¾ cups self-raising
  (self-rising) flour
10ml/2 tsp baking powder
115g/4oz/1 cup walnuts,
  finely chopped

For the topping
175g/6oz/¾ cup cream cheese
75ml/5 tbsp single (light) cream
50g/2oz/½ cup icing
  (confectioners') sugar
24 walnut halves
10ml/2 tsp unsweetened cocoa
  powder, sifted

1 Preheat the oven to 180°C/350°F/ Gas 4. Arrange 24 paper cases in muffin trays.

2 Put the butter, sugar, carrots, apples, salt, mixed spice and eggs in a mixing bowl and beat well to combine.

3 Sift together the flour and baking powder into the butter and sugar mixture. Add the chopped walnuts and fold in until evenly blended.

4 Half-fill the paper cases with the batter, then bake for 20–25 minutes, until golden, or until they spring back when pressed lightly with a finger.

5 Leave the cakes in the tins for about 5 minutes, before transferring them to a wire rack to cool completely.

6 To make the topping, put the cream cheese in a mixing bowl and beat in the cream and icing sugar until smooth.

7 Put a spoonful of the topping in the centre of each cake, then decorate with the walnuts. Dust with sifted cocoa powder and allow the icing to set before serving.

Energy 194kcal/808kJ; Protein 3.1g; Carbohydrate 18.3g, of which sugars 11.8g; Fat 12.6g, of which saturates 5.5g; Cholesterol 37mg; Calcium 38mg; Fibre 0.7g; Sodium 75mg.

Hallowe'en horrors

Children will love decorating these little chocolate cupcakes with ghostly shapes, pumpkins, witches' hats, or they can think up their own scary creations to celebrate this fun and spooky festival. Keep these for two days in an airtight container or freeze, undecorated, for three months.

MAKES 24

175g/6oz/scant 1 cup caster (superfine) sugar
175g/6oz/¾ cup soft tub margarine
3 eggs, beaten
150g/5oz/1¼ cups self-raising (self-rising) flour
5ml/1 tsp baking powder
25g/1oz/¼ cup unsweetened cocoa powder

For the icing and decoration
50g/2oz/¼ cup unsalted butter
25g/1oz/¼ cup unsweetened cocoa powder
30ml/2 tbsp milk
225g/8oz/2 cups natural icing (confectioners') sugar
500g/1¼lb sugarpaste (fondant)
orange, green, red and black paste food colourings
tubes of coloured writing icing

1 Preheat the oven to 180°C/350°F/Gas 4. Line two 12-cup muffin tins (pans) with paper cases.

2 Put the sugar, margarine and eggs in a bowl, then sift in the flour, baking powder and cocoa. Beat for 2 minutes, or until smooth and creamy.

3 Spoon the mixture into the paper cases and bake for 15–20 minutes, or until well risen and the tops spring back when lightly touched with a finger. Transfer to a wire rack to cool completely.

4 To make the icing, melt the butter with the cocoa in a small pan over low heat. Remove from the heat and add the milk, then beat in the icing sugar until smooth and glossy. Spread thickly on top of each cake.

5 Thinly roll out one third of the white sugarpaste. Cut out circles using a pastry cutter. Hold the centre and ruche up the circle to look like a ghost. Pipe black dots for eyes and a circle for the mouth using a tube of black writing icing. Make seven more.

6 Colour half of the remaining paste orange and the rest black.

7 Roll the orange paste into eight balls. Gently press a skewer at regular intervals into the side of each. Mould a green fondant stalk.

8 To make eight witches' hats, roll the black icing into equal balls, then taper into a cone. Flute the larger end. Decorate with white icing. Stick one decoration to each cake.

Energy 203kcal/859kJ; Protein 2g; Carbohydrate 42.8g, of which sugars 32.5g; Fat 3.8g, of which saturates 0.6g; Cholesterol 10mg; Calcium 72mg; Fibre 0.7g; Sodium 60mg.

Chocolate and strawberry-filled palmiers

Who could resist sweet and crisp puff pastry, with layers of chocolate, whipped cream and fresh strawberries, as a summer treat? These traditional little pastries, formed into rounded swirls, may look complicated but are actually easy to make, and they look delightful. Eat fresh.

MAKES 8

butter, for greasing
15g/½oz/2 tbsp unsweetened
    cocoa powder
375g/13oz puff pastry, thawed,
    if frozen
25g/1oz/2 tbsp golden caster
    (superfine) sugar

For the filling
300ml/½ pint/1¼ cups whipping
    cream, whipped
45ml/3 tbsp dark (bittersweet)
    chocolate spread
175g/6oz/generous 1 cup sliced
    strawberries
icing (confectioners') sugar,
    for dusting

1 Preheat the oven to 220°C/425°F/Gas 7. Grease two large baking sheets.

2 Dust a clean, dry working surface lightly with 15ml/1 tbsp cocoa powder.

3 Keeping the long side of pastry towards you, roll it out on half the cocoa powder to a rectangle 35 × 23cm/14 × 9in. Lightly brush the top of the pastry with cold water, then sprinkle over the caster sugar and remaining cocoa.

4 Measure and mark the centre of the pastry. Roll up each of the short sides like a Swiss roll (jelly roll) so that they both meet in the centre. Brush the join with a little water and press the rolls together to secure.

5 Mark and then cut the roll into 16 slices. Arrange on the baking sheets, spacing them well apart.

6 Bake for 8–10 minutes, or until risen, puffy and golden brown. Transfer to a wire rack to cool.

7 Lightly spread half the pastries with the chocolate spread.

8 To make the filling, put the cream in a piping (pastry) bag fitted with a small plain nozzle. Pipe the cream on top of the chocolate spread, then top with a few strawberry slices.

9 Top each chocolate spread cream and strawberry layer with a pastry. Dust lightly with icing sugar and serve immediately.

Energy 368kcal/1533kJ; Protein 4.2g; Carbohydrate 27g, of which sugars 9.7g; Fat 28.3g, of which saturates 10.4g; Cholesterol 40mg; Calcium 60mg; Fibre 0.5g; Sodium 180mg.

English Eccles cakes

These traditional dried fruit-filled pastry rounds taste fabulous when home-made. Make your own pastry instead of using ready-made and you'll notice the difference in its light and flaky texture and rich flavour. Inside is a warmly spiced fruit filling. These cakes keep for 1–2 days in an airtight tin.

MAKES 16

225g/8oz/2 cups plain (all-purpose) flour, plus extra for dusting
pinch of salt
200g/7oz/scant 1 cup butter, diced, plus extra for greasing
5ml/1 tsp lemon juice
100ml/3½fl oz/scant ½ cup iced water

For the filling
2.5ml/½ tsp mixed (apple pie) spice
50g/2oz/¼ cup muscovado (molasses) sugar
175g/6oz/⅔ cup currants
50g/2oz/⅓ cup mixed chopped (candied) peel
5ml/1 tsp lemon juice
finely grated rind of 1 lemon

For the glaze
1 egg, beaten
caster (superfine) sugar, for dusting

1 To make the pastry, sift the flour and salt into a bowl. Add the butter, lemon juice and iced water. Mix to a soft dough using a flat-bladed knife. Add 5–10ml/1–2 tsp extra water if it is too dry.

2 Flour your work surface and your hands, then gently knead and shape the pastry into a rectangle 28 × 13cm/11 × 5in. (The pastry will just hold together and will contain noticeable pieces of diced butter.)

3 Fold up the lower third of pastry and bring the top third down over it. Turn with the fold on the left, and press three times with the rolling pin to flatten.

4 Roll out into a rectangle and fold and roll as before. Wrap in a plastic bag and chill for 20 minutes, or freeze for 5 minutes.

5 Repeat the rolling, folding and chilling four more times. Wrap and chill for 20 minutes, or until needed.

6 Preheat the oven to 220°C/425°F/ Gas 7 and lightly grease two baking sheets.

7 Put all the filling ingredients in a bowl and stir together.

8 Roll the pastry to 5mm/¼in thick. Using a 10cm/4in round pastry (cookie) cutter, stamp out 16 rounds and place a heaped teaspoonful of the filling in the centre of each.

9 Dampen the edges with water, gather up the pastry over the filling and press to seal. Turn the pastries so the seal is underneath and roll each gently. Put on a baking sheet. Cut three slits across the top of each. Brush with beaten egg and sprinkle with sugar. Bake for 20 minutes, then cool on a wire rack.

Energy 201kcal/842kJ; Protein 1.7g; Carbohydrate 23.5g, of which sugars 12.8g; Fat 11.8g, of which saturates 7.4g; Cholesterol 30mg; Calcium 38mg; Fibre 0.8g; Sodium 96mg.

Traybakes

Versatile traybakes can be simple and plain or elaborately decorated. They are baked in square or rectangular shallow tins and the texture can be firm like a cookie or soft like a cake. Add a topping to make them even more tasty – sweet icing, a crumble or crunchy layer, or rich chocolate – and cut them into portions. Indulgent traybakes such as Millionaire's Shortbread are a special treat, but healthier slices such as Granola Squares or Marmalade Flapjacks are great to pack for school lunches or to take to the office. Traybakes are just right for feeding a large number, so they are the ideal cakes for bazaars, fêtes, coffee mornings, cake stalls, picnics and children's parties. They require little effort to prepare and are easy to transport if you leave them in the tins in which they have been baked. They usually freeze well undecorated, so you can make and freeze them ahead or bake and store them in sealed flat containers for one to two days.

Left: Almond Slices and Blueberry Coffee Cake.

Vanilla streusel bars

The crumbly topping on this cake makes a crunchy contrast to the moist vanilla-flavoured sponge underneath. A full flavour is achieved by using vanilla extract as well as vanilla sugar, which is easy to make at home. These will keep for up to four days in an airtight container.

MAKES 25 BARS

175g/6oz/¾ cup butter, softened,
   plus extra for greasing
175g/6oz/1½ cups self-raising
   (self-rising) flour
5ml/1 tsp baking powder
175g/6oz/scant 1 cup vanilla sugar
3 eggs, beaten
7.5ml/1½ tsp vanilla extract
15–30ml/1–2 tbsp milk

For the topping
115g/4oz/1 cup self-raising
   (self-rising) flour
75g/3oz/6 tbsp butter
75g/3oz/6 tbsp vanilla sugar
icing (confectioners') sugar,
   for dusting

1 Preheat the oven to 180°C/ 350°F/Gas 4. Lightly grease and line a 23 × 18cm/9 × 7in shallow tin (pan) with baking parchment.

2 To make the topping, sift the flour into a bowl and rub in the butter until the mixture resembles crumbs. Stir in the vanilla sugar. Set aside.

3 To make the base, sift the flour and baking powder into a bowl. Add the butter, vanilla sugar and eggs. Beat well until smooth, adding the vanilla extract and just enough milk to give a soft dropping consistency.

4 Spoon the mixture into the prepared tin and smooth level.

5 Sprinkle the streusel topping over the surface and press down to cover the cake batter. Bake for 45–60 minutes, or until browned and firm.

6 Cool in the tin for 5 minutes, then turn out on to a wire rack to go cold. Remove the lining paper.

7 Place on a board and dust with icing sugar. Cut into 25 bars with a sharp knife.

Energy 162kcal/680kJ; Protein 2g; Carbohydrate 19.5g, of which sugars 10.7g; Fat 9g, of which saturates 5.4g; Cholesterol 44mg; Calcium 27mg; Fibre 0.4g; Sodium 70mg.

Honey cake

The earliest form of sweetener, honey has always been an important ingredient in cooking. It adds its own distinctive aroma to foods, but there is no need to use an expensive honey for cakes, as the flavour changes slightly with baking. Keep for up to five days in an airtight container.

MAKES 16 SQUARES

175g/6oz/¾ cup butter, plus extra
   for greasing
175g/6oz/¾ cup clear honey
115g/4oz/½ cup soft light
   brown sugar
2 eggs, lightly beaten
15–30ml/1–2 tbsp milk
225g/8oz/2 cups self-raising
   (self-rising) flour

1 Grease and line a 23cm/9in square tin (pan) with baking parchment.

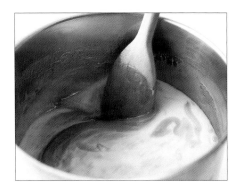

2 In a pan, gently heat the butter, honey and sugar, stirring until the sugar has dissolved and the butter has melted. Set aside to cool slightly.

3 Preheat the oven to 180°C/ 350°F/Gas 4.

4 In two batches, beat the eggs and milk into the cooled mixture in the pan, using a wooden spoon.

5 Sift the flour over the top, stir in and beat well. The batter should have a smooth pouring consistency.

6 Pour the mixture into the tin. Bake for 30 minutes, or until well risen, golden brown and firm to the touch.

7 Cool for 20 minutes, then turn on to a wire rack to go cold. Remove the paper lining and cut into squares.

Energy 152kcal/639kJ; Protein 1.9g; Carbohydrate 23.5g, of which sugars 13g; Fat 6.3g, of which saturates 3.8g; Cholesterol 26mg; Calcium 30mg; Fibre 0.4g; Sodium 49mg.

Cherry batter cake

This simple traybake is made with three contrasting layers: a cake batter, drained black cherries from a jar and a speedy brown sugar topping. It tastes lovely with a little whipped cream. This cake can be kept for up to two days in an airtight container.

3 Drain the fruit and evenly distribute it over the base.

4 Mix the remaining topping ingredients together and spoon evenly over the fruit. Bake for 40 minutes, or until golden brown and firm to the touch.

5 Leave to cool in the tin. Dust with icing sugar, cut into slices, then remove from the tin.

MAKES 12 SLICES

75g/3oz/6 tbsp butter, softened, plus extra for greasing
225g/8oz/2 cups self-raising (self-rising) flour
5ml/1 tsp baking powder
150g/5oz/⅔ cup soft light brown sugar
1 egg, lightly beaten
15–30ml/1–2 tbsp milk

For the topping
675g/1½lb jar black cherries
175g/6oz/¾ cup soft light brown sugar
50g/2oz/½ cup self-raising (self-rising) flour
50g/2oz/¼ cup butter, melted
icing (confectioners') sugar, for dusting
whipped cream, to serve (optional)

1 Preheat the oven to 190°C/375°F/Gas 5. Grease a 33 × 23cm/13 × 9in Swiss roll tin (jelly roll pan). Line the base and sides with baking parchment.

2 To make the base, sift the flour and baking powder into a large bowl. Add the butter, sugar, egg and milk. Beat the mixture until smooth, then turn into the prepared tin and smooth the surface.

Energy 314kcal/1327kJ; Protein 3.6g; Carbohydrate 57g, of which sugars 39.7g; Fat 9.5g, of which saturates 5.7g; Cholesterol 38.8mg; Calcium 74mg; Fibre 1.5g; Sodium 81mg.

Blueberry cake

This cake is studded with blueberries and has a hint of lemon zest, giving it a lovely fruity flavour and texture. It is a perfect accompaniment to a morning cup of coffee. It will keep for up to two days in an airtight container.

MAKES 12 SLICES

65g/2½oz/5 tbsp butter, at room
    temperature, plus extra
    for greasing
225g/8oz/2 cups plain
    (all-purpose) flour
15ml/1 tbsp baking powder
5ml/1 tsp salt
150g/5oz/¾ cup caster
    (superfine) sugar
1 egg
250ml/8fl oz/1 cup milk
2.5ml/½ tsp grated lemon rind
225g/8oz/2 cups fresh or frozen
    blueberries, well drained
115g/4oz/1 cup icing
    (confectioners') sugar
30ml/2 tbsp fresh lemon juice

1 Preheat the oven to 180°C/350°F/ Gas 4. Grease and line a 33 × 9cm/ 13 × 9in shallow tin (pan).

2 Sift the flour with the baking powder and salt.

3 In a large bowl, beat the butter and sugar until light and fluffy. Beat in the egg and milk. Fold in the flour mixture, then mix in the lemon rind.

4 Scrape half of the batter into the cake tin, spreading it to the edges.

5 Sprinkle with half the blueberries. Top with the remaining batter and then the remaining blueberries.

6 Bake for 35–45 minutes, or until golden brown and a skewer inserted into the centre comes out clean.

7 Allow to stand for 5 minutes in the tin, then turn out on to a wire rack to go cold. Remove the lining.

8 To make the topping, mix the icing sugar with the lemon juice to make a smooth glaze with a pouring consistency.

9 Drizzle the glaze over the top of the warm cake. Allow to set before cutting into slices and serving.

Energy 217kcal/918kJ; Protein 3.3g; Carbohydrate 41.3g, of which sugars 26.3g; Fat 5.5g, of which saturates 3.3g; Cholesterol 30mg; Calcium 66mg; Fibre 1g; Sodium 60mg.

Sticky gingerbread

The secret of this gingerbread's rich stickiness lies in the huge amount of treacle used, as well as storing the cake for two or three days to mature. Serve spread with butter or cream cheese, to contrast with the cake's taste and texture. This will keep for a week in an airtight container.

MAKES 12 SLICES

115g/4oz/½ cup butter, softened, plus extra for greasing
225g/8oz/2 cups plain (all-purpose) flour
10ml/2 tsp ground ginger
5ml/1 tsp mixed (apple pie) spice
pinch of salt
2 pieces preserved stem ginger, drained and chopped
115g/4oz/½ cup muscovado (molasses) sugar, sifted
275g/10oz/generous ⅔ cup treacle (molasses)
2 eggs, beaten
2.5ml/½ tsp bicarbonate of soda (baking soda)
30ml/2 tbsp milk, warmed
butter or cream cheese, to serve

1 Preheat the oven to 160°C/325°F/ Gas 3. Grease and line an 18cm/7in square deep cake tin (pan) with baking parchment.

2 Sift the flour, ground ginger, mixed spice and salt together into a large bowl. Add the chopped preserved ginger and toss it in the flour to coat all the pieces.

3 In a large bowl, cream the butter and sugar together until fluffy, then gradually beat in the treacle. Beat in the eggs, then the flour mixture.

4 Dissolve the bicarbonate of soda in the milk and gradually beat this into the mixture.

5 Pour the batter into the prepared tin and smooth the top level. Bake for 45 minutes. Reduce the oven temperature to 150°C/300°F/Gas 2 and bake for a further 30 minutes. The gingerbread should be dark and slightly risen. A skewer inserted into the centre should come out clean.

6 Allow to cool in the tin for 5 minutes, then turn out on to a wire rack to go cold. Remove the paper lining and slice the cake.

Energy 373kcal/1572kJ; Protein 5.2g; Carbohydrate 60.9g, of which sugars 38.7g; Fat 13.9g, of which saturates 8.1g; Cholesterol 78.5mg; Calcium 253.6mg; Fibre 0.9g; Sodium 170.5mg.

Parkin

From the north of England, parkin contains oatmeal and lots of syrup and treacle. This exceptionally moist ginger cake improves in flavour and texture when stored in a tin for several days. It is perfect for autumnal days, and will keep for up to a week in an airtight container.

MAKES 16–20 SQUARES

115g/4oz/½ cup butter, plus extra
 for greasing
300ml/½ pint/1¼ cups milk
225g/8oz/1 cup golden
 (light corn) syrup
225g/8oz/scant ¾ cup
 treacle (molasses)
50g/2oz/¼ cup soft dark
 brown sugar
450g/1lb/4 cups plain
 (all-purpose) flour
2.5ml/½ tsp bicarbonate of soda
 (baking soda)
7.5ml/1½ tsp ground ginger
350g/12oz/3 cups medium oatmeal
1 egg, beaten
icing (confectioners') sugar,
 for dusting

1 Preheat the oven to 180°C/350°F/ Gas 4. Grease and line a 20cm/8in square deep cake tin (pan).

2 Gently heat together the milk, syrup, treacle, butter and sugar, stirring until smooth; do not boil.

3 Sift the flour into a bowl, add the bicarbonate of soda, ginger and oatmeal. Make a well in the centre.

4 Allow the treacle mixture to cool in the pan slightly so that it is just warm. Add the mixture to the bowl with the egg, stirring to make a smooth batter.

5 Pour the batter into the tin and bake for 45 minutes, or until firm to the touch.

6 Cool slightly in the tin, then turn out on to a wire rack to go cold. Remove the lining paper. Dust with icing sugar and cut into squares.

COOK'S TIP
Parkin freezes well, wrapped in foil, for up to 3 months. After this the spices lose their power.

Energy 273kcal/1152kJ; Protein 5.3g; Carbohydrate 50g, of which sugars 20.1g; Fat 7.1g, of which saturates 3.3g; Cholesterol 23mg; Calcium 127mg; Fibre 1.9g; Sodium 102mg.

Marmalade flapjacks

Everyone enjoys making flapjacks because they take so little time to prepare. You don't even need a bowl – just weigh out the ingredients and mix them in the pan. These ones are fruity and tangy with orange and cranberries. Store them in an airtight container for up to five days.

5 Add the oats, sultanas and cranberries. Stir together.

6 Turn into the tin and smooth the top level. Bake for 25–30 minutes, or until firm and golden, then put the tin on a wire rack to cool. Remove the lining paper.

7 Brush the marmalade over the top of the hot flapjack, then mark into 16 slices. Leave to go cold in the tin.

MAKES 16 SLICES

115g/4oz/½ cup butter or block margarine, plus extra for greasing
1 small orange
115g/4oz/scant ⅓ cup golden (light corn) syrup
50g/2oz/½ cup soft light brown sugar
175g/6oz/scant 2 cups rolled oats
50g/2oz/⅓ cup sultanas (golden raisins)
25g/1oz/¼ cup dried cranberries
75ml/3 tbsp orange marmalade

1 Preheat the oven to 180°C/350°F/Gas 4. Grease and line a 20cm/8in square shallow tin (pan) with baking parchment.

2 Finely grate the rind from the orange. Squeeze the juice into a separate container and set aside.

3 Melt the butter or margarine, syrup and sugar together in a heavy pan over a medium heat.

4 Add the orange rind and 15ml/1 tbsp orange juice to the pan.

Energy 154kcal/646kJ; Protein 1.5g; Carbohydrate 23g, of which sugars 15g; Fat 6.8g, of which saturates 3.9g; Cholesterol 17mg; Calcium 14mg; Fibre 0.8g; Sodium 80mg.

Granola squares

These chewy treats are packed with flavour as well as lots of healthy ingredients: nuts, seeds and dried fruits. They make great lunchbox additions to keep tummies from rumbling in the afternoon. These squares keep for four days in an airtight container.

MAKES 9 SQUARES

175g/6oz/¾ cup butter, plus extra
  for greasing
150g/5oz/scant ⅔ cup clear honey
250g/9oz/generous 1 cup demerara
  (raw) sugar
350g/12oz/scant 4 cups rolled oats
5ml/1 tsp ground cinnamon
75g/3oz/¾ cup chopped pecan nuts
75g/3oz/generous ½ cup raisins
75g/3oz/½ cup dried mango,
  chopped
75g/3oz/scant ½ cup ready-to-eat
  dried apricots, chopped
50g/2oz/4 tbsp sesame seeds
75g/3oz/6 tbsp pumpkin seeds
50g/2oz/½ cup ground almonds

1 Preheat the oven to 190°C/375°F/ Gas 5. Grease and line a 23cm/9in square shallow tin (pan) with baking parchment.

2 Put the honey, butter and sugar in a heavy pan and heat gently until the sugar is dissolved.

3 Bring to the boil, then boil for 2 minutes, stirring, until a thick caramel sauce has formed. Remove from the heat.

4 Add all the remaining ingredients and stir well.

5 Spoon into the tin, then smooth the top level.

6 Bake for 15 minutes, or until just pale golden. Cool in the tin for 10 minutes, then turn out on to a wire rack. Remove the lining and mark into nine squares. Leave to go cold.

Energy 522kcal/2189kJ; Protein 8.4g; Carbohydrate 63.8g, of which sugars 40.9g; Fat 27.7g, of which saturates 8.9g; Cholesterol 31mg; Calcium 93mg; Fibre 4.3g; Sodium 108mg.

White chocolate blondies

Blondies, like brownies, are chewy and moist squares, except that they don't usually contain chocolate. These ones, however, are made with white chocolate, sticky apricots and crunchy pecan nuts, so they are extra special. Keep for up to three days in an airtight container.

MAKES 24 SQUARES

175g/6oz/¾ cup unsalted butter, softened, plus extra for greasing
300g/11oz/generous 1½ cups caster (superfine) sugar
3 eggs, beaten
5ml/1 tsp vanilla extract
200g/7oz/1¾ cups plain (all-purpose) flour
5ml/1 tsp baking powder
90g/3½oz white chocolate chips
90g/3½oz/scant 1 cup pecan nuts, roughly chopped
90g/3½oz/scant ½ cup ready-to-eat dried apricots, chopped
icing (confectioners') sugar, for dusting

1 Preheat the oven to 180°C/350°F/ Gas 4. Grease and line a 30 × 20cm/ 12 × 8in shallow tin (pan) with baking parchment.

2 Beat the butter with the sugar, then add the eggs and vanilla, beating well after each addition.

3 Sift the flour and baking powder into the bowl, then add the chocolate chips, pecan nuts and apricots, and fold into the mixture until evenly blended.

4 Spoon into the prepared tin and smooth the top level.

5 Bake for 25–30 minutes, or until just set. Mark into 24 squares and leave to cool for 10 minutes.

6 Turn out on to a wire rack to go cold. Remove the lining paper, cut into squares and dust with sugar.

COOK'S TIP
Freeze, wrapped in foil, for up to 2 months.

Energy 183kcal/767kJ; Protein 1.7g; Carbohydrate 23.3g, of which sugars 16.9g; Fat 9.9g, of which saturates 4.9g; Cholesterol 17mg; Calcium 35mg; Fibre 0.7g; Sodium 60mg.

Mint choc brownies

Chocolate and mint always make a marvellous combination, but it's quite unusual to find them in a cake. Here brownies contain crisp pieces of peppermint and are covered with a minty buttercream topping. Keep for up to three days in an airtight container.

MAKES 25 SQUARES

75g/3oz/¾ cup unsweetened
   cocoa powder
175g/6oz/¾ cup soft tub
   margarine, plus extra for greasing
75g/3oz clear peppermint boiled
   sweets (hard candies)
275g/10oz/2½ cups plain
   (all-purpose) flour
7.5ml/1½ tsp bicarbonate of soda
   (baking soda)
2.5ml/½ tsp baking powder
275g/10oz/scant 1½ cups soft
   dark brown sugar
3 eggs, beaten

For the topping
115g/4oz/½ cup unsalted
   butter, softened
225g/8oz/2 cups icing
   (confectioners') sugar
30ml/2 tbsp milk
2.5ml/½ tsp peppermint extract
a few drops of green food colouring
thin chocolate matchsticks

1 Dissolve the cocoa powder in 350ml/12fl oz/1½ cups boiling water, stir, then leave for 30 minutes.

2 Preheat the oven to 180°C/350°F/ Gas 4. Grease and line a 23cm/9in square deep cake tin (pan) with baking parchment.

3 Put the boiled mints into a strong plastic bag and tap with a rolling pin until they break into small pieces.

4 Sift the flour, bicarbonate of soda and baking powder into the cocoa.

5 Add the margarine, sugar and eggs. Beat for 2 minutes.

6 Fold in the crushed mints. Spoon into the tin. Smooth the top level.

7 Bake for 1 hour 10 minutes, or until baked through. Cool in the tin.

8 To make the topping, beat the butter with the icing sugar, milk, peppermint extract and a few drops of green food colouring. Spread over the cooled cake.

9 Cut into squares and decorate each with two small matchsticks.

Energy 331kcal/1379kJ; Protein 3.8g; Carbohydrate 30.2g, of which sugars 21.4g; Fat 22.5g, of which saturates 6.7g; Cholesterol 49mg; Calcium 37mg; Fibre 1.1g; Sodium 50mg.

Cranberry brownies

Gooey chocolate brownies are an all-time favourite, and these are packed with cranberries and crunchy nuts. Keep some dried cranberries in the store cupboard, as they will add interest to cakes and traybakes. Keep these for up to five days in an airtight container.

3 Add the beaten eggs, and sift in the flour and spice. Add the cranberries and mix well.

4 Spread half the mixture into the tin, sprinkle over the nuts, then spread the rest of the mixture on top.

MAKES 18 SLICES

225g/8oz/1 cup butter, plus extra
  for greasing
300g/11oz plain (semisweet)
  chocolate, broken into squares
275g/10oz/1¼ cups soft dark
  brown sugar
60ml/4 tbsp milk
4 eggs, beaten
225g/8oz/2 cups plain
  (all-purpose) flour
2.5ml/½ tsp ground cinnamon
75g/3oz/¾ cup dried cranberries
50g/2oz/½ cup chopped
  mixed nuts
icing (confectioners') sugar,
  for dusting

1 Preheat the oven to 180°C/350°F/ Gas 4. Grease and line a 28 × 18cm/ 7 × 11in shallow tin (pan) with baking parchment.

2 Put the chocolate, butter, sugar and milk in a pan and heat gently, stirring constantly, until melted. Leave to cool for 5 minutes.

5 Bake for 25 minutes, or until springy to the touch. Mark into squares while warm. Leave to cool in the tin on a wire rack.

Energy 290kcal/1208kJ; Protein 3.1g; Carbohydrate 20.6g, of which sugars 18.3g; Fat 22.3g, of which saturates 11.5g; Cholesterol 68mg; Calcium 35mg; Fibre 0.9g; Sodium 180mg.

Florentine slices

If you're looking for a popular cake for a cake sale or coffee morning, you'll find the colourful jewel-like topping on these fruity slices makes them a great seller – and they'll also be snapped up at home in no time. These cakes keep in an airtight container for up to four days.

MAKES 12 SLICES

150g/5oz/10 tbsp butter, plus extra
  for greasing
150g/5oz/⅔ cup golden caster
  (superfine) sugar
3 eggs
175g/6oz/1½ cups self-raising
  (self-rising) flour
275g/10oz/1⅔ cups mixed
  dried fruit
90g/3½oz/generous ½ cup glacé
  (candied) cherries, halved
a few drops of almond extract

For the topping
100g/4oz/½ cup glacé (candied)
  cherries, chopped
15ml/1 tbsp golden
  (light corn) syrup
50g/2oz/½ cup flaked
  (sliced) almonds
25g/1oz/2 tbsp angelica, chopped

1 Preheat the oven to 190°C/375°F/ Gas 5. Grease and line a 28 × 18cm/ 11 × 7in shallow cake tin (pan) with baking parchment.

2 Whisk the butter and sugar together until light and fluffy. Whisk in the eggs one at a time.

3 Fold in the flour, then set aside 30ml/2 tbsp of the mixture in a bowl.

4 Fold the dried fruit, cherries and almond extract into the remaining cake mixture, then spoon into the tin and smooth the top level.

5 Bake for 20 minutes, reduce the heat to 180°C/350°F/Gas 4. Bake for a further 15 minutes, until just set.

6 To make the topping, stir the chopped cherries into the reserved cake mixture with the syrup, almonds and angelica, and mix well.

7 Spread evenly over the cake top using a wetted spoon. Bake for 15 minutes. Leave to cool in the tin.

8 Loosen the lining papers. Cut into 12 fingers when cold.

Energy 340kcal/1429kJ; Protein 4.6g; Carbohydrate 51.7g, of which sugars 40.8g; Fat 14.2g, of which saturates 7.4g; Cholesterol 76mg; Calcium 101mg; Fibre 1.4g; Sodium 177mg.

Lamingtons

Cake that is a day old is best for coating with the chocolate icing and coconut for these tasty little squares. Bake the base the day before, then it will cut more easily into squares. Keep a slab in the deep freeze, ready for thawing, cutting and coating. Eat them fresh once decorated.

MAKES 24 SQUARES

150g/5oz/generous ½ cup butter, softened, plus extra for greasing
300g/11oz/2¾ cups self-raising (self-rising) flour, plus extra for dusting
200g/7oz/1 cup caster (superfine) sugar
3 eggs, beaten
5ml/1 tsp vanilla extract
150ml/¼ pint/⅔ cup milk

For the icing and decoration
675g/1½lb/3½ cups caster (superfine) sugar
30ml/2 tbsp unsweetened cocoa powder
150g/5oz/1⅔ cups desiccated (dry unsweetened shredded) coconut

1 Preheat the oven to 180°C/350°F/ Gas 4. Grease a 20 × 30cm/8 × 12in deep cake tin (pan) and dust it lightly with a little flour. Tap the tin and shake out any excess flour.

2 Beat the butter and sugar together until light and fluffy. Beat in the eggs in batches, adding 5ml/1 tsp flour with each addition to prevent the mixture from curdling.

3 Sift in the remaining flour, then fold into the mixture. Add the vanilla and milk, and mix to a soft, dropping consistency.

4 Spoon into the tin and smooth level, then bake for 30 minutes, or until golden and firm in the centre.

5 Cool in the tin for 5 minutes, then turn out on to a wire rack to go cold. Store, wrapped in foil, for 1 day.

6 To make the icing, put the sugar, cocoa and 250ml/8fl oz/1 cup water in a large pan. Heat over a low heat until the sugar has dissolved. Bring to the boil, then simmer, without stirring, for about 12 minutes, or until thickened into a syrup.

7 Put the coconut into a large bowl.

8 Cut the cake into 5cm/2in cubes.

9 Stab a cake cube with a fork and dip into the chocolate icing to coat all over. Coat the cube in the coconut and put on a tray to dry. Repeat with the remaining cake until all the cubes are coated.

Energy 273kcal/1140kJ; Protein 3.1g; Carbohydrate 28.7g, of which sugars 22.4g; Fat 17g, of which saturates 12.2g; Cholesterol 44mg; Calcium 59mg; Fibre 2.3g; Sodium 160mg.

Grated berry bake

Pastry layers envelop a delicious and sticky fruit filling for this traybake. If your pastry skills are zero, never fear, as the pastry is grated into the tin, so you'll still be able to make this a success. Serve this with a spoonful of cream, if you like, and keep for two days in an airtight container.

MAKES 12 BARS

275g/10oz/2½ cups plain
    (all-purpose) flour
2.5ml/½ tsp ground cinnamon
175g/6oz/¾ cup butter, diced, plus
    extra for greasing
115g/4oz/generous ½ cup golden
    caster (superfine) sugar
1 egg, beaten
icing (confectioners') sugar,
    for dusting

For the filling
350g/12oz/3 cups fresh or frozen
    fruits of the forest (mixed
    blackcurrants, redcurrants,
    raspberries, blackberries)
150g/5oz/¾ cup sugar

1 Sift the flour and cinnamon into a bowl or food processor, add the butter, then rub together.

2 Stir in the sugar and beaten egg, and mix together to form a firm dough. Put in a plastic bag and chill for 2 hours or freeze for 20 minutes, or until the pastry forms a firm block.

3 To make the filling, put the fruit in a pan with 30ml/2 tbsp water and simmer for 5 minutes to soften. Add the sugar and stir until it dissolves, then boil for 5 minutes, or until syrupy and thick. Leave to cool.

> **COOK'S TIP**
> Freeze baked or unbaked in the tin, foil-wrapped, for 2 months.

4 Preheat the oven to 200°C/400°F/ Gas 6. Grease and line a 28 × 18cm/ 11 × 7in shallow tin (pan) with baking parchment.

5 Cut the chilled dough in half and, using a coarse grater, grate one half into the tin. Spread out evenly and press down lightly.

6 Spoon the cooled fruit over the pastry. Coarsely grate the rest of the pastry over the fruit to cover completely, but do not flatten it.

7 Bake for 35 minutes, or until golden brown and firm. When cool, remove the lining paper and cut into 12 bars. Dust with icing sugar.

Energy 286kcal/1203kJ; Protein 3.3g; Carbohydrate 42.2g, of which sugars 24.8g; Fat 12.8g, of which saturates 8.1g; Cholesterol 49mg; Calcium 56mg; Fibre 1.4g; Sodium 118mg.

American apple-sauce traybake

When apples are plentiful, cook them into a purée and mix them into this delicious fruit cake mixture to make it wonderfully moist. Top it with a vanilla frosting and decorate with walnuts for a very moreish treat. These squares will keep for five days in the refrigerator.

MAKES 15 SQUARES

450g/1lb dessert apples, peeled, cored and sliced
75g/3oz/6 tbsp butter, plus extra for greasing
115g/4oz/generous ½ cup golden caster (superfine) sugar
2 eggs
175g/6oz/1½ cups plain (all-purpose) flour
10ml/2 tsp baking powder
5ml/1 tsp mixed (apple pie) spice
50g/2oz/½ cup walnut pieces, chopped
115g/4oz/scant 1 cup raisins

For the frosting
175g/6oz/1½ cups icing (confectioners') sugar
75g/3oz/6 tbsp unsalted butter, softened
1 egg white
a few drops of vanilla extract
15 walnut halves, to decorate

1 Put the sliced apples into a pan with 15ml/1 tbsp water. Cook until thick and pulpy, stirring, then pour into a bowl and leave to cool.

2 Preheat the oven to 180°C/350°F/ Gas 4. Grease and line a 28 × 18cm/ 11 × 7in shallow tin (pan) with baking parchment.

3 In a large bowl, beat the butter and sugar together until light and fluffy. Gradually beat in the eggs.

4 Stir in the cold apple purée and mix well. Sift the flour, baking powder and mixed spice into the bowl, then add the walnuts and raisins. Mix well.

5 Spoon into the tin and smooth the top level. Bake for 45 minutes, or until a skewer inserted into the centre comes out clean. Cool for 5 minutes, then turn out on to a wire rack. Peel away the lining paper.

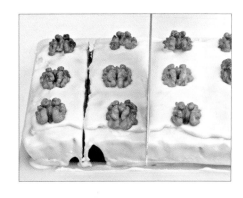

6 Put all the frosting ingredients except the walnuts into a bowl, and beat together until fluffy. Spread on top of the cake. Cut into squares and decorate each with a walnut.

Energy 255kcal/1070kJ; Protein 3g; Carbohydrate 37.4g, of which sugars 28.4g; Fat 11.4g, of which saturates 5.8g; Cholesterol 48mg; Calcium 40mg; Fibre 1.1g; Sodium 95mg.

Cornflake crunch-nut traybake

These squares have a moist, cranberry sponge base topped with a fruity and crunchy layer made with cornflakes. The combination of contrasting textures in one cake makes it hard to resist. These cakes will keep for up to two days in an airtight container.

MAKES 15 SQUARES

175g/6oz/¾ cup butter, softened, plus extra for greasing
175g/6oz/1½ cups self-raising (self-rising) flour
5ml/1 tsp baking powder
175g/6oz/scant 1 cup caster (superfine) sugar
3 eggs, beaten
75ml/5 tbsp cranberry sauce

For the topping
45ml/3 tbsp golden (light corn) syrup
75g/3oz/¾ cup dried cranberries
115g/4oz/4 cups cornflakes

1 Preheat the oven to 180°C/350°F/ Gas 4. Grease and line a 28 × 18cm/ 11 × 7in shallow tin (pan) with baking parchment.

2 Sift the flour and baking powder into a bowl and add the remaining ingredients, then beat until smooth.

COOK'S TIP
This traybake is not suitable for freezing.

3 Spoon into the tin and smooth the top level. Bake for 30 minutes, or until golden and firm in the centre.

4 To make the topping, heat the syrup and cranberries in a large pan over a low heat, then simmer for 2 minutes.

5 Add the cornflakes and gently fold in. Spoon over the cake layer and return to the oven. Bake for 10 minutes, or until lightly brown.

6 Cool in the tin for 5 minutes, then turn out on a wire rack to go cold. Remove the lining paper.

Energy 237kcal/994kJ; Protein 3.2g; Carbohydrate 33.7g, of which sugars 18.8g; Fat 10.9g, of which saturates 6.6g; Cholesterol 65mg; Calcium 35mg; Fibre 0.5g; Sodium 197mg.

Millionaire's shortbread

Shortbread topped with layers of soft caramel and set chocolate is a firm favourite with everyone, and the home-made version tastes so much better than ready-made. Give yourself plenty of time to make them, as the layers will need to set. The shortbread keeps for up to three days.

4 Bake for 20 minutes, or until light golden. Leave the shortbread base in the tin and cool on a wire rack.

5 To make the caramel, put the condensed milk, syrup, sugar and butter into a heavy pan and heat gently until the sugar has dissolved.

6 Bring the mixture to the boil and boil for 6–7 minutes, or until the mixture is light golden and thick, stirring constantly.

7 Pour the mixture straight from the pan over the cold shortbread base to cover it completely. Shake the pan to remove any air bubbles and leave until completely cold and set.

8 To make the chocolate layer, melt the chocolate in a heatproof bowl set over a pan of gently simmering water.

9 Pour the melted chocolate over the cold, set caramel and spread evenly with a metal spatula.

10 Leave to cool and set, then mark into squares with a sharp knife. Remove the lining paper.

MAKES 9 SQUARES

115g/4oz/½ cup butter, softened, plus extra for greasing
50g/2oz/generous ¼ cup caster (superfine) sugar
175g/6oz/1½ cups plain (all-purpose) flour

For the caramel layer
400g/14oz can sweetened condensed milk
30ml/2 tbsp golden (light corn) syrup
115g/4oz/generous ½ cup caster (superfine) sugar
115g/4oz/½ cup butter

For the chocolate layer
175g/6oz plain (semisweet) chocolate, broken into pieces

1 Preheat the oven to 180°C/350°F/ Gas 4. Grease and line a 20cm/8in square shallow tin (pan) with baking parchment.

2 Beat the butter and sugar together, and then mix in the flour.

3 Knead until smooth, then press into the tin using your fingers. Smooth level and prick with a fork.

Energy 587kcal/2459kJ; Protein 6.7g; Carbohydrate 74.2g, of which sugars 58.3g; Fat 31.3g, of which saturates 19.9g; Cholesterol 77mg; Calcium 178mg; Fibre 0.6g; Sodium 267mg.

Sticky toffee traybake

Dates add moisture and richness to cake mixtures, and make this traybake particularly gooey. With their luscious toffee layer these cake squares are wickedly delicious. They are perfect for toffee fans everywhere. The cakes keep for up to three days in an airtight container.

MAKES 15 SQUARES

50g/2oz/¼ cup butter, diced, plus extra for greasing
150g/5oz/scant 1 cup chopped stoned (pitted) dates
5ml/1 tsp bicarbonate of soda (baking soda)
150g/5oz/1¼ cups plain (all-purpose) flour
5ml/1 tsp baking powder
200g/7oz/1 cup caster (superfine) sugar
50g/2oz/½ cup walnuts, chopped
1 large (US extra large) egg, beaten
2.5ml/½ tsp vanilla extract

For the icing
25g/1oz/2 tbsp unsalted butter
60ml/4 tbsp soft light brown sugar
60ml/4 tbsp double (heavy) cream

1 Preheat the oven to 180°C/350°F/ Gas 4. Grease and line a 30 × 20cm/ 12 × 8in shallow baking tin (pan) with baking parchment.

2 Put the dates in a bowl with the bicarbonate of soda and pour over 250ml/8fl oz/1 cup boiling water. Stir, then leave to cool slightly while making the batter.

3 Sift the flour and baking powder into a bowl and add the butter. Rub between your fingertips until the mixture resembles fine crumbs.

4 Stir in the sugar and walnuts, and mix well. Add the egg and vanilla extract with the date mixture and beat until smooth.

5 Spoon into the baking tin and smooth the top level. Bake for 25–30 minutes, or until well risen and firm to the touch. Leave to cool in the tin for 5 minutes, then turn out to cool on a wire rack and peel away the lining paper.

6 Put the icing ingredients in a pan and stir over a low heat until the sugar dissolves. Bring to the boil and boil for 1–2 minutes, until thickened.

7 Pour over the cake. Leave to set. Cut into 15 squares.

Energy 565kcal/2356kJ; Protein 6.2g; Carbohydrate 52.8g, of which sugars 38.8g; Fat 38.1g, of which saturates 20.7g; Cholesterol 175mg; Calcium 130mg; Fibre 0.8g; Sodium 349mg.

Mincemeat and marzipan traybake

This easy fruit cake is mixed all in one go, then a crunchy almond-paste topping is added. It is ideal for Christmas parties or to make for cake sales at that time of the year. Home-made almond paste adds an edge when it comes to flavour. Keep this for up to five days in an airtight container.

MAKES 15 SQUARES

115g/4oz/½ cup butter, softened, plus extra for greasing
225g/8oz/2 cups self-raising (self-rising) flour
400g/14oz jar fruit mincemeat
115g/4oz/⅔ cup mixed dried fruit
115g/4oz/½ cup muscovado (molasses) sugar
finely grated rind of ½ lemon
5ml/1 tsp mixed (apple pie) spice
2 eggs, beaten

For the topping and icing
250g/9oz almond paste, *see page 24*
115g/4oz/1 cup icing (confectioners') sugar
15ml/1 tbsp lemon juice

1 Preheat the oven to 160°C/325°F/Gas 3. Grease and line a 28 × 18cm/11 × 7in shallow tin (pan) with baking parchment.

2 Put all the cake ingredients in a mixing bowl and beat for about 3 minutes, or until smooth. Spoon into the prepared tin and smooth the top level. Bake for 50 minutes, or until golden.

3 To make the topping, grate the almond paste using a coarse grater.

4 Sprinkle the almond paste on top of the hot cake in an even layer. Return to the oven and bake for 10 minutes, or until the almond paste is light golden. Cool in the tin for 5 minutes, then turn out on to a wire rack to go cold. Remove the lining paper.

5 To make the icing, mix the icing sugar with the lemon juice and 5–10ml/1–2 tsp water to make a drizzling consistency.

6 Fill a small paper piping (pastry) bag with icing, snip off the end, then drizzle lines over the cooled cake in a random pattern. When set, cut into 15 squares.

Energy 290kcal/1230kJ; Protein 3.6g; Carbohydrate 60.8g, of which sugars 49.4g; Fat 5g, of which saturates 1.6g; Cholesterol 29mg; Calcium 57mg; Fibre 1.3g; Sodium 60mg.

Almond slices

A light pastry base is spread with raspberry jam, topped with almond cake and a layer of flaked almonds to make elegant old-fashioned pastry slices. They are the quintessential summer tea-party cake. These cakes keep for up to three days in an airtight container.

MAKES 16

butter, for greasing
225g/8oz shortcrust or sweet
  shortcrust pastry, thawed
  if frozen
flour, for dusting
60ml/4 tbsp raspberry jam
4 egg whites
175g/6oz/1½ cups ground almonds
175g/6oz/scant 1 cup golden caster
  (superfine) sugar
a few drops of almond extract
75g/3oz/¾ cup flaked
  (sliced) almonds
15ml/1 tbsp icing (confectioners')
  sugar, for dusting (optional)

1 Preheat the oven to 180°C/350°F/ Gas 4. Grease a 28 × 18cm/11 × 7in shallow tin (pan).

2 Roll out the pastry on a lightly floured surface to a rectangle large enough to line the base and sides of the tin.

3 Lower the pastry into the tin, using a rolling pin. Press into all the corners, then trim the edges.

4 Spread the jam over the pastry.

5 Put the egg whites into a clean, grease-free bowl and whisk until they form stiff peaks.

6 Fold in the ground almonds, sugar and almond extract. Spoon into the tin, then spread the top level. Sprinkle over the flaked almonds.

7 Bake for 30–35 minutes, or until the pastry is crisp and the topping is golden and firm to the touch. Leave to cool completely in the tin.

8 Mark into 16 slices, then cut these out with a sharp knife. Dust with icing sugar, if you like.

Energy 204kcal/850kJ; Protein 4.7g; Carbohydrate 18.7g, of which sugars 12.2g; Fat 12.7g, of which saturates 0.7g; Cholesterol 0mg; Calcium 50mg; Fibre 1.4g; Sodium 41mg.

Loaf cakes

Teabreads are one of the oldest of family cakes, originally baked in a rectangular tin that fitted into the small side oven of a range cooker or wood-burning stove. There are many regional variations of loaf cakes and teabreads, such as Bara Brith, which add up to a wealth of traditional recipes. These cakes are so simple and quick to make that it's a good idea to double up the mixture and bake two at a time, then keep one in the freezer until needed. Teabreads usually keep longer if they are enriched with fruit and nuts. As they remain moist, they are useful for adding to lunch boxes: Fruit Malt Loaf, Gingerbread or Banana Bread are great for this, or for taking on a picnic. Serve them at tea time, in generously buttered slices, or if they begin to go stale, they are still delicious toasted.

Left: Raspberry and Almond Teabread and Lemon and Walnut Teabread.

Chickpea cake

Although an unusual ingredient for a cake, chickpeas add moisture and give a texture rather like Christmas pudding. Flavoured with orange and cinnamon, it tastes wonderful; try it with fresh mango or pineapple and a spoonful of yogurt. It will keep up to three days in an airtight container.

SERVES 8–10

butter, for greasing
2 × 275g/10oz cans chickpeas,
  drained and rinsed
5ml/1 tsp baking powder
grated rind and juice of 1 orange
225g/8oz/generous 1 cup caster
  (superfine) sugar
10ml/2 tsp ground cinnamon
4 eggs, beaten

For the topping
50g/2oz/scant ½ cup caster
  (superfine) sugar mixed with
  5ml/1 tsp ground cinnamon

1 Preheat the oven to 180°C/ 350°F/Gas 4. Grease and line a 450g/1lb loaf tin (pan) with baking parchment.

2 Tip the chickpeas into a colander, rinse and drain them thoroughly, then rub them between the palms of your hands to loosen and remove any skins.

3 Put the chickpeas into a food processor and process until smooth. Tip the chickpea purée into a mixing bowl, using a spatula to scrape out all the mixture.

4 Stir in the baking powder, orange rind, juice, sugar, cinnamon and eggs.

5 Pour the batter into the tin and smooth the top level. Bake for about 1½ hours, or until a skewer inserted into the centre comes out clean.

6 Leave to cool in the tin for 10 minutes, then turn out on to a wire rack. Sprinkle with cinnamon sugar, then leave to go cold.

Energy 184kcal/780kJ; Protein 5.5g; Carbohydrate 35.2g, of which sugars 28.9g; Fat 3.4g, of which saturates 0.7g; Cholesterol 76mg; Calcium 43mg; Fibre 1.6g; Sodium 118mg.

Bitter marmalade chocolate cake

Orange and chocolate always work well together, and here the cake is filled and topped with a bittersweet orange and chocolate cream, with a glistening layer of marmalade to finish. Cream is used in place of butter, giving the cake a moist and rich texture. Keep for three days, refrigerated.

SERVES 8–10

butter, for greasing
3 eggs
200g/7oz/1 cup caster
  (superfine) sugar
175ml/6fl oz/¾ cup sour cream
115g/4oz plain (semisweet)
  chocolate, melted
200g/7oz/1¾ cups self-raising
  (self-rising) flour

For the filling and glaze
175g/6oz/⅔ cup bitter
  orange marmalade
115g/4oz plain (semisweet)
  chocolate, melted
60ml/4 tbsp sour cream
shredded orange rind, to decorate

1 Preheat the oven to 180°C/
250°F/Gas 4. Grease and line a
900g/2lb loaf tin (pan) with
baking parchment.

2 In a mixing bowl, combine the eggs and sugar. Using an electric whisk, beat the mixture until thick and creamy.

3 Stir in the sour cream and cooled, melted chocolate. Fold in the flour.

4 Spoon the batter into the prepared tin. Bake for 1 hour, or until well risen and firm to the touch.

5 Cool for a few minutes in the tin, then turn out on a wire rack to go cold. Remove the lining paper.

6 To make the filling, spoon two-thirds of the marmalade into a small pan and melt over a low heat.

7 Stir the melted chocolate into the marmalade with the sour cream.

8 Slice the cake across into three layers and sandwich together with about half of the marmalade filling.

9 Spread the remainder over the top of the cake and leave to set.

10 Spoon the rest of the marmalade over the cake. Sprinkle strands of finely shredded orange rind on top.

Energy 475kcal/2004kJ; Protein 7.1g; Carbohydrate 80.1g, of which sugars 60.8g; Fat 16.3g, of which saturates 9.1g; Cholesterol 91mg; Calcium 101mg; Fibre 1.6g; Sodium 56mg.

Date and walnut loaf

This fruit loaf is lower in sugar than some cakes, but the dates and bananas add sweetness as well as depth of flavour. As they also make the loaf very moist, it keeps very well. Serve sliced and buttered. Keep it for one week in an airtight container, or freeze for up to two months.

SERVES 8–10

75g/3oz/6 tbsp butter, softened, plus extra for greasing
150g/5oz/scant 1 cup stoned (pitted), chopped, dried dates
finely grated rind and juice of 1 lemon
5ml/1 tsp bicarbonate of soda (baking soda)
50g/2oz/¼ cup soft light brown sugar
150g/5oz/½ cup sweetened condensed milk
2 eggs, beaten
150g/5oz ripe bananas, peeled and mashed
225g/8oz/2 cups self-raising (self-rising) flour
5ml/1 tsp baking powder
75g/3oz/¾ cup walnuts, chopped
butter, to serve

1 Preheat the oven to 160°C/ 325°F/Gas 3. Grease and line a 900g/2lb loaf tin (pan) with baking parchment.

2 Put the dates in a bowl with the lemon rind and juice, and 30ml/ 2 tbsp boiling water. Stir in the bicarbonate of soda. Leave to cool.

3 Put the butter, sugar and condensed milk in a bowl and whisk with an electric mixer until smooth.

4 Gradually whisk in the eggs. Stir in the bananas and the date mixture.

5 Sift the flour and baking powder into the bowl, then add the chopped nuts and stir together until smooth.

6 Spoon the mixture into the tin and smooth the top level. Bake for about 1¼ hours, or until a skewer inserted into the middle comes out clean.

7 Leave to set 10 minutes, then turn out on to a wire rack to go cold. Remove the lining paper. Serve sliced and buttered.

Energy 266kcal/1124kJ; Protein 6.1g; Carbohydrate 42.9g, of which sugars 24.3g; Fat 9g, of which saturates 1.2g; Cholesterol 1.8mg; Calcium 64mg; Fibre 3.4g; Sodium 16mg.

Quick-and-easy teabread

This succulent, fruity teabread can be served just as it is, or spread with a little butter. It is a great choice for packed lunches. Make one for picnics or simply serve it with a cup of tea. Keep for up to five days, tightly wrapped in foil, or freeze for up to two months.

SERVES 6–8

350g/12oz/2 cups luxury mixed
   dried fruit
butter, for greasing
75g/3oz/scant ⅓ cup demerara
   (raw) sugar, plus 15ml/1 tbsp
   for sprinkling
1 large (US extra large) egg
175g/6oz/1½ cups self-raising
   (self-rising) flour

1 Put the fruit in a large bowl. Add 150ml/¼ pint/⅔ cup boiling water and leave to stand for 30 minutes.

2 Preheat the oven to 180°C/350°F/ Gas 4. Grease and line a 450g/1lb loaf tin (pan) with baking parchment.

3 Stir the sugar into the fruit and then beat in the egg.

4 Sift the flour into the bowl and stir until combined.

5 Spoon into the prepared tin and level the surface. Sprinkle with the remaining 15ml/1 tbsp sugar.

6 Bake for 50 minutes, or until risen and firm to the touch; or until a skewer inserted into the centre will come out clean.

7 Leave the loaf in the tin for 10 minutes before turning out to cool on a wire rack.

Energy 236kcal/1004kJ; Protein 3.8g; Carbohydrate 56.1g, of which sugars 39.9g; Fat 1.1g, of which saturates 0.2g; Cholesterol 24mg; Calcium 117mg; Fibre 1.6g; Sodium 109mg.

Fruit malt loaf

Malt extract gives this traditional fruity loaf its wonderful chewy consistency, and wholemeal flour adds depth of flavour. Cut in slices and spread with butter, it's just right for giving to hungry children when they come home from school. Keep for up to five days in an airtight container.

2 Put the dry ingredients in a bowl.

3 Heat the malt extract and milk in a small pan, stirring until dissolved. Mix into the dry ingredients.

4 Spoon into the prepared tin. Bake for 45 minutes, or until a skewer inserted into the loaf comes out clean. Leave to stand for 5 minutes, then turn out on to a wire rack to go cold. Remove the lining paper.

SERVES 8–10

butter, for greasing
250g/9oz/2¼ cups wholemeal (whole-wheat) self-raising (self-rising) flour
pinch of salt
2.5ml/½ tsp bicarbonate of soda (baking soda)
175g/6oz/1 cup mixed dried fruit
15ml/1 tbsp malt extract
250ml/8fl oz/1 cup milk
butter, to serve

1 Preheat the oven to 160°C/325°F/Gas 3. Grease and line a 900g/2lb loaf tin (pan) with baking parchment.

Energy 260kcal/1103kJ; Protein 5.3g; Carbohydrate 58.6g, of which sugars 25.3g; Fat 2.1g, of which saturates 0.3g; Cholesterol 1mg; Calcium 97mg; Fibre 1.8g; Sodium 38mg.

Bara brith

There are many versions of this fruity Welsh teabread. The fruit is soaked in tea until it plumps up, ensuring the teabread is moist and tasty. The flavour can be varied by using a variety of teas – try Earl Grey, for example. This will keep for up to five days in an airtight container.

SERVES 8–10

225g/8oz/1⅓ cups mixed dried
   fruit and chopped mixed
   (candied) peel
250ml/8fl oz/1 cup hot strong
   tea, strained
25g/1oz/2 tbsp butter, plus extra
   for greasing
225g/8oz/2 cups self-raising
   (self-rising) flour
5ml/1 tsp mixed (apple pie) spice
100g/3¾oz/generous ½ cup soft
   light brown sugar
1 egg, lightly beaten

1 Put the fruit into a heatproof bowl and pour the hot tea over it. Cover and leave to stand at room temperature for 30 minutes.

2 Preheat the oven to 180°C/ 350°F/Gas 4. Grease and line a 900g/2lb loaf tin (pan) with baking parchment.

3 Sift the flour and the mixed spice into a large bowl. Add the butter and, with your fingertips, rub it into the flour until the mixture starts to resemble fine breadcrumbs. Alternatively, use a food processor.

4 Stir in the sugar, then add the cooled fruit and its liquid along with the beaten egg. Stir the mixture well to make a batter with a soft dropping consistency.

5 Transfer the batter to the tin and level the surface. Bake for 1 hour, or until a skewer inserted in the centre comes out clean. Turn out to cool on a wire rack. Remove the lining paper.

Energy 202kcal/858kJ; Protein 3.3g; Carbohydrate 43.2g, of which sugars 26.1g; Fat 2.9g, of which saturates 1.5g; Cholesterol 24.4mg; Calcium 56.5mg; Fibre 1.2g; Sodium 34mg.

Gingerbread

Cinnamon as well as ginger gives gingerbread its familiar warm flavouring, which couldn't be achieved by using ginger alone. Treacle and golden syrup are the essential ingredients to ensure the finished cake is soft and sticky. Store, foil-wrapped, for five days in an airtight container.

SERVES 8–10

75g/3oz/6 tbsp butter, plus extra
  for greasing
115g/4oz/½ cup soft light
  brown sugar
75g/3oz/¼ cup golden (light corn)
  syrup
75g/3oz/¼ cup treacle (molasses)
105ml/7 tbsp milk
1 egg, beaten
175g/6oz/1½ cups plain
  (all-purpose) flour
50g/2oz/½ cup gram flour
pinch of salt
10ml/2 tsp ground ginger
5ml/1 tsp ground cinnamon
7.5ml/1½ tsp baking powder

1 Preheat the oven to 160°C/ 325°F/Gas 3. Grease and line a 900g/2lb loaf tin (pan) with baking parchment.

2 Put the sugar, butter, golden syrup and treacle in a pan and heat gently until melted, stirring occasionally.

3 Remove from the heat. Cool slightly. Mix in the milk and egg.

4 Sift the flours, salt, spices and baking powder into a large bowl. Make a well in the centre and pour in the liquid mixture. Beat well.

5 Pour the batter into the tin. Bake for 1–1¼ hours, or until firm.

6 Turn out on to a wire rack to go cold. Peel off the lining.

Energy 191kcal/802kJ; Protein 1.6g; Carbohydrate 24.7g, of which sugars 24.6g; Fat 10.3g, of which saturates 6.3g; Cholesterol 45mg; Calcium 128mg; Fibre 0g; Sodium 116mg.

Banana bread

When you have some bananas that have become overripe in the fruit bowl, use them for this quick recipe. They need to be very ripe and will give the bread a lovely sweetness and fragrance as well as making it moist. Keep this for up to five days in an airtight container.

SERVES 8–10

115g/4oz/½ cup butter, plus extra
  for greasing
5ml/1 tsp bicarbonate of soda
  (baking soda)
225g/8oz/2 cups wholemeal
  (whole-wheat) flour
2 eggs, beaten
3 very ripe bananas
30–45ml/2–3 tbsp coconut milk

1 Preheat the oven to 180°C/
350°F/Gas 4. Grease and line a
900g/2lb loaf tin (pan) with
baking parchment.

2 In a large bowl, cream the butter
until it is fluffy.

3 Sift the bicarbonate of soda with
the flour, then add to the butter,
alternating with the eggs.

4 Peel the bananas and slice them
on to a plate. Mash them well, using
the back of a fork, then stir them
into the cake mixture. Mix in the
coconut milk and stir together.

5 Spoon the batter into the tin and
smooth the top level. Bake for
1¼ hours, or until golden and firm
to the touch. Cool on a wire rack.
Remove the lining paper.

Energy 226kcal/954kJ; Protein 5.1g; Carbohydrate 37.2g, of which sugars 19.5g; Fat 73.g, of which saturates 3.8g; Cholesterol 51mg; Calcium 46mg; Fibre 1.8g; Sodium 55mg.

Apricot and lemon loaf

This moreish cake has lots of flavour from apricots and nuts in the crumb itself, and is topped with a crunchy layer of flaked almonds and pistachio nuts. After baking it is soaked in a tangy lemon syrup to keep it really moist. This loaf will keep for five days in an airtight container.

SERVES 8–10

175g/6oz/¾ cup butter, softened,
 plus extra for greasing
175g/6oz/1½ cups self-raising
 (self-rising) flour, sifted
2.5ml/½ tsp baking powder
175g/6oz/scant 1 cup caster
 (superfine) sugar
3 eggs, lightly beaten
finely grated rind of 1 lemon
175g/6oz/1½ cups ready-to-eat
 dried apricots, finely chopped
75g/3oz/¾ cup ground almonds
40g/1½oz/⅓ cup pistachio
 nuts, chopped
50g/2oz/½ cup flaked almonds
15g/½oz/2 tbsp whole
 pistachio nuts

For the syrup
freshly squeezed juice of 1 lemon
45ml/3 tbsp caster (superfine)
 sugar

1 Preheat the oven to 180°C/350°F/Gas 4. Grease and line a 900g/2lb loaf tin (pan) with baking parchment.

2 Put the butter, flour and baking powder into a large bowl, then add the sugar, eggs and lemon rind. Beat for 1–2 minutes, or until smooth and glossy. Stir in the apricots, ground almonds and the chopped pistachio nuts.

3 Spoon the batter into the tin and smooth the surface. Sprinkle with the flaked almonds and whole pistachio nuts.

4 Bake for 1¼ hours, or until a skewer inserted into the centre comes out clean. Check the cake after about 45 minutes and cover with a piece of foil once the top is nicely brown.

5 Leave to cool in the tin.

6 To make the syrup, put the lemon juice and sugar into a pan and heat gently, stirring occasionally, until the sugar has dissolved.

7 Spoon the syrup over the cake. When the cake is cold, turn it out of the tin and peel off the lining paper.

Energy 436kcal/1822kJ; Protein 8.1g; Carbohydrate 44.3g, of which sugars 30.5g; Fat 26.4g, of which saturates 10.5g; Cholesterol 94mg; Calcium 96mg; Fibre 2.9g; Sodium 162mg.

Marmalade teabread

Chunky orange marmalade adds a touch of citrus zest to this spicy teabread. It is so quick and easy to make and perfect for serving with a cup of tea. Keep this cake for up to three days in an airtight container, or freeze it for up to two months wrapped in foil.

SERVES 6–8

100g/3¾oz/7 tbsp butter, diced, plus extra for greasing
200g/7oz/1¾ cups plain (all-purpose) flour
5ml/1 tsp baking powder
6.25ml/1¼ tsp ground cinnamon
50g/2oz/¼ cup soft light brown sugar
1 egg, lightly beaten
60ml/4 tbsp chunky orange marmalade
about 45ml/3 tbsp milk
60ml/4 tbsp glacé icing, to decorate
shreds of orange and lemon rind, to decorate

1 Preheat the oven to 160°C/325°F/Gas 3. Grease and line a 450g/1lb loaf tin (pan) with baking parchment.

2 Sift the flour, baking powder and cinnamon into a mixing bowl. Add the butter and rub in with your fingertips until the mixture resembles fine crumbs. Stir in the sugar.

3 In a bowl, mix the egg with the marmalade and most of the milk.

4 Stir the milk mixture into the flour, adding more milk if necessary to give a soft, dropping consistency.

5 Spoon into the prepared tin and smooth the top level. Bake for 1¼ hours, or until the cake is firm to the touch and cooked through.

6 Leave to stand in the tin for 5 minutes, then turn out to cool on a wire rack. Peel off the lining paper.

7 Drizzle the glacé icing over the top of the cake and decorate with shreds of orange and lemon rind.

Energy 287kcal/1206kJ; Protein 8.3g; Carbohydrate 34.8g, of which sugars 9.3g; Fat 13.7g, of which saturates 8.1g; Cholesterol 63mg; Calcium 68mg; Fibre 1g; Sodium 554mg.

Lemon and walnut teabread

The unusual combination of earthy walnuts and fresh zesty lemons goes together remarkably well here. Unusually for a teabread, whisked egg whites are added to the batter, making it light and airy. Keep for three days in an airtight container. Freeze for two months wrapped in foil.

SERVES 8–10

115g/4oz/½ cup butter, softened, plus extra for greasing
100g/3¾oz/generous ½ cup caster (superfine) sugar
2 eggs, separated
grated rind of 2 lemons
30ml/2 tbsp lemon juice
200g/7oz/1¾ cups plain (all-purpose) flour
10ml/2 tsp baking powder
120ml/4fl oz/½ cup milk
50g/2oz/½ cup walnuts, chopped
pinch of salt

1 Preheat the oven to 180°C/350°F/Gas 4. Grease and line a 900g/2lb loaf tin (pan) with baking parchment.

2 Beat the butter with the sugar. Beat in the egg yolks, lemon rind and juice. Set aside.

3 Sift the flour and baking powder over the butter mixture in batches, and stir well, alternating with the milk. Fold in the walnuts.

4 Put the egg whites into a clean, grease-free bowl and whisk until they form stiff peaks. Fold a large tablespoon of the egg whites into the walnut mixture to lighten it. Fold in the remaining egg whites until just blended.

5 Pour the batter into the tin and smooth the top level. Bake for 45–50 minutes, or until a skewer inserted into the centre comes out clean.

6 Leave to stand in the tin for 5 minutes then turn out on to a wire rack to go cold. Peel off the lining.

Energy 249kcal/1041kJ; Protein 4.5g; Carbohydrate 26.9g, of which sugars 10.4g; Fat 14.4g, of which saturates 6.7g; Cholesterol 63mg; Calcium 61mg; Fibre 0.8g; Sodium 90mg.

Coconut cake

Sour cream and desiccated coconut make this quick and easy cake wonderfully moist, giving it a full flavour that is lifted by a delicious lemony tang. Buy desiccated coconut as you need it for the best results. It deteriorates with storage. This cake keeps for eight days in an airtight container.

SERVES 8–10

115g/4oz/1 cup butter, softened,
   plus extra for greasing
115g/4oz/generous ½ cup caster
   (superfine) sugar
2 large (US extra large)
   eggs, beaten
115g/4oz/generous 1 cup
   desiccated (dry unsweetened
   shredded) coconut
115g/4oz/1 cup self-raising
   (self-rising) flour
75ml/5 tbsp sour cream or natural
   (plain) yogurt
15ml/1 tbsp finely grated
   lemon rind

1 Preheat the oven to 180°C/350°F/ Gas 4. Grease and line a 900g/2lb loaf tin (pan) with baking parchment.

2 In a large bowl, beat the butter and sugar together until pale and fluffy, then add the eggs in batches, beating well after each addition.

3 Add the coconut, flour, sour cream and lemon rind, and beat together until smooth.

4 Spoon into the tin. Bake for 50 minutes, or until a skewer inserted into the centre comes out clean.

5 Cool in the tin for 5 minutes, then turn out on to a wire rack to go cold. Peel off the lining paper.

COOK'S TIP
To freeze, wrap in foil and freeze for up to 3 months.

VARIATION
Add 75g/3oz/½ cup dried morello cherries at step 3.

Energy 221kcal/924kJ; Protein 3g; Carbohydrate 27.8g, of which sugars 22.1g; Fat 11.6g, of which saturates 8.2g; Cholesterol 61mg; Calcium 31mg; Fibre 1.6g; Sodium 51mg.

Raspberry and almond teabread

Fresh raspberries and almonds combine perfectly to flavour this mouthwatering loaf with its crunchy, toasted flaked-almond topping. Serve warm with a spoonful of crème fraîche for tea or to serve as a quick dessert. Eat this cake on the day it is made.

2 Sift the flour into a large bowl or the bowl of a food processor. Add the butter and rub in, or process, until the mixture resembles fine breadcrumbs.

3 Stir in the sugar and ground almonds, then gradually mix in the eggs and milk, and beat until smooth.

4 Fold in the raspberries, being careful not to crush them.

5 Spoon into the prepared tin and sprinkle over the flaked almonds.

SERVES 6–8

90g/3½oz/7 tbsp butter, plus extra
    for greasing
175g/6oz/1½ cups self-raising
    (self-rising) flour
90g/3½oz/½ cup caster
    (superfine) sugar
40g/1½oz/scant ½ cup ground
    almonds
2 eggs, beaten
30ml/2 tbsp milk
115g/4oz/1 cup fresh raspberries or
    partly thawed frozen raspberries
30ml/2 tbsp toasted flaked (sliced)
    almonds

1 Preheat the oven to 180°C/ 350°F/Gas 4. Grease and line a 450g/1lb loaf tin (pan) with baking parchment.

6 Bake for about 55 minutes, or until a skewer inserted into the centre comes out clean. Cool the cake in the tin, then turn out on to a wire rack to go cold. Remove the lining paper.

Energy 215kcal/902kJ; Protein 4.3g; Carbohydrate 24.1g, of which sugars 10.5g; Fat 12g, of which saturates 5.3g; Cholesterol 44mg; Calcium 59mg; Fibre 1.4g; Sodium 79mg.

Peanut butter teabread

Crunchy peanut butter gives this teabread richness, as well as a distinctive flavour and texture. It also adds protein to make it into a substantial snack. The topping of salted peanuts contrasts with the sweetness of the bread. This cake will keep for two days in an airtight container.

SERVES 10

50g/2oz/¼ cup butter, softened,
  plus extra for greasing
225g/8oz/2 cups plain
  (all-purpose) flour
7.5ml/1½ tsp baking powder
2.5ml/½ tsp bicarbonate of soda
  (baking soda)
175g/6oz/½ cup crunchy
  peanut butter
50g/2oz/generous ¼ cup caster
  (superfine) sugar
2 eggs, beaten
250ml/8fl oz/1 cup milk
25g/1oz/¼ cup roasted salted
  peanuts

1 Preheat the oven to 180°C/ 350°F/Gas 4. Grease and line a 900g/2lb loaf tin (pan) with baking parchment.

2 Sift the flour, baking powder and bicarbonate of soda together into a large bowl.

3 Put the butter and peanut butter in a large bowl and beat together with a wooden spoon to soften, then beat in the sugar until very light and fluffy.

4 Gradually whisk in the eggs a little at a time, then beat in the milk with the sifted flour and mix until incorporated.

5 Pour into the prepared tin and sprinkle the peanuts on top.

6 Bake for 1 hour or until a skewer inserted into the centre comes out clean. Cool in the tin for 5 minutes, then turn out on to a wire rack. Remove the lining paper.

COOK'S TIP
This teabread also works well with soup or cold meats.

Energy 214kcal/904kJ; Protein 6.4g; Carbohydrate 33.5g, of which sugars 11.4g; Fat 6.9g, of which saturates 1.7g; Cholesterol 28mg; Calcium 70mg; Fibre 1.4g; Sodium 56mg.

Crunchy pear and cherry cake

This is a great cake to make with store-cupboard ingredients. Packed with dried pears, glacé cherries and crystallized ginger, it has loads of flavour and is finished off with a crunchy demerara sugar topping. This cake keeps for up to five days in an airtight container.

SERVES 8–10

115g/4oz/½ cup butter, plus extra
   for greasing
115g/4oz/generous ½ cup caster
   (superfine) sugar
225g/8oz/2 cups plain
   (all-purpose) flour
10ml/2 tsp baking powder
2 eggs
60ml/4 tbsp milk
65g/2½oz/generous ¼ cup ready-
   to-eat dried pears, chopped
65g/2½oz/generous ¼ cup glacé
   (candied) cherries, washed
   and quartered
40g/1½oz/3 tbsp chopped
   crystallized ginger
30ml/2 tbsp demerara (raw) sugar

1 Preheat the oven to 180°C/350°F/ Gas 4. Grease and line a 900g/2lb loaf tin (pan) with baking parchment.

2 Put the butter and sugar in a bowl. Sift in the flour and baking powder.

3 Add the eggs and milk, and beat for about 2 minutes, or until smooth.

4 Fold in the pears, cherries and ginger with a large metal spoon until well combined. Spoon into the tin and smooth the top level.

5 Bake for 40 minutes, then remove from the oven and quickly sprinkle the loaf with the demerara sugar.

6 Bake for a further 15–20 minutes, or until a skewer inserted into the centre comes out clean.

7 Cool in the tin for 5 minutes, then turn out on to a wire rack to go cold. Peel off the lining paper.

COOK'S TIP
To freeze, wrap tightly in foil. Keep for up to 3 months.

Energy 257kcal/1079kJ; Protein 4.2g; Carbohydrate 37.7g, of which sugars 20.5g; Fat 11g, of which saturates 6.6g; Cholesterol 65mg; Calcium 63mg; Fibre 1.5g; Sodium 107mg.

Parsnip, banana and orange loaf

Parsnips and bananas are full of natural sugars, which add a mellow sweetness to this cake, and the orange adds a citrus tang. Keep this cake for up to five days in an airtight container, or freeze, undecorated, for two months, tightly wrapped in foil.

SERVES 8–10

250g/9oz/2¼ cups wholemeal
  (whole-wheat) self-raising
  (self-rising) flour
15ml/1 tbsp baking powder
5ml/1 tsp ground cinnamon
5ml/1 tsp freshly ground nutmeg
130g/4½oz/7 tbsp butter
130g/4½oz/generous ½ cup soft
  light brown sugar
250g/9oz parsnips, peeled and
  coarsely grated
1 medium banana, peeled
  and mashed
finely grated rind and juice of
  1 unwaxed orange

For the topping
225g/8oz cream cheese
45ml/3 tbsp icing (confectioners')
  sugar
juice and finely grated zest of
  1 small orange

1 Preheat the oven to 180°C/350°F/ Gas 4. Grease and line a 900g/2lb loaf tin (pan) with baking parchment.

2 Sift the flour, baking powder and spices into a large bowl. Add any bran remaining in the sieve (strainer).

3 Melt the butter in a pan, add the sugar and stir until dissolved.

4 Pour the melted butter and sugar into the flour mixture. Mix in the parsnips, banana, orange rind and juice.

5 Spoon the batter into the prepared tin and level the top. Bake for 45–50 minutes until a skewer inserted into the centre of the cake comes out clean. Allow to cool before removing from the tin. Peel off the lining paper.

6 For the topping, beat together the cream cheese, icing sugar, orange juice and orange zest, until smooth. Spread evenly over the cake top.

Energy 246kcal/1033kJ; Protein 5.9g; Carbohydrate 35.2g, of which sugars 13.4g; Fat 10g, of which saturates 1.2g; Cholesterol 32mg; Calcium 45mg; Fibre 2.7g; Sodium 14mg.

Fruit cakes

Cakes made using luscious fresh fruits can often double up as a pudding, but it is best that these are eaten on the day of baking, as the pieces of fruit will eventually soften. Plum Kutchen oozes with dark juicy fruits and is delicious eaten warm, whereas delicate Greek Yogurt and Fig Cake or Gooseberry Cake, are wonderful chilled, served with lashings of cream. Naturally produced vine fruits are dried in the sun and are packed with healthy goodness. They contain vitamins, minerals, iron and fibre, and supply sweetness. Adding raisins, sultanas, currants, dates and apricots to a cake gives it extra moisture, which helps it to keep for longer. Rich fruit cakes containing a large amount of dried fruits usually need to be cooked slowly at low oven temperatures for a much longer time than lighter cakes, so allow extra time for baking. As dried vine fruits have a high sugar content and the nature of a rich fruit cake mixture is dense, it is advisable, when baking, to wrap layers of brown paper or newspaper around the outside of the tin to prevent over-browning.

Left: Glacé-topped Fruit Cake and Farmhouse Apple and Sultana Cake.

Griestorte with pineapple filling

This classic continental gateau uses semolina and ground almonds for a deliciously short, crunchy texture. The filling of cream, pineapple and chocolate makes a soft, tangy contrast to the cake. Bake the base a day ahead, or bake and freeze it unfilled. Eat fresh once filled.

SERVES 8

butter, for greasing
3 eggs, separated
115g/4oz/generous ½ cup caster (superfine) sugar
juice and finely grated rind of ½ lemon
30ml/2 tbsp ground almonds
50g/2oz/⅓ cup fine semolina
icing (confectioners') sugar, for dusting
chocolate curls or flakes, to decorate, *see page 84*

For the filling

300ml/½ pint/1½ cups double (heavy) cream
4 slices canned pineapple, drained and chopped
75g/3oz dark (bittersweet) chocolate, coarsely grated

1 Preheat the oven to 180°C/350°F/ Gas 4. Grease and line a 20cm/8in round deep cake tin (pan) with baking parchment.

2 Whisk the egg yolks with the sugar and lemon rind until pale and light. Add the lemon juice. Whisk until thick and the mixture leaves a ribbon trail when the whisk is lifted.

3 Fold in the almonds and semolina.

4 Put the egg whites into a clean, grease-free bowl and whisk until they form soft peaks, then fold into the yolk mixture in three batches.

5 Spoon into the prepared tin and bake for 30–35 minutes, or until risen and pale golden.

6 Cool in the tin for 5 minutes. Turn the cake out on to a wire rack and cool completely. Remove the papers. Cut the cake in half horizontally.

7 Whip the cream until it holds its shape, then fold in the pineapple and chocolate. Use the cream to sandwich the cakes together, dust the top with icing sugar, then decorate with chocolate curls.

Energy 356kcal/1484kJ; Protein 5g; Carbohydrate 29.7g, of which sugars 24.2g; Fat 27.2g, of which saturates 13.6g; Cholesterol 121mg; Calcium 52mg; Fibre 0.5g; Sodium 44mg.

Plum kutchen

Make this spicy cake when luscious plums are in season and at their sweetest and juiciest. Don't worry if the juice from these ripe fruits drizzles down the sides, it all adds to the cake's homely charm. Serve with a dollop of thick crème fraîche. Eat this fresh on the day it is baked.

SERVES 10

275g/10oz/2½ cups self-raising
  (self-rising) flour
7.5ml/1½ tsp ground cinnamon
115g/4oz/½ cup butter, diced
115g/4oz/½ cup soft light
  brown sugar
finely grated rind and juice of
  1 small orange
2 eggs, beaten
60ml/4 tbsp milk
6 large, ripe dark plums, stoned
  (pitted) and quartered
30ml/2 tbsp demerara (raw) sugar
45ml/3 tbsp caster (superfine)
  sugar, to sprinkle

1 Preheat the oven to 180°C/350°F/Gas 4. Line the base and sides of a 20cm/8in deep round cake tin (pan) with baking parchment.

2 Sift the flour and 5ml/1 tsp cinnamon into a large bowl and add the butter. Rub the butter into the flour with your fingertips until the mixture resembles fine crumbs.

3 Stir in the soft light brown sugar and orange rind. Add the eggs and milk, and beat until smooth.

4 Spoon into the tin and smooth the top level. Arrange the plum pieces over the top of the cake, pressing them down slightly so that the fruit is half-covered by the mixture.

COOK'S TIP
Not suitable for freezing.

5 Sprinkle the orange juice over the top of the cake, then the demerara sugar and the remaining cinnamon.

6 Bake for 50 minutes to 1 hour, or until a warmed skewer inserted into the centre comes out clean.

7 Cool in the tin for 5 minutes, then turn out to cool. Sprinkle with sugar.

Energy 311kcal/1308kJ; Protein 6.4g; Carbohydrate 44.5g, of which sugars 15.9g; Fat 13.2g, of which saturates 7.4g; Cholesterol 89mg; Calcium 86mg; Fibre 2.4g; Sodium 102mg.

Apple strudel

The apfelstrudel – wafer-thin pastry layers with a luscious chopped apple filling – was first baked by the Hungarians, and then adopted by the Viennese. The longer sheets of filo are best for this recipe, but if you cannot find these, use two small sheets and overlap them. Eat fresh.

SERVES 8–10

900g/2lb cooking apples
finely grated rind and juice
  of 1 lemon
50g/2oz/½ cup caster
  (superfine) sugar
75g/3oz/½ cup sultanas
  (golden raisins)
115g/4oz/½ cup unsalted butter,
  plus extra for greasing
75g/3oz white bread made
  into crumbs
50g/2oz/¼ cup flaked
  (sliced) almonds
2.5ml/½ tsp mixed (apple pie)
  spice
400g/14oz filo pastry, thawed
  if frozen
icing (confectioners') sugar,
  for dusting

1 Peel, core and slice the apples. Put them in a pan with the lemon rind and juice and the sugar. Cook over a medium heat for 8–10 minutes, or until tender. Put in a bowl, add the sultanas and cool for 30 minutes.

2 Preheat the oven to 190°C/375°F/ Gas 5. Grease a large baking sheet.

FILO PASTRY TIPS
• If using two sheets of filo in place of one, overlap them along the short end by about 2cm/¾in after you have brushed them with butter.
• Keep any unused sheets of filo covered with a damp cloth to prevent them from drying out.

3 Melt 30ml/2 tbsp of the butter in a pan, add the breadcrumbs and cook, stirring, until golden brown. Stir in the almonds and spice. Cook for 1 minute, then set aside to cool.

4 Melt the remaining butter and brush over a large filo sheet. Reserve two sheets for decoration. Continue to butter the sheets and layer them on top of the first sheet. Brush the top layer with butter.

5 Sprinkle half the crumb mixture over, leaving a 5cm/2in border at the edges. Top with the cooked apples, then with the remaining crumbs.

6 Fold in the sides, then roll up like a Swiss roll (jelly roll) to enclose the filling. Put on the prepared baking sheet, join side down.

7 Make ruffles from the reserved filo and arrange on top. Brush all over with butter and bake for 25–30 minutes, or until light golden and crisp.

8 Cool slightly, dust with icing sugar and serve warm or cold with crème fraîche or plain (natural) yogurt.

Energy 397kcal/1676kJ; Protein 5.3g; Carbohydrate 66g, of which sugars 30.7g; Fat 14.4g, of which saturates 8.7g; Cholesterol 35mg; Calcium 82mg; Fibre 3.1g; Sodium 196mg.

Streusel-topped peach cake

When it's not the season for fresh summer fruits you can still have a hint of the warmer days of the year by making this continental cake that uses canned peaches from the store cupboard. It also works well with canned apricots or black cherries. Serve fresh with thick cream.

SERVES 8–10

75g/3oz/6 tbsp butter, softened, plus extra for greasing
225g/8oz/2 cups self-raising (self-rising) flour
5ml/1 tsp baking powder
2.5ml/½ tsp ground cinnamon
75g/3oz/6 tbsp golden caster (superfine) sugar
finely grated rind of 1 orange
1 egg, beaten
150ml/¼ pt/⅔ cup milk

For the topping
75g/3oz/⅔ cup self-raising (self-rising) flour
50g/2oz/½ cup unsalted butter, diced
25g/1oz/2 tbsp demerara (raw) sugar

For the filling
400g/14oz can peach slices in juice, drained

1 Preheat the oven to 190°C/375°F/ Gas 5. Grease the base and sides of a 20cm/8in loose-based cake tin (pan) and line with baking parchment.

2 To make the topping, put the flour in a bowl or food processor, add the butter and process or rub in until fine crumbs form, then stir in the demerara sugar.

3 To make the cake, sift the flour, baking powder and cinnamon into a large bowl.

4 Add all the remaining cake ingredients and beat together until smooth. Spoon into the tin and smooth the top level.

5 Cover the top with an even layer of drained peach slices.

6 Sprinkle the crumb topping over the peaches.

7 Bake for 40 minutes, or until golden and a skewer inserted into the centre comes out clean.

8 Cool in the tin for 5 minutes, then carefully remove the sides of the tin and cool the cake on a wire rack. Remove the lining paper.

COOK'S TIP
This cake will keep for 2 days. It is not suitable for freezing.

Energy 244kcal/1034kJ; Protein 4.7g; Carbohydrate 46.7g, of which sugars 39.4g; Fat 5g, of which saturates 0.8g; Cholesterol 71mg; Calcium 47mg; Fibre 0.9g; Sodium 32mg.

Gooseberry cake

Gooseberries can be slightly acidic, so here they are sweetened with sugar and elderflower 30 minutes before they are added to the cake batter. The elderflower infuses the batter with a light, sweet flavour. Serve this fresh as a pudding with a spoonful of crème fraîche.

SERVES 10

75g/3oz/6 tbsp butter, melted,
    plus extra for greasing
150g/5oz gooseberries
22.5ml/4½ tsp golden caster
    (superfine) sugar
15ml/1 tbsp elderflower cordial,
    plus extra for brushing
225g/8oz/2 cups plain
    (all-purpose) flour
10ml/2 tsp baking powder
150g/5oz/¾ cup golden caster
    (superfine) sugar
2.5ml/½ tsp vanilla extract
1 egg, lightly beaten
250ml/8fl oz/1 cup buttermilk
icing (confectioners') sugar,
    for dusting

1 Preheat the oven to 180°C/ 350°F/Gas 4. Grease a 23cm/9in round loose-based cake tin (pan) with butter.

2 Arrange the fruit in a single layer on a plate and sprinkle evenly with the sugar and elderflower cordial. Leave to stand for 30 minutes.

3 Sift the dry ingredients into a large bowl and make a well in the centre.

4 In a separate bowl, lightly whisk together the melted butter, vanilla extract, egg and buttermilk. Pour into the dry ingredients and fold partly together.

5 Lightly combine half the reserved gooseberries and all of the syrupy juices into the batter, then fold together with a metal spoon.

6 Spoon the mixture into the tin and sprinkle the remaining fruit on top.

7 Bake for 30 minutes, but check after 25 minutes. If the centre of the cake is springy to the touch, it is ready. Lightly brush the surface of the warm cake with elderflower cordial, if you like, and serve, dusted with icing sugar.

Energy 273kcal/1144kJ; Protein 3.9g; Carbohydrate 34.6g, of which sugars 18.1g; Fat 14.2g, of which saturates 8.3g; Cholesterol 82mg; Calcium 51mg; Fibre 1g; Sodium 112mg.

Greek yogurt and fig cake

Fresh figs, thickly sliced then baked in honey, make a delectable base that becomes a topping for a featherlight sponge. Figs that are a little on the firm side work best for this particular recipe. Keep refrigerated in an airtight container for two days.

SERVES 8–10

200g/7oz/scant 1 cup butter, softened, plus extra for greasing
6 firm fresh figs, thickly sliced
45ml/3 tbsp clear honey, plus extra for glazing
175g/6oz/scant 1 cup caster (superfine) sugar
grated rind of 1 lemon
grated rind of 1 orange
4 eggs, separated
225g/8oz/2 cups plain (all-purpose) flour
5ml/1 tsp baking powder
5ml/1 tsp bicarbonate of soda (baking soda)
250ml/8fl oz/1 cup Greek (US strained plain) yogurt

1 Preheat the oven to 180C/350°F/ Gas 4. Grease and line the base of a 23cm/9in cake tin (pan) with baking parchment.

2 Arrange the sliced figs over the base of the tin and drizzle over the honey.

3 In a large bowl, beat the butter and sugar together with the citrus rinds until pale and fluffy.

4 Gradually beat in the egg yolks.

5 Sift the dry ingredients into the creamed mixture in batches, alternating with a spoonful of yogurt. Beat well, then repeat this process until all the dry ingredients and yogurt have been incorporated.

6 Put the egg whites into a clean, grease-free bowl and whisk until they form stiff peaks.

7 Stir the egg whites into the cake batter in two batches. Pour the mixture over the figs in the tin and smooth the top level. Bake for 1¼ hours, or until golden and a skewer inserted into the centre of the cake comes out clean.

8 Turn the cake out on to a wire rack, peel off the lining paper and cool. Drizzle the fig topping with extra honey before serving.

Energy 473kcal/1982kJ; Protein 8.2g; Carbohydrate 59.5g, of which sugars 38g; Fat 24.3g, of which saturates 14g; Cholesterol 149mg; Calcium 167mg; Fibre 2g; Sodium 225mg.

Crunchy-topped fresh apricot cake

Almonds are perfect partners for fresh apricots, and this is a great way to use fruits that may be a little too firm for eating. Chopped fresh nectarines make a good alternative when apricots are not available. Serve cold as a cake, or warm with custard for a dessert. It will keep for two days.

SERVES 8

175g/6oz/¾ cup butter, softened, plus extra for greasing
175g/6oz/1½ cups self-raising (self-rising) flour
175g/6oz/¾ cup caster (superfine) sugar
115g/4oz/1 cup ground almonds
3 eggs
5ml/1 tsp almond extract
2.5ml/½ tsp baking powder
8 firm apricots, stoned (pitted) and chopped

For the topping
30ml/2 tbsp demerara (raw) sugar
50g/2oz/½ cup flaked (sliced) almonds

1 Preheat the oven to 160°C/325°F/Gas 3. Grease and line an 18cm/7in round cake tin (pan) with baking parchment.

2 Put all the ingredients, except the apricots, in a large bowl or food processor and whisk or process until light and creamy.

3 Fold the apricots into the cake batter.

4 Spoon the batter into the prepared cake tin and smooth the top level. Make a hollow in the centre with the back of a large spoon.

5 Sprinkle over 15ml/1 tbsp of the demerara sugar, then scatter the flaked almonds over the top.

6 Bake for 1½ hours, or until a skewer inserted into the centre comes out clean.

7 Sprinkle the remaining demerara sugar over the top of the cake and leave to cool for 10 minutes in the tin. Remove from the tin, peel off the paper and finish cooling on a wire rack.

Energy 414kcal/1734kJ; Protein 6.2g; Carbohydrate 46.8g, of which sugars 30.3g; Fat 23.9g, of which saturates 12.3g; Cholesterol 118mg; Calcium 126mg; Fibre 1.8g; Sodium 241mg.

Pumpkin and banana cake

Rather like a cross between a carrot cake and banana bread, this luscious cake is an excellent way of using some of the scooped-out pumpkin flesh from making Hallowe'en lanterns. A cream cheese topping provides a delicious contrast with the dense moist cake. This is best eaten fresh.

SERVES 12

225g/8oz/2 cups self-raising
  (self-rising) flour
7.5ml/1½ tsp baking powder
2.5ml/½ tsp ground cinnamon
2.5ml/½ tsp ground ginger
130g/4½oz/½ cup soft light
  brown sugar
75g/3oz/¾ cup pecan nuts or
  walnuts, chopped
115g/4oz pumpkin flesh,
  coarsely grated
2 small ripe bananas, peeled
  and mashed
2 eggs, lightly beaten
150ml/¼ pint/⅔ cup sunflower oil

For the topping
50g/2oz/¼ cup unsalted butter, at
  room temperature
150g/5oz/⅔ cup soft white
  (farmers') cheese
1.5ml/¼ tsp vanilla extract
115g/4oz/1 cup icing
  (confectioners') sugar
pecan halves, to decorate

1 Preheat the oven to 180°C/350°F/ Gas 4. Line the base and sides of a round deep 20cm/8in cake tin (pan) with baking parchment.

2 Sift the flour, baking powder, cinnamon and ginger into a large bowl to combine.

3 Stir in the sugar, chopped pecan nuts or walnuts and grated pumpkin until thoroughly mixed. Make a slight hollow in the middle of the dry ingredients.

4 In a separate bowl, combine the bananas, eggs and sunflower oil, then stir into the dry ingredients.

5 Spoon into the prepared tin and smooth the top level.

6 Bake for 45–50 minutes, or until a skewer inserted into the centre comes out clean. Cool in the tin for 10 minutes, then turn out to cool completely on a wire rack.

7 To make the topping, put the butter, soft cheese and vanilla extract into a bowl, and beat until blended and smooth. Sift in the icing sugar. Beat again until creamy.

8 Spread the topping over the cake and decorate with pecan halves. Chill for 1 hour before serving, to allow the topping to harden.

Energy 388kcal/1619kJ; Protein 4.5g; Carbohydrate 40.2g, of which sugars 25.4g; Fat 24.4g, of which saturates 7.8g; Cholesterol 53mg; Calcium 64mg; Fibre 1.1g; Sodium 83mg.

Pear and polenta cake

This light polenta sponge has a nutty corn flavour that complements the fruit perfectly. For this upside-down cake, pears and honey are added to the base of the cake tin, then the mixture is added on top. Serve as a dessert with custard or whipped cream, if you like. Eat fresh.

3 Cut the pears into chunky slices and toss them in the lemon juice.

4 Arrange the pears on the base of the cake tin. Drizzle the honey over, and set aside.

SERVES 10

butter, for greasing
175g/6oz/scant 1 cup golden caster (superfine) sugar
4 ripe pears, peeled and cored
juice of ½ lemon
30ml/2 tbsp clear honey
3 eggs
seeds from 1 vanilla pod (bean)
120ml/4fl oz/½ cup sunflower oil
115g/4oz/1 cup self-raising (self-rising) flour
50g/2oz/⅓ cup instant polenta (cornmeal)

1 Preheat the oven to 180°C/ 350°F/Gas 4. Grease and line a 20cm/8in round cake tin (pan) with baking parchment.

2 Sprinkle 30ml/2 tbsp of the sugar over the base of the prepared tin.

COOK'S TIP
To release the seeds from the vanilla pod, cut down the centre with a sharp knife, then scoop out the seeds with a teaspoon.

5 In a bowl, mix together the eggs, the seeds from the vanilla pod and the remaining sugar. Beat until thick and creamy, then gradually beat in the oil.

6 Sift the flour and polenta into the egg mixture and fold in. Pour the batter over the pears in the tin.

7 Bake for 50 minutes, or until a skewer inserted into the centre comes out clean. Cool in the tin for 10 minutes, then turn the cake out, and peel off the lining paper.

Energy 256kcal/1077kJ; Protein 3.7g; Carbohydrate 38.9g, of which sugars 26.7g; Fat 10.5g, of which saturates 1.5g; Cholesterol 57mg; Calcium 65mg; Fibre 1.8g; Sodium 66mg.

Apricot, prune and cherry cake

This moist cake has a tang of orange. As it stores well for several days, it's useful for tea-time treats during the week. It is one of the easiest cakes to make – just melt the basic ingredients together in a pan. Serve this sliced and buttered, if you like.

SERVES 8–10

175g/6oz/¾ cup butter, plus extra
   for greasing
175g/6oz/¾ cup soft dark
   muscovado (molasses) sugar
300ml/½ pint/1¼ cups
   orange juice
130g/4½oz/generous ½ cup ready-
   to-eat dried apricots, chopped
130g/4½oz/generous ½ cup
   ready-to-eat prunes, chopped
125g/4¼oz/ generous ½ cup
   glacé (candied) cherries, washed,
   dried and chopped
50g/2oz/⅓ cup chopped mixed
   (candied) peel
250g/9oz/2¼ cups plain
   (all-purpose) flour
2.5ml/½ tsp bicarbonate of soda
   (baking soda)
2 eggs, beaten
45ml/3 tbsp golden (light corn)
   syrup

1 Preheat the oven to 180°C/350°F/ Gas 4. Grease and line an 18cm/ 7in deep round cake tin (pan) with baking parchment.

2 Put the butter, sugar and orange juice in a pan and heat until the sugar dissolves. Add all the dried fruits, then simmer gently for 15 minutes. Leave to cool.

COOK'S TIP
This cake keeps for 1 week in an airtight tin. Freeze, wrapped in foil, for up to 2 months.

3 Sift the flour and bicarbonate of soda into the cooled fruit mixture with the beaten eggs.

4 Spoon into the tin and bake for 1¼ hours, until a skewer inserted into the cake centre comes out clean.

5 Leave to cool in the tin for 10 minutes, then turn out on to a wire rack, peel away the papers and cool.

6 Warm the golden syrup in a small pan, then brush it over the top of the cake to glaze before serving.

Energy 399kcal/1680kJ; Protein 5.6g; Carbohydrate 62g, of which sugars 43g; Fat 16.1g, of which saturates 9.8g; Cholesterol 78mg; Calcium 94mg; Fibre 3.7g; Sodium 182mg.

Apple cake

This recipe comes from the West of England and uses cooking apples to give the cake a moist texture and a refreshing sweet-and-sour flavour. You can use eating apples, if you prefer, for a sweeter result. This is best eaten fresh with clotted cream or vanilla ice cream.

SERVES 8

115g/4oz/½ cup butter, diced,
   plus extra for greasing
225g/8oz cooking apples, peeled,
   cored and chopped
juice of ½ lemon
225g/8oz/2 cups plain
   (all-purpose) flour
7.5ml/1½ tsp baking powder
165g/5½oz/scant ¾ cup soft
   light brown sugar
1 egg, beaten
30–45ml/2–3 tbsp milk
2.5ml/½ tsp ground cinnamon

1 Preheat the oven to 180°C/
350°F/Gas 4. Grease and line an
18cm/7in round cake tin (pan) with
baking parchment.

2 In a small bowl, toss the apples
with the lemon juice.

3 Sift the flour and baking powder
into a large bowl.

4 With cold hands, rub the butter
into the flour mixture until it
resembles fine crumbs. Stir in
115g/4oz/½ cup of the sugar, and
the apples.

5 Add the egg and enough milk to
give a soft, dropping consistency.

6 Spoon into the prepared tin and
smooth the top level.

7 Mix together the remaining sugar
with the cinnamon, then sprinkle
over the cake batter.

8 Bake for 45–50 minutes, or until
firm to the touch. Leave to cool,
then turn out on to a wire rack to go
cold. Peel off the lining paper.

COOK'S TIP
Steps 3 and 4 can be made
ahead of time and the dry
crumbs stored in the refrigerator.

Energy 476kcal/2003kJ; Protein 4.5g; Carbohydrate 74.6g, of which sugars 56.5g; Fat 19.8g, of which saturates 8.5g; Cholesterol 32.5mg; Calcium 77.1mg; Fibre 2g; Sodium 104.8mg.

Farmhouse apple and sultana cake

This is a traditional, flavourful country cake made very simply and easily using the creaming method. It has a sweet, crispy top, a lovely moist texture and a spicy apple flavour – it makes an ideal tea-time treat. Keep this cake for 2 days in an airtight container in a cool place.

SERVES 12

175g/6oz/¾ cup softened butter,
  plus extra for greasing
175g/6oz/¾ cup soft light
  brown sugar
3 eggs
225g/8oz/2 cups self-raising
  (self-rising) flour, sifted
5ml/1 tsp baking powder, sifted
10ml/2 tsp mixed (apple pie) spice
350g/12oz cooking apples, peeled,
  cored and diced
175g/6oz/generous 1 cup sultanas
  (golden raisins)
75ml/5 tbsp milk
30ml/2 tbsp demerara (raw) sugar

1 Preheat the oven to 160°C/325°F/ Gas 3. Grease and line a 20cm/8in round deep cake tin (pan) with baking parchment.

2 Put the butter in a large bowl with the sugar. Beat together until light and fluffy. Beat in the eggs. Sift in the flour, baking powder and spice, then beat until thoroughly mixed.

3 Fold in the apples, sultanas and sufficient milk to make a soft dropping consistency.

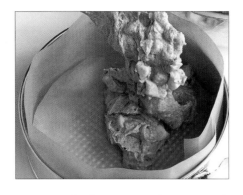

4 Spoon the batter into the prepared tin. Wet a metal spoon by running it under the tap and use the back of the wet spoon to smooth the cake top level.

5 Sprinkle with demerara sugar. Bake for about 1½ hours, or until risen, golden brown and firm to the touch. Cool in the tin for 5 minutes, then turn out on to a wire rack.

Energy 310kcal/1305kJ; Protein 4.2g; Carbohydrate 45.5g, of which sugars 31.2g; Fat 13.7g, of which saturates 8.4g; Cholesterol 81mg; Calcium 63mg; Fibre 1.3g; Sodium 135mg.

Kugelhupf

A special fluted ring mould with a chimney in the middle is a traditional tool of Austrian bakers. These tins can be used to bake rich yeasted mixtures, or this light almond sponge, which is spectacular when decorated with icing, nuts and fruits. Keep for five days in an airtight container.

3 Sift in the flour, then fold in with the orange rind, mixed peel, cranberries, sultanas, almonds and milk.

4 Spoon into the prepared tin and smooth the top level. Bake for about 1 hour, or until firm and golden. Cool in the tin for 5 minutes, then turn out to cool on a wire rack.

5 For the topping, put the honey and orange juice in a small pan and heat gently until the honey melts. Brush over the cake. Leave to cool.

6 Sift the icing sugar into a bowl, then blend in the orange juice. Spoon the icing over the cake, allowing it to drizzle down the sides. Sprinkle the fruit and nuts around the top and leave to set.

SERVES 12

225g/8oz/1 cup unsalted butter, softened (plus extra melted butter for greasing)
225g/8oz/generous 1 cup caster (superfine) sugar
3 eggs
225g/8oz/2 cups self-raising (self-rising) flour
finely grated rind of 1 orange
50g/2oz/⅓ cup chopped mixed peel
25g/1oz/¼ cup dried cranberries or dried cherries
50g/2oz/⅓ cup sultanas (golden raisins)
50g/2oz/¼ cup whole almonds, chopped
15ml/1 tbsp milk

For the topping and icing

45ml/3 tbsp clear honey
60ml/4 tbsp orange juice
115g/4oz/1 cup icing (confectioners') sugar
15ml/1 tbsp orange juice
15ml/1 tbsp dried cranberries or cherries
30ml/2 tbsp whole almonds, halved
15ml/1 tbsp whole dried orange and lemon peel, chopped

1 Preheat the oven to 190°C/375°F/ Gas 5. Brush a 1.75 litre/3 pint/ 7½ cup Kugelhupf mould well with melted butter.

2 In a bowl, beat together the butter and sugar. Beat in the eggs, adding 5ml/1 tsp flour with each egg.

Energy 319kcal/1339kJ; Protein 7g; Carbohydrate 41.8g, of which sugars 14.6g; Fat 14.6g, of which saturates 5.8g; Cholesterol 68mg; Calcium 87mg; Fibre 1.9g; Sodium 83mg.

Flourless fruit cake

Here's a really easy recipe that everyone will enjoy making. Instead of flour, the mixture contains cornflakes, so children can have fun crushing them and stirring the ingredients together. It is packed with fruity flavours too, from mincemeat to soft ready-to-eat figs.

SERVES 12–15

butter, for greasing
450g/1lb/1¼ cups mincemeat
350g/12oz/2 cups dried mixed fruit
115g/4oz/1 cup ready-to-eat dried
    apricots, chopped
115g/4oz/1 cup ready-to-eat dried
    figs, chopped
115g/4oz/½ cup glacé (candied)
    cherries, halved
115g/4oz/1 cup walnut pieces
225g/8oz/8–10 cups
    cornflakes, crushed
4 eggs, lightly beaten
400g/14oz can evaporated milk
5ml/1 tsp mixed (apple pie) spice
5ml/1 tsp baking powder
mixed glacé (candied) fruits,
    chopped, to decorate

1 Preheat the oven to 150°C/300°F/ Gas 2. Grease and line the base and sides of a 25cm/10in round cake tin (pan) with baking parchment.

2 Put all the ingredients into a large bowl and beat together well.

3 Spoon into the prepared tin and smooth the top level.

4 Bake in the centre of the oven for 1¾ hours, or until a skewer inserted into the centre of the cake comes out clean.

5 Cool in the tin for 10 minutes, then turn out to cool on a wire rack. Peel off the lining paper and leave to cool completely.

6 Decorate with the chopped glacé fruits.

COOK'S TIPS
• This cake can be kept for up to a week when stored in an airtight container.
• To crush the cornflakes, put them in a large plastic bag and tap with a rolling pin.

Energy 350kcal/1479kJ; Protein 7.4g; Carbohydrate 62.6g, of which sugars 50.38g; Fat 9.5g, of which saturates 1.5g; Cholesterol 56mg; Calcium 141mg; Fibre 2.4g; Sodium 224mg.

Currant cake

This traditional currant cake, from Norway, known as tiesen lap, uses the rubbed-in method of cake-making for combining the butter with the dry ingredients. Rather like a teabread, this cake is flavoured with nutmeg, and is light and moist with a crisp crust. It will keep for three days.

SERVES 10–12

130g/4½oz/9 tbsp butter, diced, plus extra for greasing
250g/9oz/2¼ cups plain (all-purpose) flour
7.5ml/1½ tsp baking powder
2.5ml/½ tsp freshly grated nutmeg
130g/4½oz/scant ¾ cup caster (superfine) sugar
130g/4½oz/½ cup currants or sultanas (golden raisins)
2 eggs, lightly beaten
150ml/¼ pint/⅔ cup milk or buttermilk

1 Preheat the oven to 190°C/375°F/ Gas 5. Grease a shallow 20cm/8in round cake tin (pan).

2 Sift the flour, baking powder and nutmeg into a large bowl and stir in the sugar.

3 Add the butter and, with cold fingertips, rub the butter into the flour until the mixture resembles fine breadcrumbs. Stir in the currants or sultanas.

4 Stir in the eggs with enough milk to make a soft dropping consistency.

5 Spoon the batter into the prepared tin and smooth the top level.

6 Bake for 30–40 minutes, or until risen, golden brown and cooked through, and a skewer inserted in the centre comes out clean. Cool in the tin for 5 minutes, then turn out to go cold on a wire rack.

Energy 283kcal/1190kJ; Protein 4.5g; Carbohydrate 41.9g, of which sugars 22.8g; Fat 12g, of which saturates 7g; Cholesterol 65mg; Calcium 73mg; Fibre 1g; Sodium 105mg.

Irish whiskey cake

For this light cake, Irish whiskey provides moisture and flavour. The lemon icing with its subtle hint of cloves makes a good contrast. Start preparations the night before, as the sultanas are soaked in the whiskey until plump and soft. Keep this for five days in an airtight container.

SERVES 8

225g/8oz/scant 1½ cups sultanas
   (golden raisins)
finely grated rind of 1 lemon
150ml/¼ pint/⅔ cup Irish whiskey
175g/6oz/¾ cup butter, softened,
   plus extra for greasing
175g/6oz/¾ cup soft light
   brown sugar
3 large (US extra large)
   eggs, separated
175g/6oz/1½ cups plain
   (all-purpose) flour
pinch of ground cloves
5ml/1 tsp baking powder

For the icing
juice of 1 lemon
225g/8oz/2 cups icing
   (confectioners') sugar
crystallized lemon slices, to
   decorate (optional)

1 Put the sultanas and lemon rind into a bowl with the whiskey and leave overnight to soak.

2 Preheat the oven to 180°C/ 350°F/Gas 4. Grease and line an 18cm/7in round cake tin (pan) with baking parchment.

3 In a large bowl, beat the butter and sugar until light and fluffy.

4 Beat in the egg yolks one at a time.

5 Sift over the flour, cloves and baking powder. Fold in in batches, alternating with the sultana and whiskey mixture. Do not overbeat.

6 Put the egg whites into a clean, grease-free bowl and whisk until they form stiff peaks. Fold in to the batter with a metal spoon.

7 Spoon the batter into the prepared tin and smooth the top level. Bake for 1½ hours, or until well risen. Turn out to cool on a wire rack.

8 To make the icing, mix the lemon juice with the sifted icing sugar and a few drops of cold water to make a pouring consistency. Put a plate under the cake rack to catch the drips and pour the icing over the cake a spoonful at a time, allowing it to drizzle down the side. Decorate with lemon slices, if you like.

Energy 586kcal/2466kJ; Protein 6g; Carbohydrate 88.9g, of which sugars 72.2g; Fat 20.8g, of which saturates 12.1g; Cholesterol 1mg; Calcium 91.8mg; Fibre 1.2g; Sodium 1.3mg.

Caribbean rum cake

This marvellously moist fruit cake is filled with tropical fruits – pineapple, papaya and mango – that have been soaked in rum. It is sweet and spicy with a fruity, coconut topping. Start preparations the day before for the best results. Keep this for five days in an airtight container.

2 Preheat the oven to 180°C/ 350°F/Gas 4. Grease and line a 20cm/8in round cake tin (pan) with baking parchment.

3 Cream the butter with the sugar. Beat in the eggs, a little at a time.

4 Sift over the flour and mixed spice, then fold in. Stir in the soaked fruits and mix thoroughly. Spoon into the cake tin and smooth the top level.

SERVES 10–12

50g/2oz/scant ⅓ cup sultanas (golden raisins)
175g/6oz/1 cup ready-to-eat dried pineapple, chopped
175g/6oz/1 cup ready-to-eat dried papaya, chopped
175g/6oz/1 cup ready-to-eat dried mango, chopped
60ml/4 tbsp rum
225g/8oz/1 cup butter, softened, plus extra for greasing
225g/8oz/1 cup soft light brown sugar
4 eggs, beaten
225g/8oz/2 cups plain (all-purpose) flour
10ml/2 tsp mixed (apple pie) spice

For the topping
75g/3oz/1 cup desiccated (dry unsweetened shredded) coconut
50g/2oz/⅓ cup ready-to-eat dried papaya, chopped
50g/2oz/⅓ cup ready-to-eat dried pineapple, chopped

1 Combine the sultanas with the dried pineapple, papaya and mango in a bowl. Spoon the rum over, then cover and leave for a few hours, or preferably overnight.

5 To make the topping, mix the coconut, papaya and pineapple in a small bowl. Sprinkle over the batter.

6 Bake for 1½–1¾ hours, or until a skewer inserted into the centre comes out clean. Cool in the tin for 15 minutes, then turn out on to a wire rack. Remove the lining paper.

Energy 434kcal/1826kJ; Protein 5.6g; Carbohydrate 63.2g, of which sugars 49.1g; Fat 18g, of which saturates 10.3g; Cholesterol 118mg; Calcium 86mg; Fibre 2.1g; Sodium 172mg.

Porter cake

Stout and porter are dark, full-flavoured beers and they can add real depth of flavour in cooking. This recipe originated in Ireland during the 19th century, where those drinks were popular, and it makes a fruit cake rich and tasty. Store this cake for one week before eating.

SERVES 10–12

225g/8oz/1 cup butter, at room
   temperature, plus extra
   for greasing
225g/8oz/1 cup soft dark
   brown sugar
350g/12oz/3 cups plain
   (all-purpose) flour
5ml/1 tsp baking powder
5ml/1 tsp mixed (apple pie) spice
3 eggs
450g/1lb/2⅓ cups mixed
   dried fruit
115g/4oz/½ cup glacé
   (candied) cherries
115g/4oz/⅔ cup mixed
   (candied) peel
50g/2oz/½ cup chopped almonds
   or walnuts
about 150ml/¼ pint/⅔ cup stout

1 Preheat the oven to 160°C/
325°F/Gas 3. Grease and line a
20cm/8in round cake tin (pan) with
baking parchment.

2 In a large bowl, cream the butter
and sugar until light and fluffy.

3 Sift the flour, baking powder and
spice into another bowl.

4 Add the eggs to the butter and
sugar mixture, beating well and
adding 5ml/1 tsp of the flour
mixture with each addition to
prevent the batter from curdling. Mix
well and fold in the remaining flour.

5 Add the dried fruit and nuts and
enough stout to make a soft
dropping consistency. Mix well.
Spoon into the prepared tin and
smooth the top level.

6 Bake for 1 hour. Reduce the heat
to 150°C/300°F/Gas 2 and bake for
another 1½–2 hours, or until a
skewer inserted into the centre
comes out clean. Allow to go cold
in the tin.

7 Remove the lining paper, wrap in
fresh baking parchment and store in
an airtight container.

Energy 510kcal/2150kJ; Protein 6.7g; Carbohydrate 80.4g, of which sugars 58g; Fat 20g, of which saturates 10.4g; Cholesterol 0.9mg; Calcium 0.1mg; Fibre 2.5g; Sodium 0.1mg.

Rich fruit cake

Use a food processor to chop and combine whole citrus fruits and dates to make this incredibly moist cake that is bursting with fruity and spicy flavours. This traditional cake is ideal for decorating for Christmas or special occasions. It will keep for one month in an airtight container.

SERVES 10–12

75g/3oz/scant ½ cup butter, plus
  extra for greasing
1 large orange, unpeeled, washed,
  cut into pieces and seeded
1 large lemon, unpeeled, washed,
  cut into pieces and seeded
1 large cooking apple, unpeeled,
  washed, cored and cut into pieces
90g/3½oz/generous ½ cup stoned
  (pitted) dates
75g/3oz/6 tbsp hazelnut butter
90g/3½oz/generous ½ cup raisins
90g/3½oz/generous ½ cup
  currants
90g/3½oz/generous ½ cup sultanas
  (golden raisins)
90g/3½oz/generous ½ cup
  ready-to-eat stoned (pitted)
  prunes, chopped
50g/2oz/½ cup cashew nut pieces
5ml/1 tsp ground cinnamon
5ml/1 tsp freshly grated nutmeg
2.5ml/½ tsp mace
2.5ml/½ tsp ground cloves
115g/4oz/1 cup wholemeal
  (whole-wheat) flour
7.5ml/1½tsp baking powder
115g/4oz/generous 1 cup rolled
  oats, processed until smooth
3 large (US extra large)
  eggs, beaten
45–60ml/3–4 tbsp unsweetened
  coconut milk, if needed

COOK'S TIP
Hazelnut butter is available in health-food stores and some larger supermarkets.

1 Preheat the oven to 150°F/300°C/ Gas 2. Grease and line a 20cm/8in round deep cake tin (pan) with baking parchment.

2 Put the first six ingredients in a food processor and process to make a rough purée.

3 Scrape the mixture into a bowl and stir in the raisins, currants, sultanas, prunes, nuts and spices.

4 Stir in the flour, baking powder and oats, alternating with the eggs.

5 If the mixture seems very dry, stir in the coconut milk.

6 Spoon the batter into the prepared tin and smooth the top level. Bake for 1 hour, or until a skewer inserted into the centre comes out clean. Cool for 15 minutes, then turn out to cool on a wire rack.

Energy 376kcal/1576kJ; Protein 2.4g; Carbohydrate 52.4g, of which sugars 52.4g; Fat 18.4g, of which saturates 7.9g; Cholesterol 30mg; Calcium 54mg; Fibre 1.2g; Sodium 123mg.

Glacé-topped fruit cake

This moist fruit cake is so simple to make for the festive season. It has a delightful twist of ginger and is topped with luscious glacé fruits, which take only minutes to arrange. Try to find good quality glacé fruits, for the best results. Keep for one month in an airtight container.

SERVES 12

175g/6oz/¾ cup butter, plus extra
  for greasing
300g/11oz/1¾ cups mixed
  dried fruit
50g/2oz/½ cup dried apple
  slices, chopped
75g/3oz/¾ cup dried
  apricots, chopped
75g/3oz/scant ½ cup stoned
  (pitted) prunes, chopped
50g/2oz glacé (candied)
  ginger, chopped
200g/7oz/scant 1 cup muscovado
  (molasses) sugar
200ml/7fl oz/ scant 1 cup freshly
  brewed black tea
350g/12oz/3 cups self-raising
  (self-rising) flour
5ml/1 tsp baking powder
10ml/2 tsp mixed (apple pie) spice
2 eggs, beaten
30ml/2 tbsp treacle (molasses)

For the decoration
60ml/4 tbsp ginger wine or
  ginger cordial
60ml/4 tbsp warmed and sieved
  (strained) apricot jam
450g/1lb/3 cups mixed glacé
  (candied) fruits in large pieces,
  such as pineapple rings, whole
  peel, cherries, angelica, pears,
  apricots and figs
Materials: 80cm/32in of 5cm/2in-
  wide wired ribbon

1 Preheat the oven to 160°C/325°F/ Gas 3. Grease and line the base and sides of a 23cm/9in deep round cake tin (pan) with baking parchment.

2 Put the dried mixed fruit into a large pan with the apples, apricots, prunes, ginger, sugar, butter and tea. Heat gently until the butter and sugar have melted, then stir well. Remove from the heat and leave to cool for 20 minutes.

3 Sift the flour, baking powder and spice into a large bowl and add the cooled fruit mixture.

4 Add the eggs and treacle, then beat together until smooth. Spoon into the tin. Smooth the top level.

5 Bake for 1¼ hours, or until a skewer inserted into the middle comes out clean. Leave to cool in the tin for 10 minutes, then turn out to cool on a wire rack and peel away the lining paper.

6 To decorate the cake, brush the top with the ginger wine or cordial, then brush over a little warmed apricot jam.

7 Arrange the pieces of glacé fruit on top of the cake.

8 Brush the remaining warmed glaze over the fruits on top of the cake. Decorate the sides of the cake with ribbon.

Energy 442kcal/1854kJ; Protein 5.5g; Carbohydrate 62.6g, of which sugars 48.2g; Fat 19.9g, of which saturates 10.5g; Cholesterol 103mg; Calcium 90mg; Fibre 1.6g; Sodium 159mg.

Sugar-free fruit cake

Ask your guests to guess what's in this cake. Although it tastes sweet, it contains no added sugar – all the sweetness comes from date purée and dried fruit. The cake is packed with healthy minerals and it's lower in calories than the average fruit cake, too. Keep this for two weeks.

3 Sift the flour and spice into a large bowl, then add the cooled purée and butter, eggs, dried fruit and ground almonds.

4 Beat with a wooden spoon for about 3 minutes, or until light and fluffy. Spoon into the tin and smooth the top level.

5 Sprinkle with the sliced almonds.

6 Bake for about 1¼ hours, or until a skewer inserted into the centre comes out clean.

SERVES 8–10

130g/4½oz/generous ½ cup softened butter, plus extra for greasing
175g/6oz/1 generous cup dried stoned (pitted) dates, chopped
finely grated rind of 1 small orange
225g/8oz/2 cups self-raising wholemeal (self-rising whole-wheat) flour
5ml/1 tsp mixed (apple pie) spice
3 eggs, beaten
450g/1lb/2⅔ cups mixed dried fruit
25g/1oz/¼ cup ground almonds
50g/2oz/½ cup flaked (sliced) almonds
15ml/1 tbsp clear honey, warmed, to glaze

1 Preheat the oven to 180°C/350°F/Gas 4. Grease and line a 20cm/8in round deep cake tin (pan) with baking parchment.

2 Put the dates in a heavy pan with the orange rind and 150ml/¼ pint/⅔ cup water. Simmer gently for 3–4 minutes, or until the dates form a purée, then leave to cool for 10 minutes.

7 Brush the warmed melted honey lightly over the flaked almonds on top of the cake, for a shiny glaze. Leave to cool in the tin for 15 minutes, then turn out to go cold and peel away the paper.

Energy 406kcal/1709kJ; Protein 7.1g; Carbohydrate 60.1g, of which sugars 43.2g; Fat 17g, of which saturates 7.9g; Cholesterol 87mg; Calcium 148mg; Fibre 2.9g; Sodium 224mg.

All-in-one mixed fruit cake

This cake couldn't be easier to make, as all the ingredients are added in one go. Serve it plain or use it as a base for a decorated celebration cake. If you bake it a week before you need it, the flavour will develop and the texture will improve, making it easier to cut as well.

SERVES 8–10

175g/6oz/¾ cup butter, softened, plus extra for greasing
225g/8oz/2 cups self-raising (self-rising) flour
2.5ml/½ tsp mixed (apple pie) spice
175g/6oz/¾ cup muscovado (molasses) sugar
3 eggs, beaten
350g/12oz/2 cups luxury mixed dried fruit
50g/2oz/½ cup glacé (candied) cherries, washed, dried and chopped
15ml/1 tbsp treacle (molasses)

2 Sift the flour and spice into a large bowl, then add all the remaining ingredients.

3 Beat with a wooden spoon for about 3 minutes, or until the mixture is well combined, thick and creamy.

4 Spoon into the prepared tin and smooth the top level.

5 Bake for 2–2¼ hours, or until a skewer inserted into the centre comes out clean. Leave to cool in the tin for 15 minutes, then turn out to go cold on a wire rack.

1 Preheat the oven to 160°C/325°F/ Gas 3. Grease and line the base and sides of a deep 20cm/8in round cake tin (pan) with a double layer of baking parchment snipped at the bottom edge to make a neat seal.

COOK'S TIP
This cake keeps for 1 month in an airtight tin. Freeze whole or in slices wrapped tightly in foil, for up to 4 months.

Energy 346kcal/1454kJ; Protein 4.3g; Carbohydrate 52.4g, of which sugars 39.1g; Fat 10.7g, of which saturates 6.2g; Cholesterol 62mg; Calcium 66mg; Fibre 2.1g; Sodium 90mg.

Mincemeat cake

If you have part of a jar of fruit mincemeat and a few small oranges left over after the Christmas holiday, they make a great basis for a tangy, quick and easy cake. Enrich the batter with some plain chocolate to make the cake even more special. Keep for one week in an airtight container.

SERVES 8–10

115g/4oz/½ cup soft tub
    margarine, plus extra for greasing
3 small mandarins or
    tangerines
75g/3oz/⅓ cup soft dark
    brown sugar
2 eggs, beaten
175g/6oz/1½ cups self-raising
    (self-rising) flour
2.5ml/½ tsp baking powder
15ml/1 tbsp milk
225g/8oz/⅔ cup luxury
    fruit mincemeat
50g/2oz plain (semisweet)
    chocolate, grated

For the decoration
175g/6oz/1½ cups icing
    (confectioners') sugar

1 Preheat the oven to 160°C/325°F/ Gas 3. Grease and line a 20cm/8in round deep cake tin (pan) with baking parchment.

2 Finely grate the rind from two oranges and put it in a large bowl.

3 Pare long shreds of peel from the third orange, then set aside.

4 Squeeze the juice from two oranges and keep 30ml/2 tbsp aside for the icing.

5 Put the remaining juice and all the other cake ingredients into a large bowl. Beat with a wooden spoon for about 2 minutes, or until the mixture is soft and smooth. Spoon into the tin and smooth the top level.

6 Bake for 40–45 minutes, or until firm and a warmed skewer inserted into the centre comes out clean. Cool in the tin for 10 minutes, then turn out to cool on a wire rack and peel away the papers.

7 To make the decoration, mix the icing sugar with the reserved orange juice until smooth. Spread over the top of the cold cake and allow the icing to run in drizzles down the sides. Sprinkle the orange shreds on top of the cake and leave to set for 30 minutes.

Energy 292kcal/1227kJ; Protein 2g; Carbohydrate 44.6g, of which sugars 44.4g; Fat 13g, of which saturates 7.9g; Cholesterol 66mg; Calcium 37mg; Fibre 0.5g; Sodium 135mg.

Vinegar cake

This fruit cake is sweet and moist, and not in the least sour from the white wine vinegar. It is made using an old-fashioned recipe, which contains no eggs, and the vinegar helps the mixture to rise. Keep in an airtight tin for one week and freeze whole or in slices for up to two months.

SERVES 12

150g/5oz/10 tbsp butter or block margarine, diced, plus extra for greasing
300g/11oz/2⅔ cups plain (all-purpose) flour
150g/5oz/generous ½ cup soft dark brown sugar
75g/3oz/generous ¾ cup raisins
75g/3oz/¾ cup sultanas (golden raisins)
50g/2oz/⅓ cup chopped mixed (candied) peel
2.5ml/½ tsp bicarbonate of soda (baking soda)
250ml/8fl oz/1 cup milk
25ml/1½ tbsp white wine vinegar

1 Preheat the oven to 180°C/350°F/ Gas 4. Grease and line a 20cm/8in round deep cake tin (pan).

2 Sift the flour into a large bowl. Add the butter and rub in until the mixture resembles fine breadcrumbs. Add the sugar and dried fruits, and stir together.

3 Dissolve the bicarbonate of soda in 75ml/5 tbsp of the milk and add to the dry ingredients.

4 Stir the vinegar into the remaining milk and pour into the bowl. Beat with a wooden spoon until smooth, then spoon into the prepared tin and smooth the top level. Indent the centre slightly.

5 Bake for 1 hour, then reduce the heat to 160°C/325°F/Gas 3 and bake for a further 20 minutes, or until a warmed skewer inserted into the centre comes out clean.

6 Cool in the tin for 5 minutes, then turn out to go cold on a wire rack.

Energy 276kcal/1159kJ; Protein 3.6g; Carbohydrate 43.4g, of which sugars 24.3g; Fat 11g, of which saturates 7g; Cholesterol 30mg; Calcium 78mg; Fibre 1.1g; Sodium 110mg.

Scottish black bun

The fruit for this spicy cake is soaked in whisky overnight to make it moist and rich in flavour. As the cake is traditionally served in Scotland on New Year's Day, it makes an ideal addition to a Hogmanay buffet. Make it at least two weeks ahead of time to allow it to mature.

SERVES 14

115g/4oz/½ cup butter, diced,
    plus extra for greasing
225g/8oz/2 cups plain
    (all-purpose) flour
1 egg, beaten, to glaze

For the filling
350g/12oz/generous
    1½ cups currants
350g/12oz/2½ cups raisins
50g/2oz/⅓ cup chopped
    mixed (candied) peel
50g/2oz/½ cup flaked
    (sliced) almonds
90ml/6 tbsp whisky or brandy
115g/4oz/1 cup plain
    (all-purpose) flour
5ml/1 tsp ground allspice
5ml/1 tsp ground cinnamon
5ml/1 tsp ground ginger
2.5ml/½ tsp cream of tartar
2.5ml/½ tsp bicarbonate of soda
    (baking soda)
115g/4oz/½ cup soft dark
    muscovado (molasses) sugar
1 egg, beaten

1 Put the dried fruits and nuts in a bowl with the alcohol. Soak overnight.

2 Preheat the oven to 180°C/ 350°F/Gas 4. Grease a 900g/2lb loaf tin (pan).

COOK'S TIP
Wrap in foil and store for 2 weeks in an airtight cake container, or freeze for 1 month.

3 Put the flour in a large bowl or food processor and add the fat. Rub in or process until the mixture resembles fine crumbs.

4 Add 45–60ml/3–4 tbsp cold water and mix or blend to a pliable pastry ball. Knead lightly until smooth, then wrap and chill for 30 minutes.

5 Cut off a third of the pastry and set aside. Roll out the remaining pastry and use to line the loaf tin, leaving the edges overhanging.

6 Sift the flour, spices, cream of tartar and bicarbonate of soda into a bowl, then add the sugar, the beaten egg, the soaked fruit and nuts, and the liquid from the bowl. Mix well to thoroughly combine the ingredients.

7 Spoon the fruit mixture into the pastry case and loosely fold the edges over the filling.

8 Roll out the remaining pastry to a rectangle large enough to cover the top. Moisten the pastry edges and press the rectangle on top. Trim the edges, then crimp together to make a lip.

9 With a skewer, make six holes in the top, right through the bun. Prick the pastry top with a fork, then brush all over with beaten egg.

10 Bake for 2 hours or until a skewer inserted into the centre comes out clean. If the top starts to over-brown, cover with foil. Cool in the tin for 5 minutes, then turn out to go cold on a wire rack.

Energy 435kcal/1828kJ; Protein 5.3g; Carbohydrate 67.8g, of which sugars 45.2g; Fat 14.7g, of which saturates 4.5g; Cholesterol 26mg; Calcium 101mg; Fibre 2.1g; Sodium 250mg.

Dundee cake

This classic Scottish fruit cake is made with mixed peel, dried fruit, almonds and spices. It is decorated in the traditional way, topped with whole blanched almonds. Make in advance so that the flavour can mature. Keep for one month in an airtight container.

SERVES 10–12

175g/6oz/¾ cup butter, plus
   extra for greasing
175g/6oz/¾ cup soft light
   brown sugar
3 eggs
225g/8oz/2 cups plain
   (all-purpose) flour
10ml/2 tsp baking powder
5ml/1 tsp ground cinnamon
2.5ml/½ tsp ground cloves
pinch of freshly grated nutmeg
225g/8oz/1½ cups sultanas
   (golden raisins)
175g/6oz/¾ cup glacé
   (candied) cherries
115g/4oz/⅔ cup chopped mixed
   (candied) peel
50g/2oz/½ cup blanched almonds,
   roughly chopped
grated rind of 1 lemon
30ml/2 tbsp brandy
75g/3oz/¾ cup whole blanched
   almonds, to decorate

1 Preheat the oven to 160°C/325°F/
Gas 3. Grease and line a 20cm/8in
round deep cake tin (pan).

2 Beat the butter and sugar together
in a bowl. Add each egg, beating
thoroughly after each addition.

COOK'S TIP
The flavour of this cake
improves if left in a cool place
for up to 3 weeks. Wrap it in
baking parchment and a double
layer of foil.

3 Sift the flour, baking powder and
spices together. Fold into the
creamed mixture, alternating with
the remaining ingredients. Mix until
evenly blended.

4 Spoon into the prepared tin and
smooth the top level, then make a
dip in the centre.

5 Decorate the top by arranging the
whole almonds in decreasing circles
over the entire surface. Bake in the
preheated oven for 2–2¼ hours, or
until a skewer inserted into the
centre comes out clean.

6 Cool in the tin for 30 minutes,
then turn out to cool on a wire rack.

Energy 292kcal/1229kJ; Protein 4.37g; Carbohydrate 41.5g, of which sugars 32.8g; Fat 12.9g, of which saturates 5.2g; Cholesterol 47mg; Calcium 69mg; Fibre 1.7g; Sodium 91mg.

Boiled fruit cake

The texture of this cake is quite distinctive – moist and plump as a result of boiling the dried fruit with the butter, sugar and milk prior to baking. For special occasions, arrange cherries and nuts on the surface of the batter before baking. It will keep for two weeks in an airtight container.

SERVES 10–15

225g/8oz/1 cup butter, plus
   extra for greasing
350g/12oz/2 cups mixed dried fruit
225g/8oz/1 cup soft dark
   brown sugar
400ml/14fl oz/1⅔ cups milk
450g/1lb/4 cups self-raising
   (self-rising) flour
5ml/1 tsp bicarbonate of soda
   (baking soda)
5ml/1 tsp mixed (apple pie) spice
2 eggs, beaten

1 Preheat the oven to 160°C/325°F/ Gas 3. Grease and line a 20cm/8in round cake tin (pan).

2 Put the dried fruit in a large pan and add the butter, sugar and milk. Bring to the boil. Stir occasionally.

3 When the butter has melted and the sugar has dissolved, allow the mixture to bubble gently for about 2 minutes. Remove from the heat and leave to cool slightly.

4 Sift the flour with the bicarbonate of soda and mixed spice. Stir into the fruit mixture with the eggs, and mix together well.

5 Spoon into the prepared tin and smooth the top level.

6 Bake for 1½ hours, or until firm to the touch and a skewer inserted into the centre comes out clean.

7 Cool in the tin for 20–30 minutes, then turn out to go cold on a wire rack. Remove the lining paper.

Energy 343kcal/1445kJ; Protein 4.8g; Carbohydrate 53g, of which sugars 33.2g; Fat 13.9g, of which saturates 8.3g; Cholesterol 58mg; Calcium 156mg; Fibre 1.3g; Sodium 219mg.

Dessert cakes

Many of us have been tempted to buy beautiful gateaux from a pâtisserie and serve these as a dessert for a special occasion, but you can also create these elegant specialities in your own kitchen. Gateaux do take a little more time and effort to make than many other cakes, but most can be prepared ahead or in stages. Allow plenty of time to enjoy the finishing and decorations. Although the cakes are a little more complicated, you will be surprised how simple skills can achieve a spectacular, mouthwatering centrepiece. Cheesecakes make an ideal dinner party dessert that can be made in advance. You have plenty of choice here: delicious Polish Cheesecake, Rum and Raisin Cheesecake, Baked Coffee Cheesecake, and more. There are also exquisite chocolate dessert cakes – White Chocolate Cappuccino Gateau or Chocolate Brandy-snap Gateau. You will impress friends and family with your own home-made pâtisserie.

Left: Coconut Lime Gateau and Raspberry and Hazelnut Meringue Cake.

Cassata

This traditional cake from Sicily has a rich and sweet filling of honey, Marsala and ricotta cheese studded with candied peel and chocolate chips. The cake is covered with almond paste and decorated with jewel-like glacé fruits. It is stunning to look at, and very tasty indeed.

SERVES 12

butter, for greasing
4 eggs
115g/4oz/generous ½ cup caster
  (superfine) sugar
115g/4oz/1 cup plain
  (all-purpose) flour
100ml/3½fl oz/scant ½ cup
  Marsala wine

For the filling
350g/12oz/1½ cups ricotta cheese
  30ml/2 tbsp clear honey
15ml/1 tbsp Marsala wine
1.5ml/¼ tsp vanilla extract
grated rind and juice of ½ lemon
115g/4oz/⅔ cup mixed (candied)
  peel, finely chopped
75g/3oz/½ cup plain (semisweet)
  chocolate chips

For the icing
175g/6oz/1½ cups ground
  almonds
75g/3oz/6 tbsp caster
  (superfine) sugar
75g/3oz/¾ cup icing
  (confectioners') sugar, sifted,
  plus extra for dusting
1 egg white, lightly beaten
5ml/1 tsp lemon juice
2 drops almond extract
green food colouring, optional
45ml/3 tbsp apricot jam, warmed
225g/8oz/mixed glacé
  (candied) fruits

1 Preheat the oven to 180°C/
350°F/Gas 4. Grease and line a
23cm/9in round cake tin (pan) with
baking parchment.

2 Line a 20cm/8in round cake tin
(pan) with clear film (plastic wrap).

3 Whisk the eggs and sugar in a
heatproof bowl until blended. Put
the bowl over a pan of simmering
water and whisk until thick and
pale. Remove from the heat and
continue whisking until the mixture
is cool and leaves a thick trail on the
surface when the beaters are lifted.

4 Sift the flour into the egg mixture.
Using a plastic spatula, fold the flour
into the beaten egg until smooth.

5 Pour into the larger prepared tin,
and bake for 30 minutes, or until
firm and spongy to the touch. Leave
to set in the tin for 10 minutes, then
turn out to go cold on a wire rack.
Peel away the lining papers.

6 Cut the cake into three layers.
Trim one to fit the base of the
smaller tin. Cut the second into
strips to line the tin side. Brush with
some of the Marsala. Reserve the
trimmings and the last sponge layer.

7 To make the filling, beat the
ricotta, honey, 15ml/1 tbsp Marsala,
vanilla extract and lemon rind and
juice together until very smooth.

8 Chop the sponge trimmings and
stir into the cheese mixture, with the
peel and chocolate chips. Spoon into
the sponge case, pressing into place.

COOK'S TIP
Marsala is a delicious golden
fortified dessert wine from Sicily.

Energy 380kcal/1599kJ; Protein 9.3g; Carbohydrate 50.8g, of which sugars 43.8g; Fat 13.3g, of which saturates 7.3g; Cholesterol 97mg; Calcium 72mg; Fibre 1.9g; Sodium 115mg.

9 Trim the reserved layer of sponge cake to fit tightly over the filling. Pour over the remaining Marsala and cover with clear film. Place a weight on top of the cake and chill for several hours, until firm.

10 To make the icing, combine the almonds, caster sugar and icing sugar in a bowl. Make a well in the centre.

11 Pour in the egg white, lemon juice and almond extract, and work in to form a soft pliable paste. Add a few drops of food colouring, if you like.

12 Knead the icing on a clean surface, dusted with a little icing sugar, until smooth and evenly coloured. Wrap and keep cool until required.

13 Remove the cake from the refrigerator and turn out of the tin. Remove the clear film and brush the cake with warmed apricot jam.

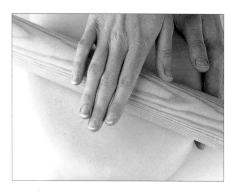

14 Roll out the almond paste to a circle a little larger than the cake and use to cover, pressing gently to the top and sides. Smooth over the icing with a metal spatula or lightly with a rolling pin. Transfer to a cake plate.

15 Make an attractive arrangement of mixed glacé fruits in the centre of the cake. Keep chilled until ready to serve. Serve with whipped cream. It will keep refrigerated, in an airtight container for 3 days.

Gateau Saint Honoré

Named after the patron saint of bakers, this spectacular dessert has a puff pastry base topped with caramel-coated choux puffs and filled with crème pâtissière. The cake is then drizzled with threads of golden caramel. Make and eat this fresh for a special occasion; do not refrigerate.

SERVES 10

175g/6oz puff pastry, thawed
  if frozen
flour, for dusting

For the choux pastry
300ml/½ pint/1¼ cups water
115g/4oz/½ cup butter, diced
130g/4½oz/generous 1 cup plain
  (all-purpose) flour, sifted
pinch of salt
4 eggs, lightly beaten
beaten egg, to glaze

For the crème pâtissière
3 egg yolks
50g/2oz/¼ cup caster
  (superfine) sugar
30ml/2 tbsp plain
  (all-purpose) flour
30ml/2 tbsp cornflour (cornstarch)
300ml/½ pint/1¼ cups milk
150ml/¼ pint/⅔ cup double
  (heavy) cream
30ml/2 tbsp orange liqueur

For the caramel
225g/8oz/generous 1 cup sugar
120ml/4fl oz/½ cup water

1 Roll out the puff pastry on a lightly floured surface, and cut out a 20cm/8in circle using a flan ring or an upturned plate as your guide.

2 Put the pastry round on a baking sheet lined with baking parchment. Prick all over with a fork and chill while you make the choux pastry.

3 To make the choux pastry, put the water and butter in a large pan. Heat until the butter has melted, then bring to the boil.

4 Add the flour and salt to the pan in one go. Remove the pan from the heat and beat vigorously until the mixture leaves the sides of the pan.

5 Beat in the eggs, a little at a time, to form a glossy paste.

6 Preheat the oven to 200°C/400°F/Gas 6.

7 Spoon the choux pastry into a piping (pastry) bag fitted with a 1cm/½in plain nozzle. Pipe a spiral of choux on to the puff pastry base, starting at the edge and working toward the centre.

8 Use the remaining choux pastry to pipe 16 small buns, using the same plain nozzle, on to a lightly greased baking sheet. Brush the buns and the choux pastry spiral with egg to glaze.

9 Bake the small buns for about 20 minutes until golden, and bake the choux-topped puff pastry on the shelf below for 35 minutes, or until well risen.

Energy 466kcal/1952kJ; Protein 7.3g; Carbohydrate 51.9g, of which sugars 30.9g; Fat 26.5g, of which saturates 12.5g; Cholesterol 186mg; Calcium 139mg; Fibre 0.5g; Sodium 221mg.

10 Pierce several holes in the top and sides of the spiral, and pierce one small hole in the side of each bun, using a skewer. Return the pastry to the oven for 5 more minutes to dry out. Cool on a wire rack.

14 To make the caramel, heat the sugar and water in a pan until dissolved, stirring occasionally. Bring to the boil and cook until it turns a rich golden colour. Remove the pan from the heat and set over a large bowl half-filled with boiling water to keep the caramel liquid.

15 Put the puff and choux pastry base on a serving plate.

16 Dip the bases of the choux buns into the caramel and arrange in a ring around the edge of the pastry.

17 Pipe the remaining crème pâtissière into the centre of the case. Drizzle the tops of the choux buns with the remaining caramel and leave to set. Keep in a cool place, but NOT the refrigerator, for up to 2 hours before serving.

11 To make the crème pâtissière, whisk the egg yolks and caster sugar until light and creamy. Whisk in the flour and cornflour.

12 Bring the milk to the boil in a pan and pour over the egg mixture, whisking all the time. Return the custard to the cleaned pan and cook for 2–3 minutes, or until thickened and smooth. Remove from the heat, cover with dampened baking parchment and leave to cool.

13 Whip the cream lightly. Remove the paper from the crème pâtissière and fold in with the orange liqueur. Spoon half into a piping bag fitted with a small plain nozzle and use it to fill the choux buns.

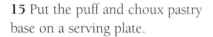

Raspberry and hazelnut meringue cake

Toasted and ground hazelnuts add a nutty flavour to this simple cake of meringue rounds sandwiched together with fresh cream and raspberries. This combination will appeal to all dessert lovers. Store the baked meringue bases, unfilled, for one week. Once filled, eat fresh.

SERVES 8

butter, for greasing
140g/5oz/1¼ cups hazelnuts
4 egg whites
200g/7oz/1 cup caster
  (superfine) sugar
2.5ml/½ tsp vanilla extract

For the filling
300ml/½ pint/1¼ cups
  whipping cream
700g/1lb 8oz/4 cups raspberries

1 Preheat the oven to 180°C/350°F/ Gas 4. Grease and line the bases of two 20cm/8in round cake tins (pans) with baking parchment.

2 Spread the hazelnuts on a baking sheet and bake for 8 minutes, or until lightly toasted. Leave to cool slightly. Rub the hazelnuts vigorously in a clean dish towel to remove the skins. Reduce the oven temperature to 150°C/ 300°F/Gas 2.

3 Grind the nuts in a food processor, until they are the consistency of coarse sand.

4 Put the egg whites into a clean, grease-free bowl and whisk until they form stiff peaks. Beat in 30ml/ 2 tbsp of the sugar, then, using a plastic spatula, fold in the remaining sugar, a few spoonfuls at a time.

5 Fold in the vanilla and hazelnuts.

6 Divide the mixture between the cake tins and smooth the top level. Bake for 1¼ hours until firm.

7 Leave to cool in the tin for 5 minutes, then run a knife around the inside edge of the tins to loosen the meringues. Turn out to go cold on a wire rack.

8 For the filling, whip the cream. Spread half on one cake round and top with half the raspberries.

9 Top with the other cake round. Spread the remaining cream on top and arrange the rest of the raspberries over the surface. Chill for 1 hour before serving.

Energy 298kcal/1252kJ; Protein 3.2g; Carbohydrate 39.5g, of which sugars 39.5g; Fat 15.3g, of which saturates 9.5g; Cholesterol 39mg; Calcium 55mg; Fibre 1.4g; Sodium 44mg.

Raspberry mousse cake

A lavish amount of raspberries gives this freezer gateau its vibrant colour and flavour. Make it at the height of summer when these deliciously scented fruits are plentiful and their flavour is at its best. Keep this cake frozen for three months. Thaw it in the refrigerator.

SERVES 8–10

2 eggs
50g/2oz/¼ cup sugar
50g/2oz/½ cup plain
  (all-purpose) flour
30ml/2 tbsp unsweetened
  cocoa powder
600g/1lb 5oz/3½ cups raspberries
115g/4oz 1 cup icing
  (confectioners') sugar
300ml/½ pint/1¼ cups
  whipping cream
2 egg whites

1 Preheat the oven to 180°C/350°F/ Gas 4. Grease and line a 23cm/9in round cake tin (pan).

2 Whisk the eggs and sugar in a bowl set over a pan of simmering water until the beaters leave a trail when lifted. Remove from the heat.

3 Sift over the flour and cocoa and fold it in with a metal spoon. Spoon into the tin. Bake for 12–15 minutes, or until just firm. Turn out to cool on a wire rack.

4 Reline the tin with baking paper and replace the cake. Freeze.

5 Set aside 175g/6oz/1 cup of raspberries.

6 Put the rest of the raspberries in a a food processor bowl, stir in the icing sugar and process to a purée.

7 Whip the cream to form soft peaks.

8 Put the egg whites into a clean, grease-free bowl and whisk until they form stiff peaks.

9 Using a large metal spoon, fold the cream, then the egg whites into the raspberry purée.

10 Spread half the raspberry mixture on to the cake. Sprinkle with the reserved raspberries. Spread the remaining raspberry mixture on top. Freeze overnight, then thaw for at least 2 hours before serving.

Energy 238kcal/996kJ; Protein 4.4g; Carbohydrate 25g, of which sugars 20.9g; Fat 14.1g, of which saturates 8.3g; Cholesterol 70mg; Calcium 58mg; Fibre 2g; Sodium 65mg.

Iced raspberry pavlova roulade

This melt-in-the-mouth meringue, rolled around vanilla cream and luscious raspberries, is a star dinner-party attraction, and is surprisingly quick and simple to make. Eat it fresh, or store it in the freezer in a rigid plastic container. Keep frozen for up to three months, and defrost for four hours.

5 Spoon the mixture into the prepared tin and smooth it level.

6 Put the meringue into a cold oven and turn the temperature to 150°C/300°F/Gas 2. Bake for 1 hour, or until the top is crisp and the meringue feels springy.

7 Turn out on to baking parchment sprinkled with sifted icing sugar, and leave to go cold.

8 Meanwhile, whip the cream and vanilla. Stir in the raspberries.

SERVES 6–8

10ml/2 tsp cornflour (cornstarch)
225g/8oz/generous 1 cup caster (superfine) sugar
4 egg whites, at room temperature
icing (confectioners') sugar, sifted, for dusting
300ml/½ pint/1¼ cups double (heavy) cream or whipping cream
a few drops of vanilla extract
175g/6oz/1 cup raspberries, partly frozen, plus extra to serve

1 Line a 33 x 23cm/13 x 9in Swiss roll tin (jelly roll pan) with baking parchment.

2 Sift the cornflour into a bowl and blend evenly with the sugar.

3 Put the egg whites into a clean, grease-free bowl and whisk until stiff peaks form.

4 Whisk in the caster sugar, a few spoonfuls at a time, until the mixture becomes stiff and glossy.

VARIATIONS
• Flavour the cream with liqueur or lemon curd.
• Fill with soft ice cream.

9 Spread the raspberry cream over the meringue, then roll up, using the paper as a support. Freeze for 1 hour before serving. Dust with icing sugar and top with more raspberries, to serve.

Energy 243kcal/1015kJ; Protein 2g; Carbohydrate 26g, of which sugars 26g; Fat 15.3g, of which saturates 9.5g; Cholesterol 39mg; Calcium 34mg; Fibre 0.5g; Sodium 33mg.

White chocolate cappuccino gateau

A fabulous dessert for a special occasion, this gateau is made with light sponge layers filled with coffee liqueur cream. On top is a fluffy coating of white chocolate and coffee liqueur frosting, with a layer of chocolate curls dusted with cocoa. This will keep chilled, for two days.

SERVES 8

butter, for greasing
4 eggs
115g/4oz/generous ½ cup caster
   (superfine) sugar
15ml/1 tbsp strong black coffee
2.5ml/½ tsp vanilla extract
115g/4oz/1 cup plain
   (all-purpose) flour
75g/3oz white chocolate, grated
white chocolate curls, to decorate,
   see page 84
unsweetened cocoa powder or
   powdered cinnamon, for dusting

For the filling
120ml/4fl oz/½ cup double
   (heavy) cream
15ml/1 tbsp coffee liqueur

For the white chocolate frosting
175g/6oz white chocolate
75g/3oz/6 tbsp unsalted butter
115g/4oz/1 cup icing
   (confectioners') sugar
90ml/6 tbsp double (heavy) cream
15ml/1 tbsp coffee liqueur

1 Preheat the oven to 180°C/350°F/Gas 4. Grease and line two 18cm/7in round shallow cake tins (pans).

2 Combine the eggs, sugar, coffee and vanilla extract in a large bowl set over a pan of hot water. Whisk until the mixture is pale and holds its shape when the beaters are lifted.

3 Sift half the flour over the mixture, and fold in. Fold in the rest of the flour with the grated chocolate.

4 Divide between the cake tins. Bake for 20–25 minutes, until golden. Turn out to cool on wire racks.

5 Whip the filling ingredients in a bowl until stiff. Spread over one cake and put the second cake on top.

6 To make the frosting, melt the chocolate with the butter in a heatproof bowl set over a pan of simmering water. Remove from the heat and beat in the icing sugar.

7 Whip the cream in another bowl until it just holds its shape, then beat into the chocolate mixture. Allow to cool, stirring occasionally. Stir in the coffee liqueur.

8 Spread over the top and sides of the cake. Top with chocolate curls and dust with cocoa or cinnamon. Serve with fresh berries. Freeze any leftover slices wrapped in foil.

Energy 337kcal/1418kJ; Protein 5.3g; Carbohydrate 50.5g, of which sugars 39.5g; Fat 13.6g, of which saturates 7.4g; Cholesterol 116mg; Calcium 61mg; Fibre 0.7g; Sodium 41mg.

Chocolate brandy-snap gateau

Savour every mouthful of this sensational dark chocolate gateau. The cake is rich with chocolate and hazelnuts, then filled and topped with ganache – a cream and chocolate icing. Crisp brandy-snap frills look wonderful and contrast beautifully with the soft cake. Eat fresh.

SERVES 8

225g/8oz/1 cup unsalted butter, softened, plus extra for greasing
225g/8oz plain (semisweet) chocolate, broken into pieces
200g/7oz/scant 1 cup muscovado (molasses) sugar
6 eggs, separated
5ml/1 tsp vanilla extract
150g/5oz/1¼ cups ground hazelnuts
60ml/4 tbsp fresh white breadcrumbs
finely grated rind of 1 large orange
icing (confectioners') sugar, for dusting

For the brandy snaps
50g/2oz/¼ cup unsalted butter
50g/2oz/¼ cup caster (superfine) sugar
75g/3oz/¼ cup golden (light corn) syrup
50g/2oz/½ cup plain (all-purpose) flour
5ml/1 tsp brandy

For the chocolate ganache
250ml/8fl oz/1 cup double (heavy) cream
225g/8oz plain (semisweet) chocolate, broken into pieces

1 Preheat the oven to 180°C/250°F/Gas 4.

2 Grease and line two 20cm/8in round shallow cake tins (pans) and two baking sheets with baking parchment.

3 To make the cake, melt the chocolate in a heatproof bowl set over a pan of gently simmering water. Stir occasionally. Remove from the heat to cool slightly.

4 Beat the butter and sugar in a large bowl until pale and fluffy. Beat in the egg yolks and vanilla extract. Add the melted chocolate and mix thoroughly.

5 Put the egg whites into a clean, grease-free bowl and whisk until they form soft peaks.

6 Fold a tablespoon of the whites into the chocolate mixture to slacken it, then fold in the rest in batches with the ground hazelnuts, breadcrumbs and orange rind.

7 Divide the cake batter between the prepared tins and smooth the tops level.

8 Bake for 25–30 minutes, or until well risen and firm, then turn out to cool on wire racks. Remove the lining paper.

9 To make the brandy snaps, melt the butter, sugar and syrup in a pan over a low heat, stirring occasionally.

10 Remove from the heat and stir in the flour and brandy until smooth.

11 Place small spoonfuls well apart on the baking sheet leaving enough space to allow each biscuit to spread out, and bake for 10–15 minutes, or until golden.

Energy 870kcal/3622kJ; Protein 10.7g; Carbohydrate 70g, of which sugars 59g; Fat 62.7g, of which saturates 31.2g; Cholesterol 244mg; Calcium 102mg; Fibre 2.3g; Sodium 424mg.

12 Cool for a few seconds until firm enough to lift.

13 Immediately pinch the edges of each brandy snap to make a frilled effect. If the biscuits become too firm, pop them back into the oven for a few minutes. Leave to set on a wire rack.

14 Meanwhile, to make the chocolate ganache, heat the cream and chocolate together in a pan over a low heat, stirring frequently until the chocolate has melted.

15 Pour into a bowl. Leave to cool, then stir until the mixture begins to hold its shape.

16 Sandwich the cake layers together with half the chocolate ganache, transfer to a plate and spread the remaining ganache on top.

17 Arrange the brandy snap frills over the gateau and dust with icing sugar. Serve immediately.

Layer cake

Three light cakes enclose one layer of crushed raspberries and another of custard, then the whole cake is covered with vanilla-flavoured cream. Make when raspberries are at their sweetest and best. Bake the cake layers the day before for the best flavour, then assemble the cake and eat it fresh.

SERVES 10–12

115g/4oz/½ cup unsalted butter,
  plus extra for greasing
200g/7oz/1 cup caster
  (superfine) sugar
4 eggs, separated
45ml/3 tbsp milk
175g/6oz/1½ cups plain
  (all-purpose) flour
25ml/1½ tbsp cornflour
  (cornstarch)
7.5ml/1½ tsp baking powder
5ml/1 tsp vanilla sugar
fresh raspberries, to decorate

For the custard filling
2 eggs
90g/3½oz/½ cup caster
  (superfine) sugar
15ml/1 tbsp cornflour (cornstarch)
350ml/12fl oz/1½ cups milk

For the cream topping
475ml/16fl oz/2 cups double
  (heavy) cream or whipping cream
25g/1oz/½ cup icing
  (confectioners') sugar
5ml/1 tsp vanilla sugar

For the raspberry filling
375g/13oz/generous 2 cups
  raspberries
sugar, to taste

COOK'S TIP
To make vanilla sugar, put a vanilla pod in a jar with a well-fitting lid, and fill with caster (superfine) sugar.

1 Preheat the oven to 230°C/450°F/ Gas 8. Lightly grease and flour three 23cm/9in shallow cake tins (pans).

2 Cream the butter with the sugar in a large bowl until light and fluffy. Beat in the egg yolks, one at a time. Stir in the milk until blended.

3 In a separate bowl, sift together the flour, cornflour, baking powder and vanilla sugar. Beat the flour mixture into the egg mixture.

4 Put the egg whites into a clean, grease-free bowl and whisk until they form stiff peaks. Gently fold the egg whites into the cake mixture.

5 Divide the batter evenly among the tins and smooth to the edges. Bake for 12 minutes. Leave the cakes to cool for 10 minutes, then turn out to go cold on a wire rack.

6 To make the custard filling, whisk together the eggs and sugar in a pan. Whisk in the cornflour and the milk. Cook over a low heat, stirring, for about 6 minutes or until thickened. Remove from the heat and leave to cool.

7 Beat the cream in a bowl until soft peaks form. Stir in the icing sugar and vanilla sugar and continue beating until stiff.

8 To make the raspberry filling, crush the raspberries in a bowl and add a little sugar to taste.

9 To assemble the cake, place one layer on a serving plate and spread with the raspberry filling.

10 Place a second cake layer over the first and spread with the cooled custard. Top with the final layer.

11 Spread whipped cream over the sides and top of the cake.

12 Chill the cake until ready to serve, and decorate with raspberries.

Energy 433kcal/1811kJ; Protein 6.1g; Carbohydrate 44.6g, of which sugars 30.4g; Fat 27g, of which saturates 15.9g; Cholesterol 157mg; Calcium 86mg; Fibre 1.2g; Sodium 109mg.

Polish cheesecake

There are many different versions of cheesecake. Unlike others, this rich, creamy baked version is not made on a biscuit base, but includes raisins and semolina, giving it sweetness and a firm texture. Keep this cheesecake refrigerated for two days, and freeze for up to two months.

SERVES 6–8

100g/3¾oz/scant ½ cup butter, softened, plus extra for greasing
500g/1¼lb/2¼ cups curd cheese
2.5ml/½ tsp vanilla extract
6 eggs, separated
150g/5½oz/scant ¾ cup caster (superfine) sugar
10ml/2 tsp grated lemon rind
15ml/1 tbsp cornflour (cornstarch)
15ml/1 tbsp semolina
50g/2oz/⅓ cup raisins
icing (confectioners') sugar, for dusting

1 Preheat the oven to 200°C/400°F/Gas 6. Grease and line the base and sides of a 20cm/8in loose-based cake tin (pan) with baking parchment.

2 In a large bowl, cream together the curd cheese, butter and vanilla extract.

3 Put the egg whites into a clean, grease-free bowl and add 15ml/1 tbsp sugar. Whisk until the whites form stiff peaks.

4 Whisk the egg yolks with the remaining sugar until thick and creamy. Add to the cheese mixture with the lemon rind, and stir to combine.

5 Gently fold in the egg whites, then fold in the cornflour, semolina and raisins.

6 Transfer to the lined tin and bake for 1 hour, or until the cake is set and golden brown.

7 Leave to cool in the tin. Remove the sides of the tin and papers, then dust with icing sugar and serve.

Energy 347kcal/1488kJ; Protein 10.8g; Carbohydrate 24.8g, of which sugars 21.6g; Fat23.6g, of which saturates 13.4g; Cholesterol 196mg; Calcium 34mg; Fibre 0g; Sodium131mg.

Baked coffee cheesecake

This rich, baked and chilled cheesecake, flavoured with coffee and orange liqueur, has a wonderfully dense, velvety texture and makes a lovely dessert served with single cream. Keep for two days refrigerated. Freeze for up to two months.

SERVES 8

75g/3oz/6 tbsp butter, plus extra
    for greasing
115g/4oz/1 cup plain
    (all-purpose) flour
5ml/1 tsp baking powder
50g/2oz/¼ cup caster
    (superfine) sugar
1 egg, lightly beaten
30ml/2 tbsp cold water
single (light) cream, to serve

For the filling
45ml/3 tbsp near-boiling water
30ml/2 tbsp ground coffee
4 eggs
225g/8oz/generous 1 cup caster
    (superfine) sugar
450g/1lb/2 cups cream cheese, at
    room temperature
30ml/2 tbsp orange liqueur
40g/1½ oz/⅓ cup plain
    (all-purpose) flour, sifted
300ml/½ pint/1¼ cups
    whipping cream
30ml/2 tbsp icing (confectioners')
    sugar, for dusting

1 Preheat the oven to 160°C/325°F/ Gas 3. Grease and line a 20cm/8in round loose-based cake tin (pan) with baking parchment.

2 Sift the flour and baking powder into a bowl. Rub in the butter until the mixture resembles fine crumbs.

3 Stir in the sugar, then add the egg and the cold water, and mix to a dough. Press the mixture into the base of the tin.

4 For the filling, pour the water over the coffee and leave for 4 minutes. Strain through a fine sieve (strainer).

5 Whisk the eggs and sugar until thick.

6 Using a wooden spoon, beat the cream cheese until softened, then beat in the liqueur, a spoonful at a time.

7 Gradually mix in the whisked eggs. Fold in the flour. Finally, stir in the whipping cream and coffee.

8 Pour over the base and bake for 1½ hours. Turn off the heat. Leave in the oven to go cold with the door ajar.

9 Chill for 1 hour. Remove from the tin and dust with icing sugar.

Energy 713kcal/2969kJ; Protein 8.4g; Carbohydrate 53.4g, of which sugars 38.6g; Fat 52.8g, of which saturates 32g; Cholesterol 233mg; Calcium 143mg; Fibre 0.6g; Sodium 301mg.

Rum and raisin cheesecake

Spectacular to look at, and superb to eat, this light, rum-flavoured cheesecake is studded with raisins and surrounded by diagonal stripes of plain and chocolate sponge. Keep this for four days refrigerated in an airtight container, or freeze for up to two months, undecorated with cream.

SERVES 8–10

115g/4oz/½ cup unsalted butter,
  melted, plus extra for greasing
2 eggs
50g/2oz/¼ cup caster
  (superfine) sugar
50g/2oz/½ cup plain (all-purpose)
  flour, sifted
5ml/1 tsp unsweetened cocoa
  powder, mixed to a paste with
  15ml/1 tbsp hot water and cooled
225g/8oz ginger biscuits
  (gingersnaps), crushed
whipped cream and sifted
  unsweetened cocoa powder,
  to decorate

For the filling
45ml/3 tbsp water
1 sachet powdered gelatine
300ml/½ pint/1¼ cups double
  (heavy) cream
30ml/2 tbsp milk
75g/3oz/generous ½ cup raisins
60ml/4 tbsp rum
50g/2oz/½ cup icing
  (confectioners') sugar, sifted
450g/1lb/2 cups curd cheese

1 Preheat the oven to 200°C/400°F/ Gas 6. Grease and line a 28 x 18cm/ 11 x 7in Swiss roll tin (jelly roll pan) with baking parchment. Also, grease and line a 20cm/8in round loose-based cake tin (pan). Cover a wire rack with baking parchment.

2 Mix the eggs and sugar in a heatproof bowl. Put over a pan of barely simmering water and whisk until the mixture forms a thick trail.

3 Fold in the sifted flour using a metal spoon.

4 Spoon half the mixture into a large piping bag fitted with a 4cm/1½in star nozzle, or use a paper piping (pastry) bag and cut the end off. Pipe diagonal stripes of the cake mixture across the tin, leaving an equal space between each row.

5 Stir the cooled cocoa paste into the remaining cake mixture until evenly mixed. Fill a piping bag with the batter and pipe as before, filling the gaps to give rows of alternating colours.

6 Bake for 10–12 minutes, then turn out the sponge on to the paper-topped wire rack. Peel off the lining paper. Leave to go cold.

7 Mix the melted butter and crushed ginger biscuits in a bowl. Spread over the bottom of the cake tin and press down firmly.

8 Cut the sponge in half lengthways and arrange the two strips around the sides of the cake tin. Set aside.

9 To make the filling, put the water into a small heatproof bowl and sprinkle over the gelatine. Leave until spongy. Put the bowl over a pan of barely simmering water and stir until the gelatine dissolves. Remove from the heat and leave to cool slightly.

10 Whisk the cream with the milk in a bowl. Fold in the raisins, rum, icing sugar and curd cheese, then stir in the cooled gelatine.

11 Spoon the filling into the prepared tin and chill until set.

12 To serve, carefully remove the cheesecake from the tin and place on a serving plate. Trim the cake level with the filling. Dust with cocoa powder and pipe whirls of cream around the edge.

Energy 467kcal/1946kJ; Protein 10.5g; Carbohydrate 34.6g, of which sugars 21.1g; Fat 33.3g, of which saturates 19.5g; Cholesterol 114mg; Calcium 121mg; Fibre 0.6g; Sodium 389mg.

Cinnamon apple gateau

Make this unusual cake for an autumn celebration. A light sponge is split and filled with a honey and cream cheese layer as well as softly cooked cinnamon apples and sultanas, then topped with glazed apples. Keep the sponge, unfilled, for two days in an airtight container; fill and eat it fresh.

SERVES 8–10

butter, for greasing
3 eggs
115g/4oz/generous ½ cup caster
　(superfine) sugar
75g/3oz/⅔ cup plain
　(all-purpose) flour
5ml/1 tsp ground cinnamon

For the filling and topping
4 large eating apples
60ml/4 tbsp clear honey
75g/3oz/generous ½ cup sultanas
　(golden raisins)
2.5ml/½ tsp ground cinnamon
350g/12oz/1½ cups soft cheese
60ml/4 tbsp fromage frais or
　crème fraîche
10ml/2 tsp lemon juice
45ml/3 tbsp apricot jam, strained
mint sprigs, to decorate

1 Preheat the oven to 190°C/
375°F/Gas 5. Grease and line a
23cm/9in round cake tin (pan) with
baking parchment.

2 Put the eggs and sugar in a bowl
and beat with an electric whisk until
thick and mousse-like and the
beaters leave a trail on the surface.

3 Sift the flour and cinnamon over
the egg mixture and carefully fold in
with a large spoon.

4 Pour into the prepared tin and
bake for 25–30 minutes, or until
the cake springs back when lightly
pressed in the centre.

5 Slide a knife between the cake and
the tin to loosen the edge, then turn
the cake on to a wire rack to cool.

6 To make the filling, peel, core and
slice three apples and put them in a
pan. Add 30ml/ 2 tbsp of the honey
and 15ml/1 tbsp water. Cover and
cook over a low heat for 10 minutes,
or until the apples have softened.

7 Add the sultanas and cinnamon,
stir, replace the lid and leave to cool.

8 Put the soft cheese in a bowl with
the remaining honey, the fromage
frais or crème fraîche and half the
lemon juice. Beat until smooth.

9 Cut the cake into two equal
rounds. Put half on a plate and
drizzle over any liquid from
the apple mixture.

10 Spread with two-thirds of the
cheese mixture, then top with the
apple filling. Fit the top of the cake
in place.

11 Swirl the remaining cheese
mixture over the top of the sponge.
Core and slice the remaining apple,
sprinkle with lemon juice and use to
decorate the edge of the cake. Brush
the apple with apricot glaze and
place mint sprigs on top to decorate.

Energy 239kcal/1010kJ; Protein 10.8g; Carbohydrate 39.9g, of which sugars 32.8g; Fat 5.8g, of which saturates 2.9g; Cholesterol 82mg; Calcium 97mg; Fibre 1.1g; Sodium 225mg.

Sponge cake with strawberries and cream

This classic treat is delicious in the summer, filled with ripe, fragrant strawberries. The sponge is exceptionally light because it is made without fat. To ensure you have a perfect sponge, have all the ingredients at room temperature. Eat this cake on the day it is made.

SERVES 8–10

oil, for greasing
115g/4oz/generous ½ cup caster (superfine) sugar, plus extra for dusting
90g/3½oz/¾ cup plain (all-purpose) flour, sifted, plus extra for dusting
4 eggs
icing (confectioners') sugar, for dusting

For the filling
300ml/½ pint/1¼ cups double (heavy) cream
about 5ml/1 tsp icing (confectioners') sugar, sifted
450g/1lb/4 cups strawberries, washed and hulled
a little orange liqueur (optional)

1 Preheat the oven to 190°C/375°F/ Gas 5. Grease a round 20cm/8in cake tin (pan). Dust the tin with 10ml/2 tsp caster sugar and flour combined. Tap out the excess.

COOK'S TIP
Freeze, unfilled, for 2 months.

2 Put the eggs and sugar into a bowl and use an electric whisk at high speed until the mixture is light and thick, and the mixture leaves a trail as it drops from the whisk. (To whisk by hand: set the bowl over a pan one quarter filled with hot water and whisk until thick and creamy, then remove from the heat.)

3 Sift the flour over the whisked eggs and carefully fold it in with a metal spoon, mixing thoroughly but losing as little volume as possible.

4 Pour the batter into the cake tin and smooth the top level. Bake for 25–30 minutes, or until the sponge feels springy to the touch.

5 Leave in the tin for 5 minutes to set slightly, then loosen the sides with a knife and invert on to a wire rack to go cold.

6 To make the filling, whip the cream with a little icing sugar until it is stiff enough to hold its shape.

7 Slice the sponge across the middle with a long sharp knife to make two even layers.

8 Divide half the cream between the two inner cut sides of the sandwich.

9 Reserve some strawberries for the cake top, and then slice the rest.

10 Put the first sponge half on a serving plate and arrange the sliced strawberries on the cream. Sprinkle with liqueur, if using.

11 Cover with the second cake half and press down gently.

12 Spread the remaining cream on top of the cake, and arrange the reserved strawberries, whole or halved according to size, on top.

13 Set aside for an hour or so for the flavours to develop, then dust lightly with icing sugar and serve.

Energy 333kcal/1387kJ; Protein 5.3g; Carbohydrate 27.8g, of which sugars 19.2g; Fat 23.1g, of which saturates 13.3g; Cholesterol 147mg; Calcium 65mg; Fibre 1g; Sodium 48mg.

Princess cake

A light sponge cake is layered and topped with vanilla custard cream, then covered with home-made marzipan to make an unusual and special dessert gateau. You can make the marzipan in advance, if you like. Serve a slice of the cake with strawberries. Keep for two days in a cool place.

SERVES 8–10

200g/7oz/scant 1 cup unsalted
   butter, plus extra for greasing
400g/14oz/2 cups caster
   (superfine) sugar
3 eggs
350g/12oz/3 cups plain
   (all-purpose) flour
5ml/1 tsp baking powder
10ml/2 tsp vanilla sugar
fresh strawberries, to serve

For the filling and topping
3 gelatine leaves
1 litre/1¾ pints/4 cups double
   (heavy) cream
10ml/2 tsp sugar
10ml/2 tsp cornflour (cornstarch)
2 egg yolks
10ml/2 tsp vanilla sugar

For the marzipan
200g/7oz/1¾ cups ground almonds
200g/7oz/1¾ cups icing
   (confectioners') sugar
1 egg white
a few drops of green food colour

1 To make the marzipan, put the ground almonds in a bowl and add the icing sugar and egg white. Mix to form a paste.

2 Add a few drops of green food colour and knead until evenly coloured. Refrigerate in a plastic bag for up to 3 days until required.

3 Preheat the oven to 180°C/350°F/ Gas 4. Grease and line a 20cm/8in round cake tin (pan).

4 Put the butter and sugar in a large bowl and beat until fluffy. Add the eggs and whisk together. Sift in the flour, baking powder and vanilla sugar and stir together.

5 Spoon the batter into the cake tin and bake for 1 hour, or until firm to the touch. Leave to cool in the tin. When cold, slice in half horizontally.

6 To make the filling, soak the gelatine in cold water according to the directions on the packet. Put half of the cream, the sugar, cornflour and egg yolks in a pan and heat gently, stirring constantly, until the mixture thickens. Do not allow it to boil or the eggs will curdle.

7 Pour into a bowl, and stir in the soaked gelatine leaves. Leave to cool.

8 Put the remaining cream with the vanilla sugar in a bowl and whisk until stiff.

9 Fold into the cooled custard and quickly spread half the mixture over the bottom layer of cake. Put the other cake layer on top and spread the remaining custard over the top and sides.

10 Put the marzipan between two sheets of foil. Roll out a thin round. Remove the top sheet of foil and, using a 30cm/12in diameter plate as a guide, cut a marzipan circle.

11 Use the foil to lift the marzipan circle over the top of the cake and smooth it down the sides. Trim the edge around the cake base. Decorate with fresh strawberries.

Energy 1326kcal/5512kJ; Protein 11.3g; Carbohydrate 112g, of which sugars 77.6g; Fat 95.7g, of which saturates 56.1g; Cholesterol 346mg; Calcium 191mg; Fibre 1.9g; Sodium 218mg.

Coconut lime gateau

American frosting is what makes this zesty lime and coconut gateau so attractive. Made by whisking egg white and a sugar mixture over heat, the frosting is like a soft meringue icing. It tastes divine scattered with toasted coconut. Eat the gateau fresh or refrigerate it for two days.

SERVES 10–12

225g/8oz/1 cup butter, at
 room temperature, plus extra
 for greasing
225g/8oz/2 cups plain
 (all-purpose) flour
12.5ml/2½ tsp baking powder
225g/8oz/generous 1 cup caster
 (superfine) sugar
grated rind of 2 limes
4 eggs
60ml/4 tbsp fresh lime juice (from
 about 2 limes)
85g/3oz/1 cup desiccated (dry
 unsweetened shredded) coconut

For the frosting
275g/10oz/scant 1½ cups caster
 (superfine) sugar
2.5ml/½ tsp cream of tartar
2 egg whites
60ml/4 tbsp cold water
15ml/1 tbsp liquid glucose
10ml/2 tsp vanilla extract

1 Preheat the oven to 180°C/350°F/ Gas 4. Grease and line two 23cm/9in round shallow cake tins (pans) with baking parchment.

2 Sift together the flour and baking powder into a bowl.

3 In another large bowl, beat the butter until soft. Add the sugar and lime rind, then beat until pale and fluffy. Beat in the eggs, one at a time, adding 5ml/1 tsp of the flour mixture with each addition to stop the batter from curdling. Beat the mixture well between each addition.

4 Using a wooden spoon, fold in the flour mixture in small batches, alternating with the lime juice. When the batter is smooth, stir in two-thirds of the coconut.

5 Divide the batter between the tins and spread it evenly to the sides.

6 Bake for 30–35 minutes, or until a skewer inserted into the centre comes out clean. Leave to cool in the tins for 10 minutes, then turn out to cool on a wire rack. Remove the lining paper. Leave to go cold.

7 Spread the remaining coconut in another cake tin. Bake until golden brown, stirring occasionally. Watch carefully so that the coconut does not get too dark. Allow to cool in the tin.

8 To make the frosting, put the sugar in a large heatproof bowl and add the cream of tartar, egg whites, water and glucose. Stir to mix.

9 Set the bowl over a pan of boiling water. Beat with an electric whisk at high speed for 7 minutes or until thick and stiff peaks form. Remove from the heat.

10 Add the vanilla extract and continue beating for 3 minutes or until the frosting has cooled slightly.

11 Invert one cake on a serving plate. Spread a layer of frosting on top.

12 Set the second cake on top. Swirl the rest of the frosting all over the cake. Sprinkle with the toasted coconut and leave to set.

Energy 732kcal/3079kJ; Protein 7.3g; Carbohydrate 111g, of which sugars 59g; Fat 32g, of which saturates 20.5g; Cholesterol 155mg; Calcium 105.7mg; Fibre 2.1g; Sodium 221mg.

Lemon chiffon cake

Split a light lemon sponge cake in half horizontally, then fill with a lovely thick layer of lemon mousse to give it a tangy centre. Top with a lemon icing and lemon zest and you have the most lemony cake. Keep this for one day in the refrigerator, or freeze for two months, undecorated.

SERVES 8

butter, for greasing
2 eggs
75g/3oz/6 tbsp caster
   (superfine) sugar
grated rind of 1 lemon
50g/2oz/1/2 cup plain (all-purpose)
   flour, sifted
lemon shreds, to decorate

For the filling
2 eggs, separated
75g/3oz/6 tbsp caster
   (superfine) sugar
grated rind and juice of 1 lemon
15ml/1 tbsp gelatine
120ml/4fl oz/1/2 cup fromage frais
   or crème fraîche

For the icing
15ml/1 tbsp lemon juice
115g/4oz/1 cup icing
   (confectioners') sugar, sifted

1 Preheat the oven to 180°C/350°F/ Gas 4. Grease and line a 20cm/8in round loose-based cake tin (pan).

2 Whisk the eggs, sugar and lemon rind until mousse-like. Fold in the flour, then pour into the cake tin.

3 Bake for 20–25 minutes, or until the cake springs back when lightly pressed in the centre. Turn on to a rack to go cold. Clean the cake tin.

4 Remove the lining paper. Split the cake in half horizontally and return the lower half to the clean cake tin.

5 To make the filling, put the egg yolks, sugar, lemon rind and juice in a bowl. Beat with an electric whisk until thick, pale and creamy.

6 Pour 30ml/2 tbsp water into a small heatproof bowl and sprinkle the gelatine on top. Leave until spongy, then set the bowl over simmering water and stir until dissolved. Cool slightly, then whisk into the yolk mixture. Fold in the fromage frais or crème fraîche.

7 When the filling mixture begins to set, whisk the egg whites in a clean, grease-free bowl until they form soft peaks. Stir a spoonful into the mousse mixture to lighten it, then fold in the rest.

8 Pour the filling over the sponge in the cake tin, spreading it to the edges. Put the second layer of sponge on top and chill until set.

9 Slide a knife dipped in hot water between the tin and the cake to loosen it, then transfer the cake to a serving plate.

10 To make the icing, add enough lemon juice to the icing sugar to make a thick, spreadable icing. Pour over the cake and spread to the edges. Decorate with lemon shreds.

Energy 356kcal/1491kJ; Protein 6.7g; Carbohydrate 43.6g, of which sugars 29.8g; Fat 18.4g, of which saturates 4g; Cholesterol 118mg; Calcium 68mg; Fibre 0.6g; Sodium 227mg.

Special occasion cakes

In this chapter you will find some fabulous cakes to help celebrate many occasions, such as family gatherings, weddings, christenings and parties, all of which call for a centrepiece. Give yourself plenty of time to make these cakes. The detailed step-by-step photographs will help to take you through the complicated techniques. A freshly baked Strawberry Shortcake couldn't be better to take to a summer barbecue party, or you could make a present of a Simnel Cake for Easter. For a christening or naming party, Lemon Daisy Christening Cake could be served with a Meringue Mountain as part of a special tea. Take the worry out of the festive season celebrations by making the Traditional Christmas Cake, Yule Log or White Christmas Cake, all of which can be prepared well ahead of time.

Left: Mother's Day Cake and Celebratory Anniversary Cake.

Lemon daisy christening cake

This delicate sponge cake is drizzled with a lemon syrup, making it moist with good keeping qualities. Use sugarpaste to give it the perfect finish, decorated with hand-moulded daisies. Make it up to four days ahead, so you have plenty of time to concentrate on decorating it.

SERVES 16–18

350g/12oz/1½ cups butter or block
   margarine, plus extra for greasing
350g/12oz/1¾ cups caster
   (superfine) sugar
6 eggs, beaten
115g/4oz/1 cup plain
   (all-purpose) flour
275g/10oz/2½ cups self-raising
   (self-rising) flour
finely grated rind and juice
   of 2 lemons

For the syrup and decorations
100g/3¼ oz/generous ½ cup caster
   (superfine) sugar
finely grated rind and juice
   of 2 lemons
1 quantity buttercream icing, *see
   page 23*
icing (confectioners') sugar,
   for dusting
1kg/2¼lb sugarpaste icing,
   see page 26
yellow and pink edible paste
   food colourings
small tube writing icing
Materials: lemon satin ribbon

1 Preheat the oven to 160°C/325°F/ Gas 3. Grease and line a 23cm/9in deep, round cake tin (pan) with baking parchment.

2 In a bowl, beat the butter and sugar together until light and fluffy.

> **COOK'S TIP**
> Keeps for 5 days, undecorated.

3 Gradually beat in the eggs a little at a time, adding 5ml/1 tsp flour with each addition to prevent the mixture from curdling.

4 Sift the flours into the bowl and fold into the egg mixture with the lemon rind and juice until smooth.

5 Spoon into the tin and smooth the top level. Bake for 1¼ hours, or until a warmed skewer inserted into the middle comes out clean.

6 Leave in the tin until just warm, then prick over the top of the cake with a skewer.

7 To make the syrup, put the sugar, lemon juice and rind in a pan and heat gently until the sugar dissolves completely. Allow to cool slightly.

8 Brush the syrup over the cake and leave to cool completely in the tin. Remove the lining paper. Wrap the cake in baking parchment, then in foil until needed.

9 Cut the cake in half horizontally, sandwich together with buttercream icing, then spread the remainder thinly around the outside.

10 Put the sugarpaste icing on a surface lightly dusted with icing sugar, and roll out to a circle large enough to cover the top and sides of the cake.

11 Lift the sugarpaste over the cake, smooth down with your hands to remove any bubbles or pleats, then trim the excess away carefully with a sharp knife.

Energy 591kcal/2503kJ; Protein 5.5g; Carbohydrate 117.6g, of which sugars 108.3g; Fat 11.6g, of which saturates 2.4g; Cholesterol 38mg; Calcium 112mg; Fibre 2g; Sodium 140mg.

12 Roll the trimmings into small pea-sized balls, then shape each one into a cone. Flatten out one edge thinly. Using clean scissors, snip the edge to represent petals. Mark the centre with the scissor points.

13 Put a dot each of yellow and pink paste colours on to a plate and, using a paintbrush, dilute slightly with water. Paint the centres of the flowers lemon and the outer petal tips pale pink. Leave to dry out.

14 Position the flowers on the cake in a daisy circle and stick each in place using a little blob of writing icing.

15 Write the name or message in the centre of the cake, if you like, and finish by tying a deep ribbon in a bow around the sides of the cake.

COOK'S TIP
To bake ahead, cool the cake, cover it with syrup and freeze, undecorated, for up to 3 months.

Celebration bow cake

Adding a little glycerine to this delicate almond cake helps it retain its moisture for longer, so you can make it ahead of time. The cake is ideal for any type of celebration, and you can vary the icing colours to suit. Small icing cutters are useful for quick-and-easy cake decorating.

SERVES 12

275g/10oz/2½ cups self-raising
  (self-rising) flour
2.5ml/½ tsp baking powder
50g/2oz/¼ cup ground almonds
275g/10oz/1¼ cups soft tub
  margarine, plus extra for greasing
275g/10oz/scant 1½ cups natural
  caster (superfine) sugar
5 eggs, beaten
a few drops of almond extract
15ml/1 tbsp milk
15ml/1 tbsp glycerine

For the decoration
90ml/6 tbsp sieved (strained)
  apricot glaze
700g/1lb 9oz almond paste
1kg/2¼lb sugarpaste icing
paste food colourings, such as
  yellow, pink and blue

1 Preheat the oven to 160°C/325°F/
Gas 3. Grease and line the base and
sides of a 20cm/8in square cake
tin (pan).

2 Sift the flour, baking powder and
almonds into a large bowl. Add the
margarine, caster sugar, eggs,
almond extract, milk and glycerine
and beat for about 2 minutes with
an electric mixer until smooth.

3 Spoon into the tin and smooth
level. Bake for 50 minutes to 1 hour,
or until well risen, golden and firm
in the middle.

4 Cool in the tin for 5 minutes, then
turn out to cool on a wire rack.

5 When cold, remove the lining
paper. Brush the cake with apricot
glaze. Roll out the almond paste
large enough to cover the cake. Lift
on to the cake, smooth down the
sides and trim. Leave for 24 hours.

6 Colour half of the sugarpaste pale
yellow and roll out to a square large
enough to cover the cake. Brush the
cake with a little cold boiled water,
then lift the icing on to the cake and
smooth down. Trim the edges neatly.

7 Colour half of the remaining
sugarpaste blue and the rest pink.

> **COOK'S TIP**
> The cake keeps for 5 days in an
> airtight container. Do not freeze.

8 Roll out the pink icing and cut
four strips 4 x 20cm/1½ x 8in and
eight strips 4 x 10cm/1½ x 4in.

9 Roll out the blue icing and cut
four strips 2.5 x 20cm/1 x 8in and
eight strips 2.5 x 10cm/1 x 4in.

10 Centre matching length blue
strips on top of the pink strips.
Using a little water, stick the longer
lengths to the cake top in a cross.

11 Form loops with four shorter
strips. Leave to dry out overnight
over the handle of a wooden spoon.

12 Trim the ends of the remaining
strips and stick to the cake top like
ribbons. Stick the loops in place.
Stamp the leftover icing into small
shapes and use to decorate the cake.

Energy 483kcal/2024kJ; Protein 4.2g; Carbohydrate 63.6g, of which sugars 49.6g; Fat 25.4g, of which saturates 15.3g; Cholesterol 124mg; Calcium 105mg; Fibre 0.6g; Sodium 265mg.

Fun kitty cake

Buttercream icing is a great way to cover a cake simply and easily. This jolly children's birthday cake is textured to look like a cat's fur and can be coloured to match the child's favourite cat. It is a simple party centrepiece – but it looks good and has a lovely citrus tang, too.

SERVES 14
350g/12oz/1½ cups soft tub margarine, plus extra for greasing
350g/12oz/1¾ cups natural caster (superfine) sugar
350g/12oz/3 cups self-raising (self-rising) flour
10ml/2 tsp baking powder
finely grated zest of 1 orange
60ml/4 tbsp orange juice
30ml/2 tbsp milk
6 eggs, beaten
60ml/4 tbsp orange marmalade

For the decoration
225g/8oz/1 cup unsalted butter
450g/1lb/4 cups natural icing (confectioners') sugar
30ml/2 tbsp warm milk
food colouring, brown or orange
bootlace liquorice, liquorice allsorts and sweets (candies)

1 Preheat the oven to 190°C/375°F/ Gas 5. Grease and line the bases of two 20cm/8in deep round cake tins (pans) with baking parchment.

2 Put the margarine and sugar in a bowl and sift in the flour and baking powder. Beat thoroughly to combine.

3 Add the orange zest, 30ml/2 tbsp of the juice, the milk and eggs. Beat for about 2 minutes, or until the mixture is smooth.

4 Spoon into the tins and bake for 30–35 minutes, or until golden. Cool in the tins for 5 minutes, then turn out to cool on a wire rack.

5 Make the buttercream with the butter, icing sugar, remaining orange juice and milk, and whisk until light. Colour the icing if required.

6 Put one cake on a board for the body. Cut the other cake into the head, ears and tail.

7 Cut the cakes in half horizontally. Sandwich together with marmalade.

8 Assemble the cake and secure with buttercream. Cover with buttercream, flicking up into a furry effect using a spatula. Make eyes, nose, mouth, whiskers and paws from liquorice.

Energy 435kcal/1828kJ; Protein 5.3g; Carbohydrate 62.6g, of which sugars 54.7g; Fat 19.9g, of which saturates 4.5g; Cholesterol 48mg; Calcium 65mg; Fibre 1.4g; Sodium 150mg.

Easy birthday cake

Make celebrating a birthday simple with this scrumptious caramel cake, which can be decorated to make it suitable for either children or adults. The fudgy icing is made in a pan then swirled over the top and sides of the cake in moments – it really couldn't be easier.

SERVES 10–12

175g/6oz/³⁄₄ cup soft tub
    margarine, plus extra for greasing
225g/8oz/2 cups self-raising
    (self-rising) flour
2.5ml/¹⁄₂ tsp baking powder
225g/8oz/1 cup soft light
    brown sugar
3 eggs, beaten
30ml/2 tbsp golden (light corn)
    syrup
60ml/4 tbsp milk
5ml/1 tbsp vanilla extract

For the caramel icing
115g/4oz/¹⁄₂ cup unsalted butter
225g/8oz/1 cup soft light
    brown sugar
60ml/4 tbsp milk
115g/4oz/1 cup icing
    (confectioners') sugar
sweets (candies) and candles,
    to decorate

1 Preheat the oven to 180°C/350°F/Gas 4. Grease and line the bases of two 20cm/8in shallow round cake tins (pans) with baking parchment.

2 Sift the flour and baking powder into a large bowl, then add the margarine, soft light brown sugar, eggs, syrup, milk and vanilla extract. Beat with an electric mixer for about 2 minutes, or until smooth, then divide between the tins.

3 Bake for 30 minutes, or until firm to the touch. Allow to cool for 5 minutes, then turn out on a wire rack. Remove the lining paper.

4 To make the icing, melt the butter in a pan, add the brown sugar and the milk, and bring to the boil. Reduce the heat and simmer for 2 minutes, then pour into a bowl and leave to cool.

5 When cold, beat in the icing sugar.

6 Swirl the icing over the top and sides of the cake. Decorate with sweets and candles or use chocolate buttons and broken flaked chocolate, as desired.

7 The undecorated cake keeps for 4 days in an airtight tin.

Energy 570kcal/2408kJ; Protein 3.8g; Carbohydrate 108.8g, of which sugars 95.1g; Fat 16.3g, of which saturates 9.6g; Cholesterol 18mg; Calcium 64mg; Fibre 0.6g; Sodium 293mg.

Mother's Day cake

Almonds, orange and vanilla give this special cake its delicate flavour, which can be further enhanced by drizzling over orange liqueur. To get the full citrus tang of the fresh orange you will need a food processor to grind the orange rind finely.

SERVES 12

200g/7oz/scant 1 cup butter,
  softened, plus extra for greasing
2 small oranges
100g/3¾oz/scant 1 cup toasted
  flaked (sliced) almonds
200g/7oz/1 cup soft light
  brown sugar
4 eggs, beaten
5ml/1 tsp vanilla extract
175g/6oz/1½ cups self-raising
  (self-rising) flour
40g/1¾oz/generous ¼ cup natural
  icing (confectioners') sugar, plus
  extra dusting
5ml/1 tbsp orange liqueur (optional)

For the decoration
½ quantity buttercream icing, *see
  page 22*
675g/1½lb sugarpaste
Materials: 1.5m/1yd fancy ribbon;
  bought sugarpaste or silk flowers

1 Preheat the oven to 180°C/350°F/
Gas 4. Grease and line a 20cm/8in
round springform cake tin (pan)
with baking parchment.

2 Peel the oranges in strips, then put
in a food processor. Process for a few
seconds until the peel forms a fine
powder, then put into a bowl.

> **COOK'S TIP**
> Store the cake undecorated in an
> airtight container for up to
> 5 days, or decorated in a cool
> place for up to 2 days.

3 Process the almonds until fine,
then mix with the powdered rind.

4 Beat the butter and sugar together
until light and fluffy. Whisk in the
eggs gradually, adding 5ml/1 tsp
flour with each addition to prevent
the mixture from curdling.

5 Fold in the remaining flour with
the almond and rind mixture until
smooth, then spoon into the tin.

6 Bake for about 40 minutes, or
until golden and firm to the touch.

7 Meanwhile, squeeze the juice from
1 orange and put in a small pan
with the icing sugar and 3 tbsp/
45ml cold water, and simmer for
10 minutes, or until syrupy. Add the
orange liqueur, if using.

8 Remove the lining paper. Prick
over the top of the cake with a
skewer and spoon the syrup over,
then leave to cool in the tin. Cut the
cake in half horizontally.

9 Spread one cut cake side with
buttercream icing. Sandwich the
other layer on top and spread thinly
all over with buttercream.

10 Roll out the sugarpaste icing
on a surface dusted with icing sugar
and use to cover the cake,
smoothing down over the top and
sides. Trim the base neatly.

11 Tie a ribbon around the sides
and into a bow. Decorate the top
with sugarpaste or silk flowers. You
can freeze the undecorated base for
up to 2 months.

Energy 573kcal/2419kJ; Protein 10.2g; Carbohydrate 98.7g, of which sugars 95.6g; Fat 18g, of which saturates 1.9g; Cholesterol 73mg; Calcium 138mg; Fibre 2.4g; Sodium 52mg.

Easter simnel cake

This cake is traditionally served at Easter. The marzipan balls on top represent the 11 faithful apostles. It is also sometimes made for Mothering Sunday, when the almond paste top is decorated with fresh or crystallized spring flowers.

SERVES 8–10

175g/6oz/¾ cup butter, plus extra
  for greasing
175g/6oz/¾ cup soft brown sugar
3 large (US extra large) eggs, beaten
225g/8oz/2 cups plain
  (all-purpose) flour
2.5ml/½ tsp ground cinnamon
2.5ml/½ tsp freshly grated nutmeg
450g/15oz/3 cups total weight
  currants, sultanas (golden
  raisins) and raisins
85g/3oz/scant ½ cup glacé
  (candied) cherries, quartered
85g/3oz/scant ½ cup chopped
  mixed (candied) peel,
grated rind of 1 large lemon
450g/1lb almond paste
icing (confectioners') sugar,
  for dusting
1 egg white, lightly beaten

1 Preheat the oven to 160°C/325°F/ Gas 3. Grease and line an 18cm/7in round cake tin (pan).

2 In a large bowl, beat the butter and sugar, then beat in the eggs. Lightly fold in the flour, spices, dried fruits, cherries, mixed peel and the lemon rind.

3 Roll half the almond paste to a 16cm/6¼in circle on a surface dusted with icing sugar.

4 Spoon half the cake batter into the prepared tin. Put the circle of almond paste on top of the mixture.

5 Spoon the remaining cake mixture on top of the almond paste and level the surface. Bake for 1 hour.

6 Reduce the temperature to 150°C/ 300°F/Gas 2 and bake for 2 more hours. Leave to cool in the tin.

7 Brush the cake with egg white. and use the remaining almond paste to cover the cake. Roll the remaining paste into 11 balls and attach with egg white. Brush the cake top with more egg white and grill (broil) until lightly browned.

Energy 810kcal/3416kJ; Protein 10.4g; Carbohydrate 132g, of which sugars 111g; Fat 30.4g, of which saturates 13.2g; Cholesterol 144mg; Calcium 156mg; Fibre 33g; Sodium 208mg.

Summer celebration shortcake

A departure from the usual summer shortcake, this crisp dessert contains crunchy almonds, which go particularly well with the juicy strawberries and cream filling. The top layer is already divided into portions, giving it an attractive appearance as well as making it easier to serve.

SERVES 8

175g/6oz/¾ cup butter, plus extra
  for greasing
150g/5oz/1¼ cups plain
  (all-purpose) flour
115g/4oz/1 cup ground almonds
50g/2oz/¼ cup caster
  (superfine) sugar
25g/1oz/¼ cup flaked
  (sliced) almonds

For the filling and decoration
450g/1lb/4 cups fresh strawberries
300ml/½ pint/1¼ cups double
  (heavy) cream
15ml/1 tbsp amaretto (optional)
icing (confectioners') sugar,
  for dusting

1 Preheat the oven to 180°C/350°F/ Gas 4. Grease two baking sheets.

2 Rub the butter into the flour until it forms fine crumbs, then stir in the ground almonds and sugar. Mix to a soft dough and knead until smooth.

3 Roll half of the dough into a 20cm/8in round and cut out neatly. Put on a baking sheet and sprinkle over half the almonds.

4 Knead the trimmings and the rest of the dough to make a second shortcake round. Sprinkle over the almonds. Prick each with a fork.

5 Bake for 20 minutes, or until pale golden. While still warm, mark the flattest one into eight even triangles and leave to cool. Cut the triangles when cold.

6 For the filling, reserve nine strawberries. Hull and chop the rest.

7 Whip the cream until it forms soft peaks. Place one quarter in a piping (pastry) bag fitted with a star nozzle.

8 Fold the berries into the remaining cream with the liqueur, if using.

9 Put the whole shortbread on a serving plate. Pile the fruit filling on top and arrange the eight triangles on top with points facing inwards.

10 Pipe a cream rosette on each one and top with a strawberry, then put the last strawberry in the centre. Dust lightly with icing sugar. Serve immediately.

Energy 364kcal/1515kJ; Protein 4.3g; Carbohydrate 29.9g, of which sugars 8.5g; Fat 25.6g, of which saturates 15.6g; Cholesterol 87mg; Calcium 70mg; Fibre 1.2g; Sodium 76mg.

Meringue mountain

A meringue can make a stunning centrepiece and is actually quite easy to make. Bake it ahead of time, if you like – it then takes just a few minutes to put together before serving. For best results bake the meringues slowly and leave them in the oven overnight to make them extra crisp.

SERVES 8–10

8 egg whites
450g/1lb/2 cups caster
 (superfine) sugar
pink food colouring
450ml/¾ pint/scant 2 cups double
 (heavy) cream
Materials: tiny rosebuds and
 candles, to decorate

1 Preheat the oven to 110°C/
225°F/Gas ½. Line three baking
sheets with baking parchment. Rinse
out a large, grease-free bowl with
boiling water, then dry completely.

2 Put the egg whites into the bowl
of an electric mixer. Whisk the
egg whites until they form soft
peaks. Whisk in the sugar, 15ml/
1 tbsp at a time, until the mixture
forms stiff peaks.

COOK'S TIPS
• Bake the meringues ahead and
store in an airtight tin in a dry
place for up to a week.
• This cake is not suitable
for freezing.

3 Remove a quarter of the mixture
and put it into a clean bowl. Colour
it a pale pink with food colouring.

4 Spoon the pink meringue
mixture into a piping (pastry) bag
fitted with a star nozzle and pipe
15 pink rosettes.

5 Spoon the remaining white
mixture into a piping bag fitted
with a star nozzle and pipe a thin
20cm/8in circle on to one of the
baking sheets. Pipe about 15
small white rosettes with the
remaining meringue.

6 Bake for 4 hours, swapping the
trays over in the oven halfway
through. Turn off the heat and
allow the meringues to dry out in
the oven overnight if possible.

7 To assemble, whip the cream until
it forms soft peaks, then spoon into
a piping bag.

8 Pipe a cone shape of cream on to
the circular base. Pipe a little cream
on the base of each meringue
rosette, then assemble them in a
conical shape.

9 Decorate with rosebuds and
candles, and serve immediately.

Energy 389kcal/1628kJ; Protein 3.3g; Carbohydrate 48.2g, of which sugars 48.2g; Fat 24.2g, of which saturates 13.5g; Cholesterol 59mg; Calcium 48mg; Fibre 0g; Sodium 68mg.

Croquembouche

This stunning tower is made from tiny, light-as-air choux buns filled with cream and delicately drizzled with caramel. Croquembouche is served in France for special occasions such as weddings and tastes wonderful. Be careful when you make the caramel, as it can easily burn.

SERVES 10

75g/3oz/6 tbsp unsalted butter,
  plus extra for greasing
115g/4oz/1 cup plain (all-purpose)
  flour, sifted
3 eggs

For the filling
600ml/1 pint/2¼ cups double
  (heavy) cream
60ml/4 tbsp caster (superfine) sugar

For the caramel
115g/4oz/generous ½ cup caster
  (superfine) sugar

1 Preheat the oven to 200°C/400°F/
Gas 6. Grease four baking sheets.

2 Melt the butter in a pan with
250ml/8fl oz/1 cup water and bring
to the boil. Remove from the heat.

3 Sift the flour on to a paper sheet
and immediately pour into the pan.

COOK'S TIP
Bake the buns a day ahead and
store unfilled in an airtight box.

4 Quickly beat together until the
mixture forms a ball.

5 Transfer to a bowl and whisk in
the eggs, using an electric whisk,
until a smooth, thick paste forms.

6 Fill a piping (pastry) bag fitted
with a 1cm/½in plain nozzle and
pipe small balls about 2.5cm/1in
wide on to the baking sheets,
spaced well apart.

COOK'S TIP
Freeze unfilled buns in a plastic
box. Keep for 2 months. Thaw,
then re-heat in the oven at 180°C/
350°F/Gas 4 for 10 minutes.
Cool, then fill as step 9.

7 Bake for 20 minutes, or until
golden. Pierce a large hole in the
base of each to release the steam,
then return to the oven for a further
5 minutes. Cool on a wire rack.

8 To make the filling, whip the
cream together with the 60ml/4 tbsp
sugar, until it forms soft peaks.

9 Spoon into a piping bag fitted
with a 5mm/¼in nozzle and pipe
cream into each bun through the
hole in the base.

10 Arrange the buns in a pyramid.

11 To make the caramel, slowly heat
the sugar until liquid in a pan.

12 Drizzle the hot caramel over the
pyramid, allowing it to drizzle down
over the buns. Serve immediately.

Energy 579kcal/2400kJ; Protein 6g; Carbohydrate 32.6g, of which sugars 24.4g; Fat 46.8g, of which saturates 28.3g; Cholesterol 159mg; Calcium 123mg; Fibre 0.3g; Sodium 138mg.

Celebratory anniversary cake

Sugarpaste makes a perfectly smooth finish for a celebration cake and can also be used to mould decorations, as for these delicate arum lilies. When you colour the centre of the lilies, use silver to indicate 25 years of marriage or gold for 50 years.

SERVES 30

175g/6oz/¾ cup butter, plus extra for greasing
450g/1lb/2⅔ cups mixed dried fruit
50g/2oz/¼ cup glacé (candied) cherries, chopped
150g/5oz/generous ½ cup ready-to-eat dried apricots, chopped
115g/4oz/scant 1 cup dried, stoned (pitted) dates, chopped
165g/5½oz/scant 1½ cups dried, stoned (pitted) prunes, chopped
50g/2oz/¼ cup dried peaches, chopped
175g/6oz/¾ cup muscovado (molasses) sugar
2 oranges and 1 lemon
15ml/1 tbsp mixed (apple pie) spice
15ml/1 tbsp treacle (molasses)
4 eggs, beaten
250g/9oz/2¼ cups plain (all-purpose) flour
5ml/1 tsp baking powder

For the decoration
60ml/4 tbsp apricot glaze
900g/2lb almond paste
1.2kg/2½lb ivory-coloured sugarpaste
Materials: 8 strands of green floristry wire; gold or silver food colouring or dusting powder; 10 strands of bear grass; 1.5m/1¾yd silver or gold fine net ribbon

1 Put the butter in a large, heavy pan and add the dried fruits and the muscovado sugar.

2 Grate in the rind from one orange and the lemon. Squeeze in the juice from both oranges and the lemon with 75ml/2½fl oz/⅓ cup water. Heat gently, stirring, for 10 minutes, or until the butter melts and the sugar dissolves.

3 Pour into a large bowl, stir in the mixed spice and treacle, and leave to stand overnight.

4 Preheat the oven to 160°C/325°F/Gas 3. Grease and triple-line a 20cm/8in square tin (pan) or a 23cm/9in round cake tin, and wrap four layers of newspaper around the outside.

5 Add the eggs to the fruit mixture, then sift in the flour and baking powder. Mix until smooth.

6 Pour into the prepared tin and level the top. Cover with two layers of baking parchment to prevent over-browning.

7 Bake for 2 hours, then lower the temperature to 150°C/300°F/Gas 2 and bake for a further 1¾ –2 hours. Test with a skewer inserted into the centre; it will come out clean when the cake is cooked. Cool in the tin, then turn out and wrap in foil to mature for 2–3 months.

8 Remove the lining paper. To decorate the cake, brush with the apricot glaze and cover with almond paste. Leave for 24 hours.

9 Roll out the sugarpaste icing to a square large enough to cover the cake. Brush the cake with cooled boiled water, position the sugarpaste on the cake, smooth over the top and sides, and trim neatly.

COOK'S TIP
Keep for 4–6 months, wrapped in foil in an airtight tin. Freeze undecorated for up to 4 months.

Energy 224kcal/936kJ; Protein 2.4g; Carbohydrate 26.7g, of which sugars 20.5g; Fat 12.6g, of which saturates 7.6g; Cholesterol 17mg; Calcium 26mg; Fibre 0.7g; Sodium 168mg.

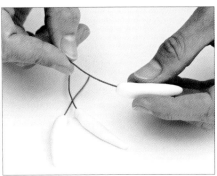

10 Make a small flat loop at the top of each piece of floristry wire. The loop helps the sugarpaste adhere to the wire. Re-roll the sugarpaste scraps to make 8 thin sausages and wrap these around the floristry wires. Leave to dry for 24 hours on waxed or non-stick paper.

11 Roll out the remaining sugarpaste thinly and cut into small rectangles 10 × 9cm/4 × 3in. Wrap each rectangle into a cone around the centre as shown, leaving a long, pointed tip. Flute out the edges to soften. Leave to dry out upside down in egg boxes for 24 hours.

12 Paint the tips of the lily stamens silver or gold, or dust the powder over with a dry paintbrush. Arrange a bunch of lilies with a few strands of bear grass and tie this together with a ribbon to secure. Arrange the flowers on the cake. Trim the sides with matching ribbon.

Rose-petal wedding cake

This special two-tiered cake looks very dainty with its pink and white glossy buttercream icing decorated with rose petals. You can bake the cake bases a day or two before you need them, then decorate them with the simple icing on the day.

SERVES 18

For the small cake
115g/4oz/½ cup butter, softened,
    plus extra for greasing
115/4oz/1 cup self-raising
    (self-rising) flour
2.5ml/½ tsp baking powder
115g/4oz/generous ½ cup natural
    caster (superfine) sugar
2 eggs, beaten
15ml/1 tbsp milk
a few drops of rose water

For the large cake
350g/12oz/1½ cups butter,
    softened, plus extra for greasing
350g/12oz/3 cups self-raising
    (self-rising) flour
5ml/1 tsp baking powder
350g/12oz/1½ cups natural caster
    (superfine) sugar
6 eggs, beaten
30ml/2 tbsp milk
a few drops of rose water

For the decoration
4 egg whites
275g/10oz/ 2½ cups icing
    (confectioners') sugar
275g/10 oz/1¼ cups unsalted
    butter, beaten
a few drops of rose water
pink food colouring
120ml/4fl oz/½ cup apricot jam
crystallized rose petals

1 Make and bake the two cakes separately. Preheat the oven to 160°C/325°F/Gas 3. Grease and line a 15cm/6in round deep cake tin (pan) with baking parchment.

2 To make the small cake, sift the flour and baking powder into a bowl. Add the sugar, butter, eggs, milk and rose water. Beat for 2 minutes, until smooth. Spoon into the cake tin and smooth the top.

3 Bake for 30–40 minutes, until firm and golden. Turn out to cool on a wire rack.

4 Repeat steps 1–3 to make the large cake, using a 25cm/10in round cake tin. Bake for 1 hour 5–10 minutes.

5 Whisk the egg whites and icing sugar in a bowl set over a pan of hot water until the beaters leave a trail when lifted. Remove from the heat. Continue whisking until soft peaks form. Cool slightly, then beat into the softened butter and rose water.

6 Put 45ml/3 tbsp of the mixture into a piping (pastry) bag and snip a tiny hole off the end.

7 Colour one-third of the remaining icing pale pink and put 60ml/4 tbsp in another paper icing bag, then snip off the end.

8 Remove the paper linings. Slice each cake in half horizontally and sandwich together with apricot jam.

COOK'S TIPS
• Cover in foil for up to 3 days until ready to decorate.
• Freeze the undecorated sponge cake bases, wrapped in foil or strong plastic bags, for up to 2 months.

Energy 253kcal/1071kJ; Protein 2.5g; Carbohydrate 48.8g, of which sugars 44.6g; Fat 5.5g, of which saturates 1.1g; Cholesterol 17mg; Calcium 49mg; Fibre 0.9g; Sodium 63mg.

9 Cover the small cake with pink icing and smooth flat with a metal spatula. Cover the large cake with white icing and smooth it flat.

10 Using a metal spatula, put the small cake on top of the large one. Remove the spatula carefully to avoid spreading cake crumbs.

11 Pipe tiny beads around the base of each cake. Sprinkle crystallized rose petals over the cakes and around the base, and serve.

Traditional Christmas cake

Make this cake four to six weeks before Christmas to give it time to mature. Once or twice during this time, pierce the cake with a skewer and spoon over 30–45ml/2–3 tbsp brandy to make it beautifully moist and rich. Top it with almond paste and sugarpaste just before eating.

SERVES 20

225g/8oz/1⅓ cups sultanas
   (golden raisins)
225g/8oz/1 cup currants
225g/8oz/1⅓ cups raisins
115g/4oz/½ cup prunes, stoned
   (pitted) and chopped
50g/2oz/¼ cup glacé (candied)
   cherries, halved
50g/2oz/⅓ cup chopped mixed
   (candied) peel,
45ml/3 tbsp brandy or sherry
225g/8oz/1 cup butter, plus extra
   for greasing
225g/8oz/2 cups plain
   (all-purpose) flour
pinch of salt
2.5ml/½ tsp ground cinnamon
2.5ml/½ tsp freshly grated nutmeg
15ml/1 tbsp unsweetened
   cocoa powder
225g/8oz/1 cup soft dark
   brown sugar
4 large (US extra large) eggs
finely grated rind of 1 orange
   or 1 lemon
50g/2oz/½ cup ground almonds
50g/2oz/½ cup chopped almonds

For the decoration
60ml/4 tbsp apricot jam
icing (confectioners') sugar
   for dusting
450g/1lb almond paste, *see page 24*
30ml/2 tbsp Kirsch or brandy
450g/1lb white sugarpaste icing,
   see page 26
225g/8oz royal icing, *see page 25*
Materials: red or green ribbon

1 The day before you want to bake the cake, put all the dried fruit in a large bowl. Pour in the brandy or sherry, cover with clear film (plastic wrap) and leave overnight.

2 Preheat the oven to 170°C/325°F/ Gas 3. Grease and line the base and sides of a 20cm/8in round cake tin (pan) with a double thickness of baking parchment.

3 Sift together the flour, salt, spices and cocoa powder into a large bowl.

4 In a large bowl, beat the butter and sugar together until light and fluffy, then beat in each egg.

5 Mix in the citrus rind, both almonds, dried fruits (with any liquid) and the flour mixture.

6 Spoon into the prepared tin and smooth the surface level. Give the cake tin a gentle tap on the work surface to settle the batter and disperse any air bubbles.

7 Bake for 3 hours, or until a skewer inserted into the centre comes out clean.

8 Leave the cake to cool in the tin for an hour. Turn the cake out on to a wire rack, but leave the paper on, as it will help to keep the cake moist during storage. When the cake is cold, wrap it tightly in foil and store in a cool place until ready to decorate.

9 Put the apricot jam in a pan and heat to warm, then sieve (strain) it to make a glaze.

Energy 6637kcal/28042kJ; Protein 60.6g; Carbohydrate 1245.8g, of which sugars 1129.2g; Fat 166.7g, of which saturates 85.9g; Cholesterol 940mg; Calcium 1515mg; Fibre 31.1g; Sodium 1896mg.

10 Remove the lining paper and centre the cake on a cake board.

11 Brush the cake with hot jam.

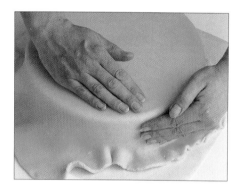

12 Dust the work surface with sifted icing sugar. Roll out the almond paste until large enough to cover the top and sides of the cake. Pick the almond paste up on the rolling pin and fit over the surface. Smooth out any air bubbles with your hands. Trim away any excess.

13 Brush 2 tbsp Kirsch over the almond paste. Roll out the sugarpaste as before and use to cover the cake. Trim the excess.

14 Roll out any sugarpaste trimmings and stamp out festive decorations using cutters. Lift in place with a small palette knife, then stick them in place with a little royal icing.

15 Use a star nozzle in a piping (pastry) bag and one-third fill it with royal icing. Pipe a border of rosettes around the base of the cake. Leave to dry thoroughly. Tie a ribbon around the sides of the cake.

Festive Yule log

The chocolate-covered Yule log has its origins in France. It makes a good alternative for those who don't like the traditional rich fruit cake, or it can be served during the Christmas holidays as a dessert with a fresh fruit compote. Eat this fresh or freeze it, unfilled, for two months.

SERVES 8

butter, for greasing
90g/3½oz/¾ cup self-raising
   (self-rising) flour
30ml/2 tbsp unsweetened
   cocoa powder
pinch of salt
4 eggs
115g/4oz/generous ½ cup golden
   caster (superfine) sugar, plus
   extra for dusting

For the filling and icing
150ml/¼ pint/⅔ cup double
   (heavy) cream
50g/2oz plain (semisweet)
   chocolate
30ml/2 tbsp unsweetened
   cocoa powder
15ml/2 tbsp boiling water
115g/4oz/½ cup unsalted
   butter, softened
225g/8oz/2 cups natural icing
   (confectioners') sugar, sifted,
   plus extra for dusting
almond paste or chocolate holly
   leaves, to decorate

1 Preheat the oven to 220°C/425°F/ Gas 7. Grease and line a 33 x 23cm/ 13 x 9in Swiss roll tin (jelly roll pan).

2 Sift the flour, cocoa and salt into a bowl.

> **COOK'S TIP**
> The sponge mixture for a Swiss roll is rolled up while it is still hot, to avoid it cracking.

3 Put the eggs and sugar into a large heatproof bowl and place this over a pan of hot water. Whisk for 10 minutes, or until the mixture is thick. Remove the bowl from the water and whisk until the mixture is thick and pale, and leaves a trail when the beaters are lifted away.

4 Using a large metal spoon, gently fold in half the flour and cocoa using a figure-of-eight movement. Fold in the remaining flour with 15ml/1 tbsp cold water. Pour the mixture into the prepared tin and smooth level.

5 Bake for 10 minutes, or until springy to the touch. Sprinkle a sheet of baking parchment with caster sugar and place this on a clean dish towel.

6 Turn the hot sponge out on to the paper.

7 Peel away the lining paper. Trim away the crusty sponge edges. Using the dish towel, roll up the sponge loosely, with the paper inside, then leave to cool on a wire rack.

8 Carefully unwrap the cold sponge cake and remove the paper. Whip the cream until stiff, spread over the sponge, then roll up and chill until needed.

9 Melt the chocolate in a heatproof bowl over a pan of gently simmering water, then leave to cool.

10 Dissolve the cocoa in the boiling water, stir until blended, then leave to cool.

Energy 478kcal/2003kJ; Protein 7.1g; Carbohydrate 55.4g, of which sugars 44.1g; Fat 26.1g, of which saturates 15g; Cholesterol 130mg; Calcium 75mg; Fibre 1.4g; Sodium 47mg.

11 Beat the butter until fluffy, then beat in the icing sugar and cooled cocoa with the melted chocolate.

12 Put the cake on a long serving dish. Spread the chocolate icing over the top and sides of the cake with a metal spatula, in deep swirls and ridges.

13 Decorate the top with almond paste or chocolate holly leaves and dust very lightly with a sprinkle of icing sugar before serving.

White Christmas cake

This light and zesty cake makes a refreshing change to a traditional heavy fruit cake. Make the moist sponge bases a day ahead, or bake and freeze them to make life simple over the holiday, so that all you have to do is add the very easy filling and decoration. Eat on the day it is made.

SERVES 12

225g/8oz/1 cup unsalted butter,
  softened, plus extra for greasing
finely grated rind and juice
  of 2 limes
75g/3oz block creamed coconut,
  grated or 150ml coconut cream
225g/8oz/generous 1 cup caster
  (superfine) sugar
4 large (US extra large) eggs
225g/8oz/2 cups self-raising
  (self-rising) flour

For the filling and decoration
200g/7oz/scant ¾ cup lemon curd
 225g/8oz/1 cup cream cheese
75g/3oz/6 tbsp unsalted butter
275g/10oz/2½ cups icing
  (confectioners') sugar
finely grated rind of 1 lime
175g/6oz/2 cups shredded coconut
crystallized sprigs of bay leaf,
  rosemary and cranberries,
  or silver Christmas baubles
  or snowflake ornaments,
  to decorate

1 Preheat the oven to 180°C/350°F/
Gas 4. Grease and line two 20cm/
8in round cake tins (pans).

COOK'S TIP
To make frosted leaves and
berries, whisk 1 egg white until
frothy, then brush it over a bay
leaf, sprigs of rosemary and a
few cranberries. Put on a wire
rack. Dust with plenty of caster
(superfine) sugar. Leave to dry.

2 Put the lime juice and 30ml/2 tbsp water in a small pan with the creamed coconut and heat gently to dissolve, then cool.

3 Put the lime rind, butter, sugar, eggs, flour and cooled coconut mixture into a bowl and whisk for 2–3 minutes, or until smooth and soft.

4 Divide the batter equally between the cake tins and smooth the tops level.

5 Bake for 20–25 minutes, or until golden and risen, and firm to the touch in the centre.

6 Cool in the tin for 5 minutes, then turn out to cool on a wire rack and peel away the lining papers.

7 Cut each cake in half horizontally with a sharp knife, then sandwich each together with lemon curd. Put one cake on a plate, spread the top with the remaining lemon curd and sandwich both cakes together.

8 To make the coating, put the cream cheese, butter, icing sugar and lime rind in a bowl and beat until smooth. Spread the coating over the top and sides of the cake.

9 Sprinkle the coconut over the top and pat on to the sides, then tidy the base.

10 Decorate the centre of the cake with sprigs of rosemary and cranberries, or bought silver Christmas baubles or snowflake ornaments, if you like.

Energy 698kcal/2912kJ; Protein 8.9g; Carbohydrate 63g, of which sugars 51.8g; Fat 47.5g, of which saturates 34.7g; Cholesterol 193mg; Calcium 78mg; Fibre 6.4g; Sodium 188mg.

Index

This edition is published by Lorenz Books, an imprint of Anness Publishing Ltd, Blaby Road, Wigston, Leicestershire LE18 4SE

info@anness.com

www.lorenzbooks.com;
www.annesspublishing.com

If you like the images in this book and would like to investigate using them for publishing, promotions or advertising, please visit our website www.practicalpictures.com for more information.

A CIP catalogue record for this book is available from the British Library.

Publisher: Joanna Lorenz
Editorial Director: Helen Sudell
Editor: Simona Hill
Photographer: William Lingwood
Stylist: Liz Hippisley
Home Economist: Lucy McKelvie
Designer: Nigel Partridge
Production Controller: Pirong Wang

Main front cover image shows Meringue Mountain – for recipe, see page 240

PUBLISHER'S NOTE
Although the advice and information in this book are believed to be accurate and true at the time of going to press, neither the authors nor the publisher can accept any legal responsibility or liability for any errors or omissions that may have been made nor for any inaccuracies nor for any loss, harm or injury that comes about from following instructions or advice in this book.

NOTES
Bracketed terms are intended for American readers.
• For all recipes, quantities are given in both metric and imperial measures and, where appropriate, in standard cups and spoons. Follow one set of measures, but not a mixture, because they are not interchangeable.
• Standard spoon and cup measures are level. 1 tsp = 5ml, 1 tbsp = 15ml, 1 cup = 250ml/8fl oz.
• Australian standard tablespoons are 20ml. Australian readers should use 3 tsp in place of 1 tbsp for measuring small quantities.
• American pints are 16fl oz/ 2 cups. American readers should use 20fl oz/2.5 cups in place of 1 pint when measuring liquids.
• Electric oven temperatures in this book are for conventional ovens. When using a fan oven, the temperature will probably need to be reduced by about 10–20°C/ 20–40°F. Since ovens vary, check with your manufacturer's instruction book for guidance.
• The nutritional analysis given for each recipe is calculated per portion (i.e. serving or item), unless otherwise stated. If the recipe gives a range, such as Serves 4–6, then the nutritional analysis will be for the smaller portion size, i.e. 6 servings. The analysis does not include optional ingredients, such as salt added to taste.
• Medium (US large) eggs are used unless stated.
• Recipes containing raw eggs should not be eaten by pregnant women, babies, the very young and elderly people. You can use dried egg whites instead which give excellent results and can be substituted in recipes.

The following companies provide an excellent postal service for all cake decorating and baking supplies.
For all cake decorating supplies:
Squires Kitchen
www.squires-group.co.uk
www.squires-shop.com
For all baking supplies:
Lakeland
www.lakeland.co.uk